Great Natural Areas in Western Pennsylvania

Great Natural Areas in Western Pennsylvania

Stephen J. Ostrander

STACKPOLE
BOOKS

Copyright © 2000 by Stackpole Books

Published by
STACKPOLE BOOKS
5067 Ritter Road
Mechanicsburg, PA 17055
www.stackpolebooks.com

Printed in the United States of America

10 9 8 7 6 5 4 3 2 1

FIRST EDITION

Cover design by Caroline Stover
Cover photo by Stephen J. Ostrander

Library of Congress Cataloging-in-Publication Data

Ostrander, Stephen.
    Great natural areas in western Pennsylvania / Stephen J. Ostrander.
    — 1st ed.
        p.   cm.
    ISBN 0–8117–2778–5
    1. Natural history—Pennsylvania—Guidebooks. 2. Pennsylvania—
Guidebooks. I. Title.
QH105.P4 O88 2000
508.748 21—dc21
                                                            99–045680
                                                            CIP

To my parents,
who gave me life
and showed me there
is more to life than me.

N

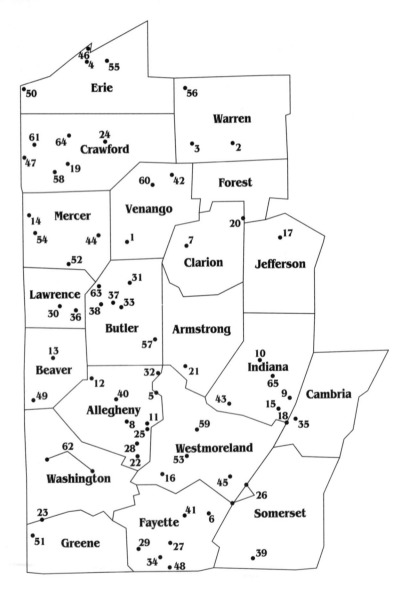

46
4 55

50

Erie

61 64 24
Crawford

47

58 19

56

Warren

3 2

60 42

Forest

14 Mercer

54

Venango

44 1

52

20

7

17

Clarion

Jefferson

Lawrence

31

63 37 33

30 36 38

Butler

57

Armstrong

13

Beaver

12

49

40 5

Allegheny

8 11

25

28

22

32 21

43

10

Indiana

65

9

15

18 35

Cambria

59

Westmoreland

53

62

Washington

16

45

26

23

41 6

Fayette

Somerset

51 Greene

29 27

34 48

39

Contents

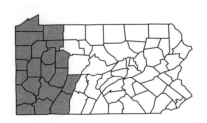

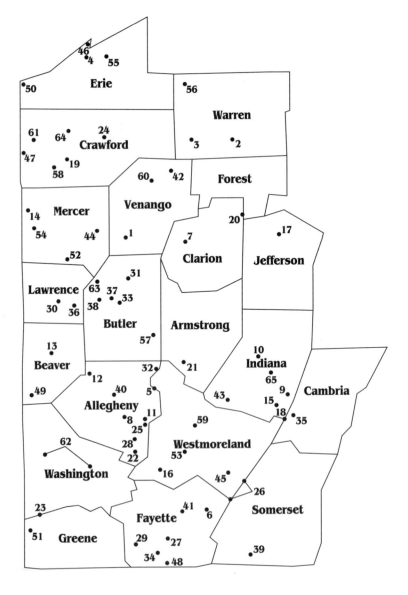

Erie

46
4   55

50

56

Warren

61   64   24
         Crawford   3   2

47   19
   58

Forest

60   42

Venango

14   Mercer

54   44   1

52

20

17

7

Clarion   Jefferson

31

Lawrence 63 37
          38 33

30   36

Butler   Armstrong

57

13

Beaver

12

49

40   5

Allegheny

8   11

25

62

28

22

Washington

16

32   21

43

59

Westmoreland

53

45

10

Indiana

65

9   Cambria

15

18   35

26

Somerset

23

51   Greene

41   6

Fayette

29   27

34   48

39

Contents _____ ix

Acknowledgments

Writing a book is a euphoric and humbling journey. Like every literary adventurer, I am indebted to the kindness of strangers—the many people who helped me with research. This book is partly the product of their labor and love. I am also indebted to the many scientists and writers whose studies and books on Pennsylvania's natural history proved invaluable.

The following people and their staffs deserve my thanks: Dan Devlin, Mark Bodamer, and Chris Firestone, Pennsylvania Department of Conservation and Natural Resources, Bureau of Forestry; Rick Keen, Bureau of Topographic and Geologic Survey; Michael J. Cummings, Rich Akers, John Derby, Ed Schwinn, and Pat Kline, U.S. Army Corps of Engineers; Dr. Stephen J. Tonsor and Debra A. Miller, University of Pittsburgh, Pymatuning Laboratory of Ecology; Randy A. Meyer, Presque Isle State Park; Jean Stull, Waterford, Pennsylvania; Dr. Joseph Merritt, Powdermill Nature Reserve, Carnegie Museum of Natural History; Pat Adams, Raccoon Creek State Park; Shayne Hoachlander, Regis Senko, and Dennis Jones, Pennsylvania Game Commission; Meg Scanlon, Tammy Watychowicz, and Mike Diehl, Allegheny Department of Parks, Recreation and Conservation; Marcia G. Baker, Oil Creek State Park; the entire helpful and friendly crew at Allegheny National Forest; Michael Kuzemchak, Indiana County Parks; Brian Winslow and Heather Zimmerman, Asbury Woods Nature Center; Roy Boyle, Two Mile Run County Park; Ed Rhoades and Jim Danmit, Westmoreland County Department of Parks and Recreation; Dr. Joseph Cruzan, Geneva College; Julie Lalo, Western Pennsylvania Conservancy; Bernie Sposia, U.S. Department of Agriculture, Clarion Conservation District; Tingle Barnes, Beechwood Farms Nature Reserve; Tom Mountain, Erie National Wildlife Refuge; Wayne Minnich, Cook Forest State Park; Barb Darbal, Ohiopyle State Park; and Kyle Weaver of Stackpole Books, who safely guided this book to a soft landing.

Introduction

I want you to know, right up front, that I am a writer with a mission. I wrote this book to arouse your curiosity so that you will explore the natural wonders of Western Pennsylvania. Consider it the first step of an ambitious adventure to recapture lost treasure. To save the land, you must understand it. To understand it, you must be in it.

More practically, this volume serves as a natural-history and travel guide, a companion for ecotourists. It points you to many of the state's natural attractions and explains what's so special about them. The special places in this book—selected state and county parks, nature preserves, state game lands, sites in national and state forests, historic places, U.S. Army Corps of Engineers projects, scientific field stations, scenic rivers, and national wildlife refuges—present a brief picture of the natural history of western Pennsylvania. The list is not complete, certainly. I had to draw the line somewhere.

Natural areas are places for preserving wildlife, especially endangered species and habitats, and for showing off natural beauty. Here, natural processes continue without human interference. William Shakespeare was right when he wrote, "One touch of nature makes the whole world kin." In nature preserves, we accept biological diversity, which will help us respect human diversity as well.

Most of the natural places in this book are open to the public year-round and are free. Preserves typically have something to offer any time of year. Spring is the best time to view wildflowers and migratory birds. Summer displays nature's full abundance, but it's not the best time to see forest animals or geological formations. Fall is a good time for birding and wildlife observation, and Pennsylvania's autumn colors rival those of New England. Winter is quiet and bare, and the best time to view geological formations.

Wildlife, of course, does not punch a precise time clock, and certain flora or fauna may not appear when you visit a locale for any of a hundred reasons. That's the case with me and black bears. I've yet to encounter this noble beast, though claw marks and scat assure me of their existence. But bears or not, there's always some form of life to captivate me.

The common names of animals and plants used in this text are those found in major field guides. Throughout the book, I have noted the status of imperiled plants and animals. Endangered species are those in danger of extirpation (statewide extinction) or extinction unless their habitat is restored. Threatened species are experiencing rapid decline and habitat degradation. They may be abundant in one place but generally suffering throughout their range. To simplify classifications, I have rated all other "listed" species as rare, these being life forms endemic (exclusive to an area), disjunct (separated from the main population), or considered at risk of being imperiled.

When planning to hike in one of these areas, dress appropriately and wear sturdy footwear. I recommend slacks rather than shorts to avoid poison ivy, insect bites, scrapes, and other posthike discomforts. Wear a full-brimmed hat or cap for protection from bugs, sun, rain, and debris that falls from the canopy. Use insect repellent in summer. Take drinking water and toilet paper.

Carry out all litter, including cigarette butts. Slow, quiet, and alert hikers always see the most wildlife. Don't play a radio, shout, talk incessantly, run, jog, or bicycle on foot trails. These activities disturb other visitors and frighten wildlife. For the same reasons, dogs are prohibited in most sites.

Though you're not likely to get lost, it's always good to obtain a trail map before hiking. In remote areas, like Forbes State Forest, don't stray from the trail unless you are familiar with the territory, can read a topographical map, or are skilled in orienteering. The maps in this book are merely escorts. The rest of the journey is up to you.

Best Picks

ALL-AROUND FAVORITES
Every place has its charm, but these charmed me. Your list may differ from mine.
* Presque Isle State Park
* Erie National Wildlife Refuge
* Ohiopyle State Park
* Allegheny National Forest
* Raccoon Creek *and* McConnells Mill State Parks

BIRDING HOT SPOTS
These are rewarding realms for birders with binoculars.
* Todd Sanctuary
* Erie National Wildlife Refuge
* Presque Isle State Park
* Pymatuning Wetlands
* Glade Dam Lake

TOP WILDFLOWER PRESERVES
Visit in spring and summer when blossoms are ablaze.
* Wildflower Preserve, Raccoon Creek State Park
* Ferncliff Peninsula, Ohiopyle State Park
* Flower and Wildlife Preserve (Trillium Trail)
* Wolf Creek Narrows Natural Area
* Jennings Environmental Education Center

BEST SCENIC OVERLOOKS
Enjoy the view, but watch your step.
* Jake's Rocks, Allegheny National Forest
* David M. Roderick Wildlife Reserve, State Game Lands 314
* Allegheny Gorge, Kittaning State Forest
* Harrison Hills Park
* Forbes State Forest (Mount Davis, Wolf Rocks)

GREAT GEOLOGICAL SITES
* Presque Isle State Park (sand spit, dunes)
* Youghiogheny River Gorge, Ohiopyle State Park
* McConnells Mill State Park *and* Miller Esker

- Laurel Caverns
- Oil Creek State Park

SOLITUDE AND SILENCE
These are the best places to avoid other people.
- Allegheny National Forest
- Erie National Wildlife Refuge
- Roaring Run Natural Area (Forbes State Forest)
- Enlow Fork Natural Area
- Quebec Run Wild Area

BEST OUTINGS FOR CHILDREN
When your kids tire of nature centers, try these places.
- Presque Isle State Park (but not the beaches)
- Ferncliff Peninsula, Ohiopyle State Park
- Laurel Caverns (unlighted passages)
- Heart's Content Scenic Area, Allegheny National Forest
- Raccoon Creek State Park

BEST EASYGOING TRAILS
These trails are easy to find, easy to walk, and always rewarding.
- Youghiogheny Bike and Hike Trail, Ohiopyle State Park
- Schollard's Run Wetland
- Erie National Wildlife Refuge
- Heart's Content Scenic Area, Allegheny National Forest
- Bear Run Nature Reserve

BEST SURPRISES
These places surpassed my expectations.
- Crooked Creek Lake
- Allegheny Gorge
- Pymatuning Wetlands
- Schollard's Run Wetland
- Glade Dam Lake

1

Allegheny Gorge

This steep and forested tract angles up the western bank of the Allegheny River for nearly 7 miles in southwestern Venango County. Trails parallel the river, crisscross hemlock-shrouded runs, climb to vistas with panoramic views 500 feet above the Allegheny River, and descend to the ruins of an old iron furnace.

Ownership. Pennsylvania Department of Conservation and Natural Resources, Bureau of Forestry.

Size. The Allegheny River Tract of Kittaning State Forest comprises 3,165 acres.

Physiographic Region. Pittsburgh Low Plateau.

Nearby Natural Attractions. Oil Creek State Park, Two Mile Run County Park, and State Game Lands 39, 45, and 47.

Features. There are four points of entry. From I-80 (Clintonville exit), go north on PA 308 nearly 4 miles. (Southbound travelers on PA 8, get off at PA 308 and head southeasterly.) Just south of Bullion, turn right (east) on SR 3008, toward Kennerdell. Drive 4 miles and watch for state forest boundary signs. The River Trail, southeastern access, starts at a gated lane on the north side of SR 3008, before the Kennerdell bridge, on the west bank of the river. You must park at a pulloff on the south side of the road 100 feet back. The River Trail is the main drag through the gorge. An easy, scenic route covers 4.5 miles from the Kennerdell Bridge to the Danner Camping Area and back. North of the primitive camp, the River Trail becomes tougher and more demanding. It merges with the Fishermans Cove Trail and goes to the northern boundary. Round-trip between the camp and northern line is about 10 miles.

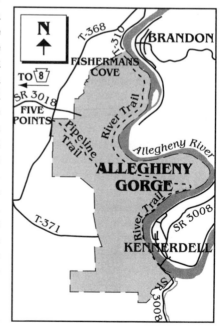

The Pipeline, Ridge, Fishermans Cove, and Iron Furnace Trails start

1

on the west side of the tract, from parking areas on township roads. To get to these spots, return to PA 308 and head north (right) to Bullion, less than a mile. Here, bear right on Bullion Road, heading north. Turn right (east) on Dennison Run Road (T368). In half a mile, T368 turns sharply left, heading north. Just before the bend, take T371, which branches right to a parking lot for State Game Lands 39. Follow the abandoned road heading southbound at the right. In a quarter mile, take the trail going left. This old lane enters the state forest and meets the Dennison Run Trail (first left), Overlook Trail (second left), and Iron Furnace Trail (stay right). Stay left at upcoming junctions to reach the iron furnace.

Continuing north on T368, you will reach two parking areas for state forest trails. The southernmost area is the western terminus of the Ridge Trail, which heads east to the Dennison Run, Pipeline, and River Trails. The second pulloff at Five Points is for the Pipeline Trail, an eastbound path to the river.

For the Fishermans Cove Trail, continue north on T368 to Five Points and turn right on SR 3018. Just past the state forest boundary (at a right bend), follow the Fishermans Cove Trail, branching left (northeast) behind a gated woods road. This merges with the River Trail and goes upstream to the northern border of the tract. To reach the northern terminus of the River/Fishermans Cove Trail, follow T368 (Fishermans Cove Road) north from Five Points to its end, then turn right on T310 to its conclusion.

This selected hike takes the shortcut to Dennison Run Overlook, which features an expansive view of the Allegheny River. From the Kennerdell bridge, follow the River Trail upstream a mile to Dennison Run, rated an exceptional value stream for its purity and native trout hatchery. Turn left (west) on Dennison Run Trail. In a little less than half a mile, take the steep and rubbly Overlook Trail, a.k.a Lookout Trail, which branches left (south) from Dennison Run Trail. This route rises 400 feet in a quarter mile, a real cardiac challenge. Loose debris and some quirky detours add to the adventure. Closely follow the red blazes. On the summit, a side trail heading left (east) leads to a viewing deck with interpretive signs. The exertion is worth the view. Take a breather and enjoy the scene.

From here, you can backtrack to Dennison Run, the river, and the bridge or return via another route. If you choose the latter, go back to the Overlook Trail and turn left (southwest). At the first intersection, go left on the Kennerdell Trail, which merges with the South Trail at a peak above the Allegheny River. The route's end needs reworking and clarifying by trail blazers. Essentially, you must descend the slope and follow a red-blazed path along the forest boundary. You'll eventually reach an old logging trail that angles down to SR 3008, a few hundred yards from the parking spot.

An easier and simpler hike is a 4.5-mile round-trip on the River Trail from the bridge to Danner Camping Area. From the camp, ambitious hikers can continue upstream on the River Trail to the Fishermans Cove Trail and northern border of the tract (T310). This leg over tough terrain measures 12 miles round-trip. A 10-mile round-trip via the River and Pipeline Trails goes between the bridge and Five Points entry. Trails are marked by red blazes.

The trail map printed by the forestry bureau is highly recommended for this area. Primitive camping is allowed at the Danner Camping Area, off the River Trail, 2 miles north of the Kennerdell Bridge.

Geology. The overlook perches nearly 500 feet above a bend in the Allegheny River. Bedrock consists of layers of sandstone, shale, limestone, and coal, representing members of the Cuyahoga Formation (310 million years old) at the river level, overlain by the Pottsville and Allegheny Formations (310 to 280 million years old).

According to scientists Chet and Maureen Raymo, the transition from the Mesozoic to Cenozoic Eras, roughly 70 million years, was marked by a general uplifting in this region. The flex caused rivers like the preglacial Allegheny current to begin entrenching, thus exposing the underlying bedrock. This erosion accelerated during the ice age, when the Allegheny River served as the drainage basin for glacial meltwater.

The cottage-size sandstone boulders visible along the river broke from the gorge wall due to weathering and slid to their current positions. These boulders have become minihabitats for plants and animals.

Wildlife. White pine and hemlock dominated the early postglacial forest, roughly 12,000 years ago. The major hardwoods associated with those conifers were oaks, chestnuts, beeches, birches, sugar maple, and black cherry. The activities of Euro-American settlers drastically altered the original forest. The Dennison Point Overlook information board explains that "uncontrolled logging, the spread of chestnut blight, wildfires, and a general lack of concern for the resources caused the changes."

Hikers exploring the tract will notice dramatic changes in vegetation, depending on elevation, slope-facing direction, and soil. The River Trail starts with a hemlock and rhododendron grove on the left and sugar maples on the right. When the trail drops into the floodplain, sycamores, willows, and red maples, all water-tolerant species, take over. Much of the Dennison Run Trail tracks through a ravine of hemlocks, which thrive in cool, moist, north-looking slopes. Climbing to the overlook, you will pass mountain laurels, the state flower, and lowbush blueberries, which grow in higher and drier places. The woods also have American beech, some white pine, cucumber magnolia, tulip tree, flowering dogwood, shagbark hickory, white and red oaks (near the iron furnace), red maple, yellow birch, and black cherry.

Warm weather brings wildflowers called foamflower and hepatica, as well as maidenhair, New York, Christmas, evergreen wood, and common polypody ferns, the last growing like whiskers from cracks in boulders.

Birders should be alert for woodland songbirds and waterbirds. Around 176 varieties have been spotted, including the hooded, black-and-white, Cape May, cerulean, parula, Canada, wormeating, blackpoll, and Tennessee warblers, plus the black-capped chickadee, dark-eyed junco, ruffed grouse (in blueberry patches), scarlet tanager, American bittern (PA threatened) yellow-bellied cuckoo, eastern pewees (along Dennison Run), and red-eyed vireos. Owls are represented by the great horned, screech, saw-whet, barn, and long-eared (the last three PA rare). Raptors glide the gorge, notably the osprey (PA endangered), northern goshawk (PA rare), and sharp-shinned hawk. Flocks of wild turkeys scratch for autumn acorns on the oak summit. A flock of eight bluejays followed my progress down the River Trail for a quarter mile.

Fur-bearing vertebrates number forty-seven species, including the bobcat, small-footed myotis (PA threatened), silver-haired bat (PA rare), porcupine, short-tailed weasel (also known as ermine), southern bog lemming, and snowshoe hare.

Amphibians such as the hellbender, mudpuppy, pickerel and northern leopard frogs, redspotted newt, and Jefferson, northern two-lined, and spotted salamanders live here. Timber rattlesnakes (PA endangered) and copperheads lurk around the ledges. Turtles include the stinkpot, spotted, and wood.

History. An information board at the Dennison Point Overlook notes that the area's first human inhabitants were the so-called Archaic Indians, who lived here about 8,000 years ago. Petroglyphs carved in sandstone by ancient inhabitants once decorated Indian God Rock on the east bank of the Allegheny River, 5 miles south of Franklin. Erosion and vandalism destroyed the historic etchings, but a reproduction appears at the overlook.

Allegheny is thought to derive from *Alli-gawi-sipu,* a native people who the Lenni-Lenape (Delaware Nation) said lived along the river. In 1611 missionary Louis Hennepina, a Franciscan friar and explorer, was the first European to penetrate into the river valley. The Seneca people, members of the Iroquois Confederacy, resided here when white settlers arrived in the 1740s. The overlook stands on land first owned by John Hovis, whose father was a native of Russia. These industrious pioneers established farms, sawmills, gristmills, woolen mills, blacksmith foundries, iron furnaces, and oil wells in the valley. Keelboats began hauling cargo and passengers in the 1790s. Steamboats plied the Allegheny by 1828.

Stonecutters erected Bullion Iron Furnace in 1840, using neighborhood sandstone. No mortar was used to bond the blocks. During its ten years of operation, more than 1,000 acres of the forest was shaved to make charcoal for the blast furnace. The furnace bore 3 tons of pig iron a day at its peak. Timber rafts on the Allegheny River floated the iron to Pittsburgh.

Forestry maps in the 1970s had this tract marked as Allegheny River State Park, and natural area status once was considered for Dennison Run. Those designations never materialized.

Allegheny National Forest

Heart's Content Scenic Area
Hickory Creek Wilderness Area
Allegheny River Islands Wilderness Area
Jake's Rocks
Little Drummer Historical Pathway
Tionesta Scenic Area

Allegheny National Forest encourages the free flow of hyperbole. Like a great city, everything you've heard about it is true. Its mosaic of habitats, some carefully cultivated, houses an amazing array of creatures. There are 800 square miles of playland, a lake with 90 miles of shoreline, two national scenic rivers, and a menu of outdoor activities that can't be consumed in just a few days.

The Forest Service dubs it the "Land of Many Uses," but I call it a land of juxtaposition. In golden protected places noble, old-growth hemlocks, pines, and beeches that have stood longer than castles connect us soothingly with primeval times. But in 1985 some of these

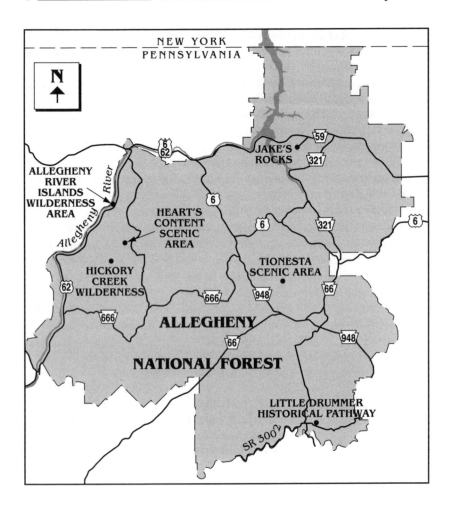

ancients were tossed like toothpicks by a tornado, reminding us of our vulnerability to natural forces. There is vastness for solitude here, as well as 1,300 miles of roadways for returning to human civilization. It is simultaneously savage and wild and managed to timidity. Abandoned railroads, overgrown logging roads, and rust-encrusted oil wells remind us of the short-sighted, hot-for-profit drive that razed the forest a century ago. The growl of chain saws and the grassy gashes cut through the forest for pipelines are evidence that the energy of those bygone days has not been abandoned.

Ownership. U.S. Department of Agriculture, Forest Service.
Size. 513,000 acres.
Physiographic Region. High Plateau.

Nearby Natural Attractions. Cook Forest, Clear Creek, and Chapman State Parks; Kittaning and Cornplanter State Forests; and Anders Run Natural Area.

Features. *Heart's Content Scenic Area* spares a 121-acre grove of ancient hemlocks and white pines from the sawmill. A flat, easy loop path wanders a little more than a mile among coniferous giants that stretch straight up for 150 feet. Folks opting for the quarter-mile Short Loop get only a glimpse of this sacred place. Many behemoths here have swayed in the wind for 350 years and have diameters of 40 inches or more. Many consider the cathedral-like trees in Heart's Content and nearby Cook Forest State Park the symbolic equivalents of the redwoods and sequoias of the western United States.

The majesty of the grove even awed the axmen of the Wheeler and Dusenbury Lumber Company, who refrained from cutting a 20-acre patch of virgin timber and gave it to the U.S. Forest Service in 1922. The U.S. Department of the Interior designated this place a National Natural Landmark in May 1973.

The parking area for Heart's Content, on SR 2002, also serves as the departure point for the 11.3-mile hiking trail into *Hickory Creek Wilderness,* the only federally designated wilderness area east of the Mississippi River. The yellow-blazed trail begins on the north side of the parking area, but it quickly turns west and crosses the road. Just past the campground for Heart's Content Recreation Area, the trail splits into the legs of its loop. The route crosses moderately steep terrain, most of it forested with hardwoods within the branches of East Hickory Creek and Middle Hickory Creek. This is the only maintained trail in the 8,663-acre wilderness. This is the place to go for solitude. Backpackers should be prepared for a possible food raid by black bears.

Allegheny River Wilderness Islands, part of the Hickory Creek Wilderness, consists of seven islands in the Allegheny River amounting to 368 acres. The islands are scattered between the Buckaloons Recreation Area and Tionesta (pronounced Ty-NES-ta). You can reach the islands only by boat, but once you're there, you can explore them to your heart's content. Don't expect trails. From Buckaloons heading downstream, island hoppers go from Crull's Island (96 acres), to Thompson's Island (30 acres), the site of the only Revolutionary War battle in northwestern Pennsylvania, Courson Island (62 acres), King Island (36 acres), Baker Island (67 acres), which had its trees flattened on May 31, 1985, by a tornado, and No-Name Island (10 acres). Camping is permitted. Pick up a forest service brochure showing the location of wilderness islands and privately owned islands.

Jake's Rocks looks as if monster-size dump trucks deposited gigantic blocks and slabs of boulders atop Coal Knob Ridge. This "rock city" of jumbled conglomerate was created by natural forces, however. A paved trail leads to a ledge and a striking overlook framing Allegheny Reservoir. This vantage helps you imagine ancient Lake Carll, the ice-age lake now occupied by the man-made reservoir. Mountain laurels and great rhododendrons decorate the place. Just east of the Kinzua Point Visitor Center on SR 59, turn south on Forest Road 262 and follow signs to the attraction.

Tionesta Scenic Area and its old-growth forest became a National Natural Landmark in May 1973. The celebrated spot consists of 300- to 400-year-old beech, hemlock, and sugar maple stands. The remote, 4,135-acre tract includes the adjacent Tionesta Research Natural Area. Carefully follow FR 133 and destination signs stemming south from US 6 in Ludlow. The 1.5-mile nature trail begins from the loop road serving as the only auto access. Follow the meandering path to a clear swath hiding a gas pipeline. Here the nature trail meets the North Country National Scenic Trail (NCT). I suggest walking left (south) a few hundred yards to see the devastating natural clear-cut done by a tornado on May 31, 1985. The twister toppled several hundred acres of old-growth. Return to the junction and head right (north) along the pipeline a few hundred yards. The NCT/nature trail turns right (east) and goes back to the loop road. Retrace your route to US 6.

From SR 3002 (Spring Creek Road) in the southeastern corner of the Allegheny National Forest, the *Little Drummer Historical Pathway* twists for 3.5 miles in a figure-eight route. Write in advance for an informative and colorful forty-two-page trail guide. Forty interpretive stops explain the natural and human history of the site. Roughly half of the trail follows the bed of an abandoned narrow-gauge railroad once used by loggers; vegetation has hidden all but a few reminders. "Little Drummer" refers to the ruffed grouse that usually flush when hikers approach. The Ruffed Grouse Society, National Wild Turkey Federation, Eastern National Forest Interpretive Association, Boot Jack Snow Gliders, Elk County Visitors Bureau, and Pennsylvania Department of Transportation all participated in blazing this trail.

The Beaver Meadows, Buzzard Swamp, and Twin Lakes Recreation Areas also have hiking loops ideal for wildlife watching and natural study. Besides these attractions, Allegheny National Forest offers eleven family campgrounds (615 sites), five boating camps (85 sites), 230 miles of hiking trails, paths for mountain bikes and off-road vehicles, swimming, boating, hunting, fishing, orienteering, Nordic skiing, and picnicking. More than 87 miles of the North Country National Scenic Trail runs across the Allegheny National Forest.

Two state and national scenic rivers, the Allegheny and Clarion Rivers, wash the forest's western and southern borders, and Tionesta Creek, a waterway proposed for state scenic status, runs through the middle of it. Kinzua Dam impounds Allegheny Reservoir, a 27-mile-long lake that stretches north into New York.

For more information, contact Allegheny National Forest, 222 Liberty St., P.O. Box 847, Warren, PA 16365, telephone (814) 723-5150, e-mail anf@penn.com, web site http://www.penn.com/~anf. A visitors center is located at Kinzua Point, 10 miles east of Warren on PA 59 (summer only). The U.S. Army Corps of Engineers operates the Big Bend Visitor Center at Kinzua Dam, also on PA 59.

Geology. The national forest stands atop the Allegheny Plateau, which covers most of western Pennsylvania and western New York. Crustal action hundreds of millions of years ago created a dome-shaped uplift in the Allegheny Plateau centered over McKean and Potter Counties. During the ice age, starting a million years ago, glaciers edged partway up the dome but were unable to surmount it.

Some 20,000 years ago, Kinzua Dam was a dam of a different kind. Back then the margin of the last glacier, the Wisconsinan, loomed to the north and west. Glacial meltwater pooled in front of the glacier, creating Lake Carll, an impoundment similar to the contemporary Allegheny Reservoir. The southwestern plug of the ancient lake was located at a saddle-shaped ridge near a natural bottleneck (Kinzua Pass). Icebergs drifted on the lake like tall ships, and snow crystals whisked across ridges, even in summer. Over the centuries, as the ice mountain melted, Lake Carll swelled with meltwater from the northern slope, and waves spilled over the shallow pass. Trickles became torrents of water, the valley deepened, and the lake shrank to the Allegheny River. Kinzua Dam restored the scene of old Lake Carll.

The ice mass also rerouted the preglacial Allegheny River and its tributaries. The three branches of the ancient stream once drained northward into the Atlantic Ocean via an old route through Lakes Erie and Ontario and the St. Lawrence River. The watershed now empties into the Gulf of Mexico. A terminal moraine, a ridge of sediment that piled up at the front of the glacier, cut off the Conewango Creek, which enters the Allegheny River at Warren, from its preglacial path along Cattaraugus Creek in New York.

The overlook at Jake's Rocks, above Kinzua Point, is an ideal spot to envision Lake Carll. This rock city once was a solid caprock of heavy, resistant conglomerate, aged during the Pennsylvanian Period (300 million years ago). It sprawled horizontally atop weaker layers of shale and siltstone. Hillside erosion erased the underlying shales faster than the conglomerate. Consequently, overhanging ledges of conglomerate broke along joints, or fractures. Slabs then slid down the slope, piling into each other. Frost and tree roots hastened the process by widening joints and jostling boulders.

Geologists joke that the area has no hills, just valleys. The entire forest lies within the Allegheny High Plateau, a region of horizontal sedimentary rocks that was lifted some 250 million years ago during the Allegheny orogeny. Downcutting rivers and streams have created the relief in this elevated tableland. In deeply gouged valleys, 330 to 390 million-year-old sedimentary rock from the Mississippian and Devonian periods has been exposed.

The Allegheny National Forest is smack in the middle of Pennsylvania's oil and gas field, where some 6,000 wells still extract these fossil fuels. The fuel's high paraffin content makes it prized as a lubricant. Roughly 100,000 wells have been emptied, and most of these remain unplugged.

Wildlife. Two centuries ago, hemlock and beech covered 58 percent of the forest. Sugar maple filled 13 percent of the canopy, and white pine occupied 6 percent, mostly along river bottoms. Today, hemlocks and beeches compose just 7 percent of the trees, sugar maple 7 percent, and white pine less than one-tenth of a percent. Black cherry and red maple, trees virtually nonexistent in the original forest, are now dominant, spreading over 60 percent of the forest. Eighty percent of the world's black cherry timber stands in Allegheny National Forest. The hallowed hemlocks and white pines at Heart's Content are really anomalous to the whole picture.

Though many giant pines at Heart's Content appear vigorous, their glory years may be behind them. Pine sprouts need direct sunlight and open space and cannot grow in the shadow of their parents. Self-perpetuating climax trees such as hemlock, whose seedlings rise everywhere, and some hardwoods are gradually taking over the site.

Humans are to blame for changing the composition of the forest. The original thatch was wiped out during the industrial revolution to fuel railroads, mines, leather making, charcoal, and lumber and chemical industries. Wood was also needed by the burgeoning human populations for shelter and farms. By 1920 the slopes were depleted. Wildfires burned for weeks, flooding became common, woodland creatures disappeared. Gone were shade-tolerant and long-living trees like hemlocks and beeches. Sun-loving, short-lived newcomers like black cherry, red maple, and black birch grew quickly on the barren slopes. Oaks and aspens also improved their lot. A diminished deer herd at the time also abetted the newcomers. The forest service tries to maintain the new composition.

The Allegheny now has fifty species of trees, including yellow birch, cucumber magnolia, shagbark hickory, speckled alder, aspen, mountain holly, butternut, hazelnut, sycamore, basswood, hawthorn, and witch hazel. Many beeches at Heart's Content succumb to a fungal disease called beech bark scale, which appears as tiny white dots on the smooth bark.

This immense national forest supports a vast number of plants and animals, including 217 bird species, 46 mammals, and 71 kinds of fish. Imperiled raptors such as the bald eagle, goshawk, and Cooper's, red-shouldered, and sharp-shinned hawks nest here. Ospreys, endangered birds, stop during their migrations. Other fliers, all local rarities, include the saw-whet owl, great blue heron, American bittern, great egret, Swainson's thrush, eastern bluebird, grasshopper sparrow, raven, yellow-bellied flycatcher, and bobolink. According to the Allegheny National Forest's bird checklist, the cedar waxwing, scarlet tanager, wild turkey, wood thrush, ruffed grouse, American redstart, and rufous-sided towhee are abundant. Two dozen kinds of wood warblers nest here, notably the common yellowthroat, northern parula, and chestnut-sided, black-throated green, and black-throated blue warblers.

In some locations, deer have become a nuisance, devouring much of the understory, except for ferns, and creating a browse line about 6 feet off the ground. Their overabundance may be causing declines in the populations of bear, turkey, and grouse, which depend on a flourishing understory for shelter, concealment, and food. Oak, ash, cherry, tulip tree, hemlock, and maple seedlings are all deer favorites, and their absence makes space for less tasty plants like ferns, striped maple, sedges, and beeches. For all its grandeur, Heart's Content Scenic Area lacks a thriving understory of trees to replace the giants that fall.

Aside from deer, keen observers might see a beaver, bobcat, mink, red fox, weasel, snowshoe hare, mole, or black bear, which is a midnight raider around campgrounds. River otters and fishers were reintroduced in the 1990s.

At least eighteen species of amphibians and reptiles slink through the forest, including the poisonous timber rattlesnake (PA rare) and copperhead. Northern water snakes and various ribbon snakes hang out near streams. Watery habitats attract the dusky salamander, pickerel frog, and bullfrog. Wooded areas are favored by the slimy salamander, coal skink, and box turtle.

In the forest's streams, lakes, and ponds, fishermen go for trout, walleye, smallmouth bass, muskellunge, salmon, channel catfish, crappie, northern pike, and yellow perch. The Allegheny brook lamprey, Tippecanoe darter, long-headed darter, slenderhead darter, brook stickleback, and southern redbelly dace, all imperiled in Pennsylvania, are also found in the Allegheny River watershed. Two federally endangered freshwater mussels, northern riffleshell and club-shell, survive in some of the forest's streams. The Allegheny National Forest has 770 miles of year-round cold-water streams and 43 miles of warm-water streams.

Deer haven't eaten all the wildflowers. Look for jack-in-the-pulpit, blue cohosh, Dutchman's breeches, carrion flower, Indian cucumber root, wood sorrel, Solomon's seal, and chickweed. Along the Little Drummer Historical Pathway, look for nannyberry, purple-fringed orchid, ox-eye daisy, sticktights, green orchis, marsh marigold, pick-erelweed, blueberry, bird's-foot trefoil, and bunchberry. In places, ferns grow in thick patches. Common varieties are maidenhair, bracken, hay-scented, cinnamon, marginal shield, and sensitive ferns.

A peculiar by-product of earlier logging has been the develop-ment of wet savannas, which now constitute about 4 percent of the Allegheny National Forest. The underground water once transpired back into the atmosphere via the big trees. When flat areas were clear-cut a century ago, the water table rose to the topsoil level or higher. Tree seedlings could not regenerate in the soggy openings, but grasses, ferns, shrubs, and wetland vegetation thrived. Young trees encroaching from the edge are slowly reclaiming the savannas, but the forest service plans to maintain some of these areas because they support unique biological communities.

History. When Europeans first entered the region now called the Allegheny National Forest, people of the Seneca tribe, one of the nations in the Iroquois Confederacy, had established settlements along the Allegheny River and its tributaries. Refugees from other war-torn tribes, the Munsees and Delawares, also settled among the Senecas, whose stronghold was Goshgoshing, at the confluence of the Allegheny River and Hickory Creek.

During the American Revolution, the Iroquois sided with the British. To shatter the confederacy, the Americans sent raiders from New York and Fort Pitt in the summer of 1779. The main force, led by Gen. John Sullivan ransacked towns and massacred villagers in western New York. A diversionary force commanded by Col. Daniel Brodhead burned a town near Goshgoshing where lived Gyantwahia, or Cornplanter, the son of a Dutch trader and Seneca royalty. Brod-head's men also torched 500 acres of corn, skirmished with Indian and British forces at Thompson's Island (now part of Allegheny River Islands Wilderness), and retreated before the Senecas could rally. Brodhead's probe was the only military action during the Revolution in northwestern Pennsylvania.

After the war, Cornplanter, also known as John Abeel or O'Bail, helped restore peace between the tribes and the United States. For his diplomacy, Pennsylvania gave the chief three tracts of land on the upper Allegheny. He sold two tracts and lived on the third, roughly 600 acres along the river south of the New York border. His village, Jenuchshadego, and two islands he owned disappeared when Kinzua Dam created the Allegheny Reservoir. Cornplanter's descendants live on the Seneca Nation Reservation in New York.

Cornplanter's death at age eighty-six in 1836 roughly marked the start of exploitation in the Allegheny Valley. The area's natural resources both above and below ground were plundered during the industrial revolution, reducing the forest to stumps, changing its composition, causing wildfires, fouling rivers and streams, and wiping out some wildlife species, such as deer. It also inspired reform. The Allegheny National Forest was created in 1923.

Cornplanter's old realm has rebounded under the management of the forest service. In the 1930s workers hired by the Civilian Conservation Corps built much of the recreation infrastructure and reforested slopes in the national forest. The U.S. Army Corps of Engineers finished Kinzua Dam in 1965, creating the 12,000-acre Allegheny Reservoir across two states. Ecological improvements led to national natural landmark designations for the Heart's Content and Tionesta Scenic Areas in the 1970s, followed by national scenic river titles for the Allegheny and Clarion Rivers. The forest service estimated that in 1997 people spent 3.3 million recreation visitor days in the Allegheny National Forest (one recreation visitor day equals twelve hours' use by one person).

3

Anders Run Natural Area

Think of the conifers here as heirs apparent. In a century or so, the eastern white pines flanking this creek will be as impressive as those standing today in nearby Allegheny National Forest and Cook Forest State Park. Already, many of these second-growth evergreens would qualify as main masts for tall wooden ships. Barring disease, natural catastrophe, or a change in human heart, these will be the big trees gawked at by our great-great-grandchildren and their descendents.

Ownership. Pennsylvania Department of Conservation and Natural Resources, Bureau of Forestry.

Size. 96 acres.

Physiographic Region. High Plateau.

Nearby Natural Attractions. Allegheny National Forest, the Allegheny River, and Tamarack Bog National Natural Landmark (State Game Lands 197).

Features. Three parking areas provide access to a 2-mile loop trail. My journey started at the easternmost lot, located on Dunn's Eddy Road, just north of the junction with Allegheny Springs Road, which runs parallel to Anders Run and has two parking locations. The well-marked trail, blazed by yellow diamonds, stays close to Anders Run and features wooden bridges and benches for rest and wildlife

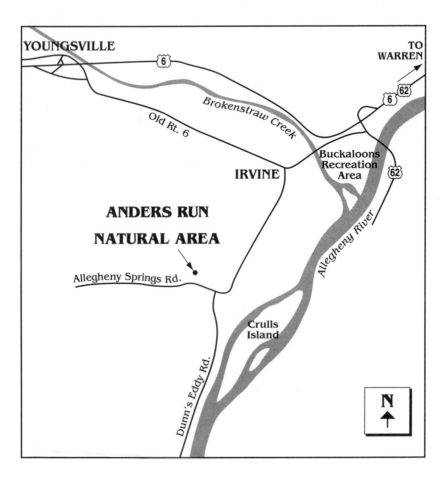

observation. At one point, the trail edges close to private property owned by local lumber interests. Compare the skinny trees on their side of the line to the beasts in the natural area. Not surprisingly, chain saws revved beyond the boundary during my mid-July hike.

Anders Run is part of Cornplanter State Forest. Another segment of the state forest is located in Forest County, near Tionesta. For more information, contact the Pennsylvania Bureau of Forestry, Cornplanter State Forest, 323 N. State St., North Warren, PA 16365, telephone (814) 723-0262.

Geology. Torrents of meltwater flowing from the Wisconsinan glacier some 15,000 years ago created the Allegheny and many of its local tributaries. Anders Run, which flows east just 4 miles from York Mountain to the river, may be an exception. It appears to be a young side-cut tributary that deepened headward, from mouth to source, as the Allegheny also deepened. The boulders along the trail are sandstone made in the Devonian Period about 375 million years ago.

Wildlife. The Bureau of Forestry's pamphlet on the preserve sets the stage: "The tract was logged sometime during the first two decades of the 1800s for the first and last time. Today, this second-growth forest has white pine and hemlock trees 170 years old, many standing 120 feet high with trunk diameters of over 40 inches. . . . If the [original] trees of Anders Run Natural Area had never been cut, the white pines [today] would be dead or dying, being replaced inexorably by climax species of hemlock and northern hardwoods, a process now occurring in the virgin timber stands at Heart's Content Scenic Area (Allegheny National Forest) and Cook Forest State Park. Left alone over the next several centuries, the Anders Run Natural Area will serve for future generations as a remnant window to what much of Pennsylvania looked like."

The key words are "looked like." The bureau's forthright experiment in "restoration forestry" will probably give us pines that "look like" the ones in Penn's Woods, but it won't be the reconstituted primeval forest, complete with all its biological baggage. The site is too small and too disturbed for that—and naturalists and foresters know that. Still, we preserve what we can, regenerate what we can, and hope for the best.

Anders Run has more than pines and hemlocks. Growing rates are faster than average in the hollow, thanks to fertile soil, and acorns from its robust red oaks are sent to state tree nurseries for seedlings. The preserve also has white oak, beeches, hickories, sassafras, and black cherry.

Life on the forest floor is enriched by many plant species, including skunk cabbage, foamflower, painted and red trilliums, pink lady's slipper, Solomon's seal, white Clintonia, several kinds of violets, wild ginger, bunchberry, Indian cucumber root, white baneberry, and blue cohosh. Clusters of Indian pipe, a drooping, white saprophytic plant, are easy to see on the dark woodland ground. Look for lush colonies of ferns in summer, notably New York, Christmas, sensitive, cinnamon, maidenhair, common polypody, and several wood ferns. Use a powerful hand lens or a 50mm camera lens to get a close-up look at the moss on boulders.

In spite of the preserve's billing as a haven for the raucous red squirrel, I heard only one bark at me. Nevertheless, evidence of their presence—the shucks and husks of pine cones at favorite feeding spots—is everywhere. The red squirrel is the smallest of the diurnal tree squirrels. (The smaller flying squirrels are nocturnal.) Unlike gray and fox squirrels, which bury each prize, red squirrels store food in large caches, such as hollow logs. Anders Run is ideal for red squirrels, which bed down in conifers and gorge themselves on the ripening cones of white pines. Chipmunks also are abundant. Birders will find pine siskins and red crossbills in the evergreens, plus brown creepers and black-capped chickadees.

The Western Pennsylvania Conservancy purchased the adjacent Irvine Flats Tract, a 295-acre parcel bordering the Allegheny River between Anders Run and Brokenstraw Creek. This broad, alluvial floodplain, mostly former farmland, has forest buffers of sycamores, silver maple, black cherry, and black walnut.

History. The former homestead of William Irvine, a Revolutionary War general, congressman, and Constitutional Convention delegate, still stands on Dunn's Eddy Road. Irvine, for whom the nearby village was named, surveyed Warren and Erie Counties and most of the areas around Franklin and Waterford. The home is a private residence today.

Preservation of the site began in 1963, when landowner National Forge Company announced a timber sale. The news prompted the Northern Allegheny Conservation Association to ask the local business firm to spare the noble pines along Anders Run. The company agreed and in 1987 sold the place at half the market price to the Western Pennsylvania Conservancy. Funds totaling more than a quarter of the sale were provided by the DeFrees Family Foundation and Northern Allegheny Conservation Association, both based in Warren. Ownership was later transferred to the Pennsylvania Department of Conservation and Natural Resources, Bureau of Forestry, which designated the site a natural area.

Asbury Woods Nature Center

Many wealthy people bequeath their fortunes to the arts or to charitable causes. Otto Behrend, on the other hand, gave much of his booty to benefit the school kids of Millcreek Township, near Erie. The property has changed from dairyland to woodland since the papermill magnate bought it in 1921. Today more than 60,000 visitors take advantage of Behrend's generosity.

Ownership. Millcreek Township School District.

Size. 50 acres.

Physiographic Region. Coastal Lowland.

Nearby Natural Attractions. Presque Isle State Park, the David M. Roderick Wildlife Reserve, and Siegel Marsh.

Features. First-time visitors usually start their journey at the Interpretive Cottage, the former vacation home of Dr. Otto Behrend. It features changing nature exhibits, a wildlife room with live amphibians and reptiles, a gift shop, and offices. Gardeners should check out the colonial-style herb and flower gardens outside the building. A large picnic shelter doubles as an outdoor classroom.

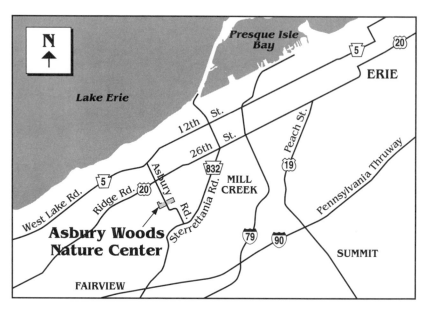

Six interconnecting trails totaling 2 miles wind through woods, wetlands, and meadows. One popular path, Grandfather Tree Trail, passes a 200-year-old red oak. A one-third-mile barrier-free board-walk path stops at a vernal pond. A 200-acre greenway trail will soon link the nature center to the James Wildlife Preserve of Mercyhurst College, Asbury Community Park, two school campuses, and the nature center's adjunct site, Brown's Farm, on Sterrettania Road.

The nature center is open from 9 A.M. to 5 P.M. Monday through Saturday and noon to 5 P.M. Sunday, April 1 through October 31. It closes at 4 P.M. November 1 through March 31 and is closed on holidays. Trails are open every day. Nature-related programs are offered for adults as well as schoolchildren. For more information, contact Asbury Woods Nature Center, 4105 Asbury Rd., Erie, PA 16506, telephone (814) 835-5356.

Geology. The coastal lowland, or Lake Erie Plains, is a ribbon of turf several miles wide along Lake Erie. It is a speck of a larger flatland known as the Central Lowland, which encompasses the Great Lakes basin, the St. Lawrence River, Lake Champlain, the Mohawk-Hudson Valleys, and the Great Plains from Saskatchewan to Texas. In northwestern Pennsylvania, this glaciated plain rises gently from 570 feet at lake level to 800 feet at the base of the Erie escarpment. The incline is interrupted by the beach ridges of ice-age lakes Warren and Whittlesey.

Asbury Woods continues a little deception to pique interest. A landmark rock once thought to be a meteorite turned out to be a common Canadian erratic orphaned by the Wisconsinan glacier 10,000 years ago. In 1969 a geologist declared that the odd lump was hornblende, an igneous rock from the Canadian Shield.

Wildlife. Asbury Woods has diverse habitats ranging from field to forest, with small ponds, swamps and creeks. Birders have spotted seventy-three species, including the American bittern, Cooper's hawk, screech owl, wild turkey, chimney swift, pileated and red-bellied woodpeckers, great-crested flycatcher, tree swallow, white-breasted nuthatch, Swainson's thrush, indigo bunting, Baltimore oriole, scarlet tanager, goldfinch, and yellow-rumped, blue-winged, cerulean, hooded, and black-and-white warblers.

Ten amphibians and nine reptiles reside here. Snapping and painted turtles inhabit the pond, along with bullfrogs, green frogs, and leopard frogs. The woods are home to the spotted salamander, gray tree frog, American toad, and the common black rat, eastern milk, and northern water snakes.

Twenty-three kinds of mammals have been seen, notably the coyote, short-tailed shrew, longtail weasel, muskrat, little brown bat, northern flying squirrel, and the omnipresent white-tailed deer.

The woods contains sixty-eight species of trees and shrubs. Many are pioneers in reverting fields, such as four varieties of dogwood, staghorn sumac, redbud, European buckthorn, hawthorn, honey locust, eastern red cedar, and bigtooth aspen. The evergreens, apples, and Chinese chestnuts were planted during Behrend's reign. Look for black, white, green, and pumpkin ashes; red, white, scarlet, and pin oaks; sugar, red, silver, and Norway maples; chokecherry and black, pin, and fire cherries; and American, English and slippery elms. Other trees include sycamores, cottonwood, beeches, hemlocks, shagbark hickory, basswood, black walnut, and butternut. Trillium, trout lily, jack-in-the-pulpit, witch hazel, and wild grape thrive in the understory, and duckweed and cattail grace the wetlands.

History. The Eriez people lived here until they were driven away by invading Iroquois in the mid-seventeenth century. From 1797 to 1915 this property was owned by the Nicholson family and managed as a farm. Martha Thompson of Detroit bought the place in 1915, but in 1921 she sold it to Dr. Otto Frederick Behrend, cofounder of the Hammermill Paper Company. Behrend used the farm as a summer retreat and to plant native and imported trees, notably Chinese chestnuts.

Behrend bequeathed his 110-acre farm to the Millcreek Township School District when he died in 1957. Development of half the site as a nature education center got under way in the late 1960s, following a National Audubon Society land-use study. In 1995 the school district received 25 acres of adjoining land.

<hr/>

5

Barking Slopes Wildlife Preserve

Fourteenmile Islands

The Allegheny River looks like a moat beneath this citadel of rock and trees. Preservationists say the site protects the last and best cliffside habitat along the lower Allegheny River. An island in the moving moat may become a beachhead for returning mollusks, now that the river is getting cleaner.

Ownership. Allegheny Land Trust owns Barking Slopes. Fourteenmile Islands (Upper and Lower) are owned by the Pennsylvania General Services Administration.

Size. The preserve is 77 acres, the islands about 50 acres.

Physiographic Region. Pittsburgh Low Plateau.

Nearby Natural Attractions. Beechwood Farms Nature Reserve, Dead Man's Hollow Wildlife Preserve, Boyce Park, Todd Sanctuary, and Frick Woods Nature Reserve.

Features. Access is tricky. From the Hulton Road–Coxcomb Road traffic signal in Oakmont, go east on Coxcomb Road 1.3 miles to a pulloff in front of a Duquesne Power substation and farm market. Don't block the service road. Walk to the substation. Just before the fence, take a service road left to the back of the substation. Look for the improved trail begun by the land trust in 1998. The path leads to the cliffs above the Allegheny River, then turns left (west) following the edge of the bluff nearly to the golf course in Oakmont. To the east, Coxcomb Road (SR 2082) merges with Shady Road and Logans Ferry Road. Climbing the cliffs is unlawful and foolhardy. No facilities are present.

Upper and Lower Fourteenmile Islands can be reached by boat, if necessary. They are separated by Lock and Dam Number 3, operated by the U.S. Army Corps of Engineers. They also can be observed from the cliff or along the shore. The pillars of I-76 and railroad bridges sink in the lower island.

For more information, contact the Allegheny Land Trust, 425 Sixth Ave., Suite 800, Pittsburgh, PA 15219, telephone (412) 350-4666.

Geology. Barking Slopes is characterized by near-vertical north-facing slopes fronting the Allegheny River. The slopes run for several miles. Elevation ranges from 780 feet at river level to 1,300 feet. Black's

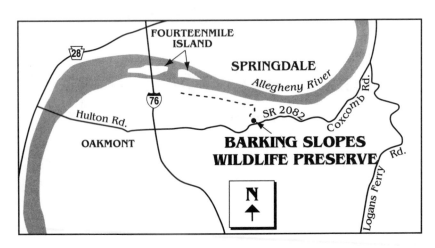

Run has ground a zigzagging, 2.5-mile slit through the bluff, angling southeast to northwest. The creek discharges into the Allegheny River by Upper Fourteenmile Island and a little upstream from Lock and Dam Number 3. Construction of this lock and dam in the 1950s divided Fourteenmile Island into upper and lower islands. Their foundations consist of gravel, cobble, and sand piled by shifting river sediments.

Other short creeks, cut perpendicular to the Allegheny, tumble over waterfalls composed of 300-million-year-old sandstone slabs that date back to the Pennsylvanian Period.

Wildlife. American beech, red and white oaks, sugar maple, eastern hemlock, ironwood, American basswood, hickories, white ash, mountain laurel, and hornbeam are represented in the preserve's blended woodland. Herbaceous species beneath the forest canopy include large-flowered trillium, red trillium, blue cohosh, hepatica, and jack-in-the-pulpit. Wild columbine indicates alkaline soils derived from limestone or dolomite.

Previous owners selectively logged Black's Run in the last two decades. Trees on the north-facing slope are small due to the extremely steep terrain and long-ago fires set by ember-spitting railroad engines.

Rock outcrops festooned with ferns and mosses seem to be worlds unto themselves. Before entering the woods, hikers pass burdock, teasel, multiflora rose, and goldenrod stalks bearing galls, rounded growths in which larval midges develop.

The upper island hosts floodplain plants such as silver maple, willows, silky dogwood, false nettle, Jerusalem artichoke, and pale jewelweed. Cottonwood dominates the canopy of the lower island, but sycamores and silver maple are making headway. The shores and shoals of these islands will provide habitats for the small fish and mussels that return to the less polluted river.

Birders may spot birds riding thermals near the cliff, such as hawks, geese, and vultures. Woodland songbirds can be seen and heard in the forest. The islands attract gulls and other waterbirds. Share your findings with the land trust.

History. In early 1997 Property Venture, a subsidiary of DQE, Inc., donated this 77-acre parcel, which was a farm three decades ago, to the land trust. The land trust was converting an old farm lane into a hiking trail. A plant inventory is under way.

Bear Run Nature Reserve

Fallingwater

This sprawling reserve protects one of Pennsylvania's most pristine streams and one of the world's most celebrated homes. Come here in early July, when great rhododendron and mountain laurel, in full regalia, escort the water of Bear Run and Beaver Run into the Youghiogheny River. While thousands descend upon Fallingwater, an architectural mecca within the reserve, the trails branching from a nature center half a mile away remain uncrowded, quiet, and rewarding.

Ownership. Western Pennsylvania Conservancy.

Size. 5,000 acres. The grounds include Fallingwater, the landmark home designed by architect Frank Lloyd Wright.

Physiographic Region. Allegheny Mountains.

Nearby Natural Attractions. Ohiopyle State Park, Fort Necessity National Battlefield, Friendship Hill National Historic Site, Quebec Run Wild Area, and Laurel Caverns.

Features. Bear Run Nature Reserve begins half a mile north of Fallingwater on PA 381. Nineteen color-and-shape-coded trails totaling 20 miles explore the property. Most of them are easy to moderate in difficulty, with stretches of soggy and rocky terrain. Well-crafted, easy-to-read trail guides are available in the parking lot above the nature education center. The routes wander through hardwood ridges and pine groves, along mountain creeks, across meadows, and through fragrant thickets of rhododendron and mountain laurel.

Hike the Arbutus, Laurel Run, and Rhododendron Trails when the rhododendrons bloom in early July. The Arbutus path crosses tumbling Bear Run four times via wooden bridges. For glimpses of the Youghiogheny River gorge, follow the 2.5-mile Peninsula Trail on the west side of PA 381. It leads to two vistas in Ohiopyle State Park, where you can watch—and hear—boaters running Dimple Rapids. Laurel Run and

Bear Run Trails follow their namesakes. Laurel Run Trail boasts impressive rock outcrops on the east side of PA 381 and peeks into Laurel Glen, a steep-walled gorge and waterfall graced by mountain laurel and rhododendron on the west side of the highway. Both scenic streams wash off the western slope of Laurel Ridge. The Rhododendron and Bear Run paths follow overgrown jeep trails. Backpackers can pitch tents at campsites on the Peninsula, Warbler, Ridge, Snow Bunny, and Hemlock Trails. Sign the registry at the parking lot before camping. Reservations are required for the group camp on Snow Bunny Trail.

For more information, contact Bear Run Nature Reserve, Mill Run, PA 15464, telephone (724) 329-8501, e-mail fallingwater@paconserve.org. (Same address and phone number for Fallingwater.)

Geology. The clear, chilly, spring-fed water of Bear Run, a state scenic river, begins to gurgle atop Laurel Ridge, at an elevation of roughly 2,400 feet. By the time it reaches PA 381, having traveled 3 miles, it has descended 1,000 feet, sometimes rushing over small stairways of cascades. It drops nearly 300 feet in its final mile, the most precipitous leap being the one at Fallingwater. Beaver Run, a tributary, is also a state scenic river.

Laurel Ridge is an anticline, or elongated ridge, stretching from West Virginia to north of Johnstown. The collision of continental plates that formed the Appalachian Mountains to the east 290 million years ago, known as the Alleghenian Orogeny, also lifted and folded land to the west. Technically, the ridge is considered part of the Allegheny Plateau, not the Valley and Ridge Province, because its sedimentary bedrock, though wrinkled and slanted, essentially remained stacked in its original beds. Erosion since the orogeny has produced the mountainous terrain typical of the area.

The sandstone used in the construction of Fallingwater came from quarries nearby. Most of it is Pottsville sandstone dating back 300 million years to the Pennsylvanian Era.

Paradise Overlook on the Peninsula Trail shines on Dimple and Swimmers Rapids in the Youghiogheny River. The dimple is a large chunk of sandstone with frothy water crashing and splashing into it. Boaters have to bear right of the rock, then navigate Class III to IV rapids.

Wildlife. Bear Run's watershed is the focal point of this preserve. Occasionally a black bear drinks from Bear Run, but the sightings are few and far between. Beavers once colonized Beaver Run, but I saw no signs of this furbearing rodent. Brook trout look like ghostly shadows in the calm pools. In narrow places, the brooks rush through tunnels of mountain laurel and great rhododendrons.

White, red, black, and chestnut oaks thrive in their likely habitats, as do black birch, eastern hemlock, American beech, red maple, tulip tree, striped maple, sassafras, black gum, cucumber magnolia, bigtooth aspen, and white pine. The place is brightened by wildflowers such as the painted trillium, pink lady's slipper, trailing arbutus, Canada mayflower, halbert-leaved violet, spring beauty, and wintergreen, or teaberry.

Songbirds trill from the boughs above Bear Run. Look and listen for hooded and black-throated blue warblers, northern waterthrush, scarlet tanager, red-eyed vireo, ruby-throated hummingbird, golden-crowned kinglet, black-capped chickadee, cardinal, and wood thrush. Barred owls and great horned owls sometimes hoot from the dark pines during the day. Acorns attract wild turkeys, brush supports ruffed grouse, and woodcocks nest in the meadows. The overlooks on the Peninsula Trail offer views of migrating birds.

Rocky ledges along Laurel Run are suitable habitats for bobcats, bears, eastern wood rats, and snakes. White-tailed deer leave their prints just about everywhere.

History. In 1936, at the height of the Great Depression, a department store tycoon and an influential and flamboyant architect wrapped a rich man's residence around Bear Run's waterfalls. The home, Fallingwater, and its creator, Frank Lloyd Wright, became better known than the cascade. But a quarter century later, the owners abandoned their wooded realm to a caretaker conservancy.

These slopes had been logged, mined, and farmed by the time Edgar J. Kaufmann, owner of a Pittsburgh department store, bought them. Faint remnants of these activities can be seen along trails that once served as logging and wagon roads. During his reign, Kaufmann reforested some slopes with conifers, such as the pines by the nature center, and thinned out some hardwood stands.

In 1936 Kaufmann hired the acclaimed architect Frank Lloyd Wright to design a weekend retreat at Bear Run Falls. Kaufmann imagined a cottage looking at the falls, but Wright daringly put it horizontally atop the falls, to symbolically integrate humanity and nature.

The place served as a family residence until 1963, when Edgar Kaufmann, Jr., presented the house, contents, and grounds to the Western Pennsylvania Conservancy. Since then, the conservancy has constructed a visitors center, nature center for education programs, and trail system.

Bear Run and Beaver Run have been declared state scenic waterways by the Pennsylvania Department of Conservation and Natural Resources, and the U.S. Department of the Interior has designated Fallingwater a national historic landmark.

7

Beaver Creek Nature Area

Two decades ago, half a dozen conservation groups began transforming exhausted and abandoned farmland into wildlife sanctuary. Today, sixteen wetlands straddling Beaver Creek make this an inviting place for waterfowl and marsh creatures, including the beaver. Only 20 bird species showed up here in the early 1980s. Now 150 kinds stop for a visit. Consider this place an unfinished canvas.

Ownership. Clarion Conservation District. The Alliance for Wetlands and Wildlife, a nonprofit organization, maintains the site.

Size. 850 acres

Physiographic Region. Pittsburgh Low Plateau.

Nearby Natural Attractions. The Clarion River, a state scenic river, and Cook Forest State Park.

Features. Your landmarks are a large pavilion and parking lot on the north side of PA 208. From here, a mowed trail leads a few hundred yards to a wildlife observation blind. Before reaching the platform, a path breaking west hooks around a pond. Both paths total half a mile tops.

A better trail is south of the state highway. A path across the road takes you to twin ponds. Stay on the west embankment of the ponds. At the south end of the second pond, the trail goes into woods and climbs a hill to a picnic spot. At the summit, either backtrack or trace the sometimes mowed route that winds across the grassy slope back to the highway.

The site is open daily. For more information, contact Clarion Conservation District, RR 3, P.O. Box 265, Clarion, PA 16214, telephone (814) 226-6126.

Geology. Beaver Creek is a 7-mile waterway that feeds the Clarion River a few miles east of its merger with the Allegheny River. The wetland is flanked by round-shouldered, open farmland. The bedrock beneath the creek dates back 300 million years to the Pennsylvanian Period.

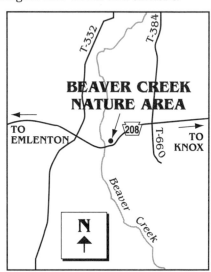

25

Wildlife. Beaver Creek is a pilot project to show landowners how to take land of little agricultural value and develop it into a wildlife area. Plaques on the north side of the nature area explain the advantages of contour farming, preventing streambank erosion, and conservation tillage. The demonstration project also stresses how to increase water quantity and improve its quality. To that end, sixteen ponds amounting to more than 199 acres have been constructed.

Beaver Creek caters to wetland, woodland, and meadow creatures. Furbearers include mink, muskrats, and beavers. White-tailed deer, black bear, wild turkeys, gray squirrels, and ruffed grouse use all the habitats here.

Birders can search for the wood duck, Canada goose, eastern bluebird, and barred, great horned, and screech owls. Rarities like the endangered osprey and bald eagle occasionally perch and hunt by the ponds. With these birds in mind, nesting platforms have been placed in several ponds. Wood duck and bluebird boxes are scattered throughout the area. Woodland warblers grow in diversity and number yearly. Local Audubon members keep tabs on the avian visitors.

Aquatic habitats have been enriched with plantings of sago pond weed, duck potato, wild celery, wild bulrush, buttonbush, and arrowhead. Cattails, black birch, and white pine also grow here. Several trees cradle the cottony cribs of tent caterpillars. The Pennsylvania Fish and Boat Commission stocks the ponds with largemouth bass and bluegills. Hunting and fishing are permitted, but trapping is prohibited.

History. The Alliance for Wetlands and Wildlife, Knox Nature Club, and Clarion Conservation District began this undertaking with the U.S. Department of Agriculture's Natural Resources Conservation Service (NRCS) in the early 1980s. The local groups raised funds and negotiated with landowners, while the NRCS prepared designs and supervised construction of water control structures, or ponds and wetlands. Later, the Seneca Rock Audubon Society started monitoring birds on the improved habitat. The U.S. Fish and Wildlife Service and the Pennsylvania Bureau of Forestry also have gotten into the act. More than $1.5 million has been raised for land purchases. A large barn at the edge of the property is being converted into a classroom and workshop. Future plans call for the creation of a 90-acre lake that will serve recreationists as well as wildlife such as ospreys and bald eagles. A cold-water spill that will cool Beaver Creek into a trout fishery is also in the works.

8

Beechwood Farms
Nature Reserve

This old farm is a refreshing oasis in the sprawling suburbia of Pittsburgh. It serves as a clubhouse for local birdwatchers, a nature education center, a wildlife sanctuary, and a respite for thousands of visitors annually. Several short trails lead to varied habitats, including a pond, pine grove, meadows, and hardwoods.

Ownership. The reserve is owned by the Western Pennsylvania Conservancy, except for 4 acres that serve as headquarters for the Audubon Society of Western Pennsylvania, the site manager.

Size. 134 acres.

Physiographic Region. Pittsburgh Low Plateau.

Nearby Natural Attractions. Flower and Wildlife Preserve (Trillium Trail), Frick Woods Nature Reserve, Boyce Park, North Park, Harrison Hills Park, Barking Slopes Preserve, Dead Man's Hollow Wildlife Preserve, and Bradford Woods (State Game Lands 203).

Features. First stop is the Evans Nature Center, the home of the Flynn family in the 1870s. Today the house and adjoining building contain meeting rooms, offices, a gift shop, a library, nature exhibits, a wildlife observation area, an auditorium, and rest rooms. Outdoors there's an herb garden. At the nature center, you can obtain a map, trail guides, and other information on the sanctuary. The center is open Tuesday to Saturday 9 A.M. to 5 P.M., and Sunday 1 to 5 P.M. Trails totaling 5 miles depart from this learning center.

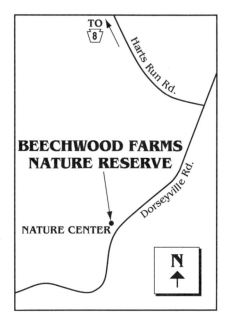

A recommended route along the perimeter, starting and ending at the nature center, includes portions of the Spring Hollow, Woodland, Meadowview, and Pine Hollow Trails, roughly 2 miles. Consult the trail map and signposts. A worthwhile

27

detour is the TreeTop on the Spring Hollow Trail, a unique wooden platform in the forest canopy. Side paths from the Woodland and Meadowview Trails lead to vistas of the neighborhood's rolling terrain. Pine Hollow Trail, the least trodden track, features solitude and a diminutive waterfall on Pine Hollow Run. Meadowview Trail crosses a lane to private homes and passes beside a windmill that produces electricity for the nature center. If children in your group enjoy interpretive hikes, stick to the Spring Hollow Walk and take along a written guide that can be purchased in the nature center. Staff naturalists also lead nature hikes for schools and groups. Trails stay open dawn to dusk.

For more information, contact Beechwood Farms Nature Reserve, 614 Dorseyville Rd., Pittsburgh, PA 15238, telephone (412) 963-6100.

Geology. The terrain here is undulating due to etching by the intermittent headwaters of Harts Run, draining from the pond behind the nature center, and Pine Hollow Run. Harts Run trickles into Little Pine Creek and the Allegheny River. Relief changes 150 feet within the property, the high points being the Woodland Trail vista and the nature center.

Wildlife. This pastoral land is recovering from past agricultural use. A young, second-growth deciduous forest is rising on former cropland and is slowly overtaking a pine plantation on the southwestern portion of the property. Reverting meadows, shrub thickets, orchards, and mowed open areas add to the natural diversity of the site.

A 40-acre native plant sanctuary established in 1985 provides a refuge for indigenous plants. The reserve has hundreds of bloomers and berry makers. Look for flowers on dogwood, Hercules' club, and apple trees. Meadows produce milkweed, the host plant for monarch butterflies, plus goldenrod, butterfly weed, bindweed, and Canada thistle, whose seeds are prized by goldfinches. Forests along Spring Hollow Walk and Oak Forest Footpath reveal large-flowered and purple trillium, rue anemone, jack-in-the-pulpit, wild geranium, mayapple, Virginia creeper, spring beauty, Solomon's seal, skunk cabbage, and several kinds of violets. By summer, these are overshadowed by the plumes of spinulose woodfern and Christmas fern. Try to find a colorful slime mold draped across a fallen pine.

Towering above the scene are white, black, and red oaks, tulip tree; black cherry; red, silver, and sugar maples; beech; sycamore; hemlock; shagbark hickory; arrow-leaved viburnum; spicebush; buckthorn; staghorn sumac; witch hazel; elm; aspen; hawthorn; red, white, and scotch pines; spruces; sour gum; elderberry; white ash; and sassafras. Gypsy moth infestation has taken victims.

Such habitat diversity attracts a wide range of birds. Mixed oak groves shelter the wood thrush, scarlet tanager, yellow-shafted flicker, rufous-sided towhee, blue-gray gnatcatcher, ovenbird, hooded warblers, and American redstart. Other warblers include the yellow, Kentucky, and common yellowthroat, which nest here, and the black-throated green, yellow-rumped, bay-breasted, and chestnut-sided, all migrants. Multiflora rose in the meadows, which is cut on a three-year rotation, conceals the prairie warbler and yellow-breasted chat. The pond and rills bring the great blue heron (PA threatened), green heron, belted kingfisher, and spotted sandpiper within easily spotting distance. The finch-size pine siskins sometimes nest and visit feeders with cardinals, nuthatches, chickadees, sparrows, and blue jays. Hawks occasionally circle above the reserve, ready to prey on the smaller songbirds Red-tailed hawks have nested atop oaks on the Spring Hollow Walk.

Trail guides encourage hikers to find tent caterpillars, American toads, fall webworms, daddy longlegs spiders, katydids, dragonflies, sow bugs, chipmunks, and the tracks of raccoons and white-tailed deer. An overweight herd of these ungulates roams casually through the grounds, even to the bird feeders behind the nature center. Quiet, slow-moving walkers can approach within 25 yards.

History. A century ago Beechwood was a 400-acre dairy farm owned by Sen. William Flynn. In 1976 the Western Pennsylvania Conservancy acquired the original 90 acres as a gift from Mrs. John F. Walton, Jr., and Mr. and Mrs. Joshua Whetzel. Additional purchases increased the parcel to its present size. The conservancy deeded 4 acres and the farmhouse–turned–nature center to the longtime site manager, Audubon Society of Western Pennsylvania, in 1989.

9

Blacklick Valley Natural Area

Blacklick Creek cuts through the slumping northern shoulders of Laurel Ridge and Chestnut Ridge and then across generous rolling farmland before delivering its water into arteries that will carry it to a tropical sea. Given time, this chunk of newly preserved land will recover some of its former glory.

Ownership. Indiana County Parks.

Size. 675 acres.

Physiographic Region. Allegheny Mountains.

Nearby Natural Attractions. Yellow Creek State Park, Buttermilk Falls Natural Area, Conemaugh Gorge, Blue Spruce, Hemlock Lake, and Pine Ridge County Parks.

Features. Blacklick Valley Natural Area consists of three tracts. The contiguous Caldwell and Clarke Run tracts, which total 413 acres and are north of Blacklick Creek, are undeveloped and are closed to the public except for the county's 12-mile Ghost Town Trail, a rail-to-trail greenway for hiking and biking that passes between the north creek bank and SR 2012. Dilltown, roughly 2 miles west of the preserve at the junction of SR 2012 and PA 403, is the western terminus of the hike-bike trail. The 262-acre Parker Tract, straddling the south bank of Blacklick Creek at the end of McFeaters Road, features nearly 5 miles of trails that visit a bottomland forest, creek, wet meadows, beech-maple upland forest, and Christmas tree farms.

From the crushed stone parking lot, most folks head for the stream via the blue-blazed Blacklick Trail. The 0.9-mile path hugs the south bank of the creek until it reaches a grove of Christmas spruces and pines, a lingering commercial venture in the preserve.

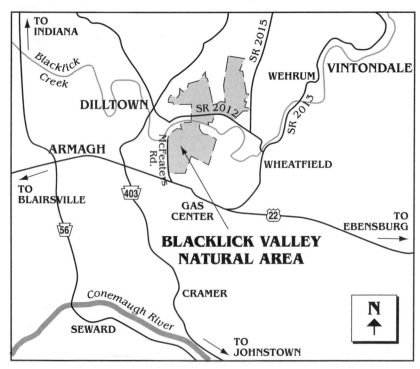

The 0.4 mile-long Candlestick Trail surrounds the stand. Continue ahead to Parker Lane, an abandoned road that once led to the homestead of a former landowner but now goes back to the parking area.

Collier Trail, 2.6 miles, branches from Parker Lane 100 yards past the evergreens and at its terminus at the parking lot. This orange-blazed path climbs a hardwood ridge to views 300 feet above the creek. The overlook is beside a charcoal flat, where colliers made charcoal for local iron furnaces.

In spring, the bottomland trails (Blacklick, Parker Lane, and connectors) become soggy, so many hikers choose the higher and drier Collier Trail, which is better for wildflowers anyway, until summer dries out the lower routes. Look for interpretive trail guides in a wooden box at the parking lot. Trails are open from sunrise to sunset.

For more information, contact Indiana County Parks, Blue Spruce Park Rd., Indiana, PA 15701, telephone (724) 463-8636.

Geology. Like the Conemaugh River to the south, Blacklick Creek cuts perpendicularly across parallel ridges named Chestnut and Laurel, formed about 290 million years ago during a mountain-building event called the Allegheny Orogeny. Blacklick joins the Conemaugh River west of Blairsville.

Each spring, Blacklick Creek typically floods its banks, abandons silted-over channels, and flows into new ones. Keen observers tramping the floodplain trails will notice a network of winding troughs, the former routes of Blacklick Creek. Wetland vegetation now occupies these oxbows, which often become shallow vernal ponds in spring.

When I explored Blacklick Creek in early autumn, it was sleepy, shallow, and wide. The water, however, had an orangish tint due to "yellow boy," an acidic pollutant from past coal mining. The poison has killed most aquatic life, making the creek one of the most severely damaged in the state. Restoration of wetlands on both sides of the stream may alleviate the problem.

Wildlife. Though Shawnee and Lenni-Lenape people settled, hunted, fished, and canoed in the Blacklick Valley, their use of its natural resources was gentle compared with the exploitation by conquering Euro-Americans in the eighteenth century. The original forest, probably an Appalachian oak-hickory community, was wiped out to support various human endeavors. Today second- and third-growth forest dominated by sugar maple and American beech covers most of the Parker Tract.

The natural area nearly straddles two forest communities. At the time of European settlement, it likely could have been described as an Appalachian oak forest dominated by white, chestnut, scarlet, and black oaks, along with tulip tree, bitternut hickory, and smatterings of sugar maple and beeches. Just a few miles east, on the slopes of

Laurel and Chestnut Ridges, a northern hardwood forest thrived, with sugar maple, beeches, white ash, and hemlocks ruling the canopy. Blacklick Valley Natural Area may be fluctuating between these biological communities.

Canopy vegetation in the floodplain consists of American beech, black cherry, red oak, yellow birch, and red maple. Black gum, white ash, and black birch stand on the rim of abandoned creek channels. The subcanopy is occupied by ironwood, spicebush, witch hazel, arrowwood, or maple-leaved viburnum, and hawthorn. Mayapple, skunk cabbage, club moss, and sensitive, wood, and New York ferns spread across the ground.

Low-lying farmland and Christmas tree stands abandoned twenty years ago are returning to successional meadows. The evergreens, now 10 to 20 feet high, share their plot with clusters of black cherry, crab apple, swamp white oak, black locust, and shingle oak. Taller Scotch and red pines, 50 to 60 feet, have dug in here too. Wild multiflora rose, hawthorns, arrowwood, red maple, wild grape, blackberry, and dewberry have created dense, colorful thickets. A colony of green dragon, a rare member of the arum family, grows in this moist location along with its cousin, jack-in-the-pulpit.

In the forested heights reached by the Collier Trail, sugar maple, black cherry, American beech, tulip tree, shagbark hickory, and red oak dominate the canopy. The easternmost turn in the trail passes through a beech-maple climax forest. Ground observers will see an abundant wildflower called lady's thumb, Virginia creeper, jumpseed, Indian cucumber root, rough bedstraw, Pennsylvania smartweed, and Christmas, hay-scented, and wood ferns.

Forty-three bird species were counted in the spring of 1996, including the scarlet tanager, indigo bunting, blue-gray gnatcatcher, wood thrush, wild turkey, woodcock, Baltimore oriole, American redstart, and yellow-rumped, blue-winged, Kentucky, and chestnut-sided warblers. My brief expedition added the goldfinch and belted kingfisher to the list.

Deer seem plentiful. One boldly drank in midstream when I arrived at the creek. Creekside beaches were heavily pocked with deer tracks. The outermost extent of their tracks marked the acorn shower line. Four does scampered from me, including two that bolted 10 yards ahead of me on the Parker Lane Trail. Tracks also revealed the presence of raccoons, squirrels, and canines. Black bears have been seen in the woods.

Indiana County became an important Christmas tree producer in the 1930s. By 1960, 200 tree growers in the county sold more than a million trees annually. Farmers turned to this lucrative pursuit when conventional crop farming declined. William Stephens, former owner of the Parker Tract, was one of the earliest commercial growers in the county. Several Christmas tree plantations survive in the preserve, notably the one encircled by the Candlestick Trail. The trail name refers to the new growth on top of an evergreen, called a candlestick.

History. The hunting-and-gathering culture of Native Americans gave way to an agricultural and industrial economy when William Bracken arrived and built a gristmill here in 1786. Hugh Parker, the Parker Tract's namesake, acquired the land in 1856. His family held it until 1908. Luke Swank, a Pittsburgh photographer, held it briefly in the early 1900s. He built a home on an existing foundation, which can still be detected along Parker Lane. Members of the John Stephens family owned the place from 1914 to 1995. Blacklick Valley Natural Area was donated to Indiana County Parks in November 1995 by David and Marion (Penny) Stephens Russell of Dilltown, the last of the many individual property owners.

10

Blue Spruce County Park

This land is on the mend after centuries of use as farmland, timber forest, coal field, and railroad yard. Early successional growth is healing the ravaged slopes above Getty Run. In a century or so, if left alone, mature hardwoods will again cover the slopes. Today city-torn and work-weary humans can find a pleasant playground around a lake originally made for steam engines.

Ownership. Indiana County Parks.

Size. 420 acres.

Physiographic Region. Pittsburgh Low Plateau.

Nearby Natural Attractions. Blacklick Valley and Buttermilk Falls Natural Areas, Pine Ridge and Hemlock Lake County Parks, Yellow Creek State Park, and sites encompassing the Conemaugh Gorge.

Features. Blue Spruce Park boasts a 6.1-mile trail system flanking its 12-acre centerpiece, Cummings Dam Lake. The trailhead for the featured route of the Overlook and Vista Ridge Trails is a parking lot on Groft Road, which runs along the north shore of Cummings

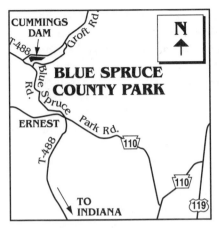

Lake. Groft Road (TR 494) branches from Blue Spruce Road (TR 488) and the main park road. A shady picnic area is adjacent to the trail, and a latrine is available.

Overlook Trail parallels the road a piece, then turns left into the woods. Midway, the blue-blazed trail follows an old jeep road and merges with the northern leg of the orange-blazed Vista Ridge Trail. The path swings by an overgrown homestead, past a couple of gas wells, and across some reverting meadows. On its descent, bear right at the fork (the left trail is the lower leg of the Vista Ridge Trail) and follow the path to the picnic area.

Getty Run Trail, 1.3 miles, wanders up Getty Run from the east side of the park lake. The PCC (Pennsylvania Conservation Corps), Trillium, Aspen, and Swinging Bridge Trails branch into the southern half of the park. The mile-long PCC Trail, off the Aspen Trail, ventures to southern heights above the lake. Children enjoy the quarter-mile Swinging Bridge Trail for its 40-foot-long suspension bridge above a coal bank. Trail maps are available at the park office on Blue Spruce Park Road.

Other human comforts include picnic shelters, playgrounds, boat rental, horseshoe and volleyball courts, fishing, and a day-use lodge. For more information, contact Indiana County Parks, Blue Spruce Park Rd., Indiana, PA 15701, telephone (724) 463-8636.

Geology. The park is situated in the Pittsburgh Low Plateau of the Allegheny Plateau, a region dissected by small streams. Tiny Getty Run has eroded a relatively wide and steep valley some 400 feet below the highest point in the park. It drains westward into Crooked Creek and the Allegheny River. During dry summers, the current shrinks to a dribble or disappears altogether. This, in turn, lowers the park lake behind Cummings Dam. Lake water may escape through shale layers on the lake bed and into nearby abandoned coal mines. Most of the sedimentary bedrock dates back to the Pennsylvanian Period, 300 million years ago.

Wildlife. The vegetation reveals the park's agricultural past. Pioneer tree species such as black cherry, bigtooth aspen, sassafras, black locust, staghorn sumac, and black birch grow in areas changing from farmland to meadow-forest. Saplings of various oaks, maples, and beeches will slowly succeed these early settlers. The ground cover is likely to be thickets of black raspberry, bedstraw, blackberry, and greenbrier. Club moss spreads over acres at the start of the Overlook Trail, indicating previously disturbed land and soil low in fertility. A mature red oak and tulip tree forest grips a slope in the southwest corner. Sugar and red maples in the lower canopy eventually will take over. Spicebush and witch hazel occupy the understory.

The bottomland flanking Getty Run holds the most diversity. Red oak, black cherry, and red maple presently rule this realm, with flowering dogwood, ninebark (a showy flowering shrub), and black cherry saplings in the subcanopy. This is the place to go for wildflowers. Seventy species brighten the site, the most common being tall meadow rue, goldenrod, common cinquefoil, jewelweed, sweet cicely, and violets.

A marshy wetland is developing where silt from Getty Run fills the eastern end of the lake. Wetland plants here provide nesting sites for waterfowl. Park officials have installed a silt bar in the lake to prevent it from being suffocated by silt.

Trillium Trail bears clusters of nodding trillium and other spring beauties. Naturalists have recorded 170 wildflowers in the park, from skunk cabbage in late February to asters in late September. Also look for purple bergamot, dame's rocket, mad dog skullcap, butterfly weed, blue flag, pink turtlehead, boneset, and cleavers. The blossoms mix with the fronds of eleven varieties of ferns, including cinnamon, rattlesnake, sensitive and ebony spleenwort.

Birders affiliated with the Todd Sanctuary in southeastern Butler County have listed 137 avian species. The lake attracts buffleheads, mallards, old-squaws, lesser scaups, and ring-necked and black ducks, as well as Canada geese, green herons, and double-crested cormorants. Warblers include the bay-breasted, chestnut-sided, blue-winged, black-and-white, black-throated, Kentucky, Nashville, Tennessee, Connecticut, and Canada. The place gets fliers as small as the ruby-throated hummingbird and as large as the turkey vulture, and those as quiet as the mute swan and as melodious as the wood thrush. Swainson's thrush, considered a candidate at risk by the Pennsylvania Biological Survey, has been glassed. A bird list can be found in the park's inventory, available at the office.

On one hike on the Vista Ridge Trail, I saw a woodchuck climbing a tree. The fat furball was about 4 feet above terra firma. It froze and clung hard to the bark with all fours as I investigated from the path. Besides woodchucks, the park is home to deer, black bears, raccoons, opossums, skunks, squirrels, rabbits, chipmunks, bats, and various kinds of mice. In the lake, stocked trout swim with smallmouth bass, bluegill, crappie, carp, and catfish.

History. The Buffalo, Rochester, and Pittsburgh Railway constructed a dam here in 1908. It was the time of steam locomotives, which needed lots of water daily. Engineers discovered that the acidic water pumped from coal mines into tanks for locomotives ate through the boilers—and their profits. Though Getty Run flowed through a mining area, it contained no corrosive sulfuric acid, so the railroad dammed Getty Run for its fresh water supply. A dozen company-owned houses lodged workers who maintained the dam and railyard. The dam and yard were named after A. E. Cummings, an early landowner.

Getty Run derives its name from the Getty family, who lived here into the early 1900s. The overgrown foundation of the Getty homestead can be discerned along the Getty Trail. In 1981 the park district bought Lezanic Farm, a 41-acre parcel on the northern slope of Getty Run. Though covered by vegetation, remnants of the Lezanic homestead are visible along the Overlook Trail. Before Indiana County ownership, coal was removed below the property via underground shafts by the Rochester and Pittsburgh Coal Company. Active gas wells still dot the place.

Boyce Park

This is rehab land—terrain on the mend after bouts of mining and farming. New floral and faunal pioneers, humans included, are healing the wounds. A nature center and budding greenhouse are nurturing stewards and seeds for the next revival.

Ownership. Allegheny County Department of Parks, Recreation and Conservation.

Size. 1,096 acres.

Physiographic Region. Pittsburgh Low Plateau.

Nearby Natural Attractions. Frick Woods and Beechwood Farms Nature Reserves, the Flower and Wildlife Preserve, Barking Slopes and Dead Man's Hollow Wildlife Preserves, Bradford Woods, and Harrison Hills and North Parks.

Features. Youngsters like to start at the nature center on Old Frankstown Road, which displays touchables like fossils and bones, plus exhibits on animals, bugs, birds, flowers, and seeds, and a big, stuffed elk head near the entrance. The center also offers trail maps, rest rooms, a small library, and information.

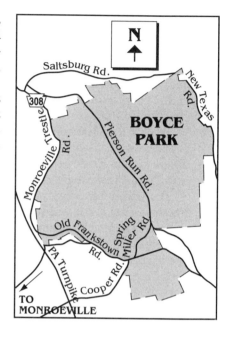

Trails beside the center are short and sweet. On the Sensory Trail, just a couple hundred yards long, school-children—or anybody, really—can use their senses to learn about nature. The Cucumber Trail, a half-mile loop around the Sensory Trail, visits forests, fields, reverting meadows, and gardens for butterflies, medicinal plants, and herbs. The 1.6-mile Indian Hill Trail loops around Indian Hill from branches on Cucumber Trail. Stop by the greenhouse, next to the nature center, where native plants for park use are cultivated. The park's administrative building is next door.

Boyce Park has another 10 miles of hiking trails, the best being alongside and east of Pierson Run Road. Start at the Carpenter Log House, a restored early-1800s cabin on Pierson Run Road. From the parking area, a gated gravel road leads to the trailheads to the 3-mile Carpenter Trail and 4.6-mile Outer Trail.

Carpenter Trail winds northerly across recovering strip mines to a recreation complex in the northeastern corner of the park. From there it goes west along Deever Drive, then southerly along Pierson Run (west of the road) back to the start. Outer Trail essentially overlaps portions of the Carpenter, Center, and Indian Hill Trails to form a perimeter loop connecting the log cabin, recreation complex, nature center, ski slopes, and Four Seasons Lodge. Center Trail, 2.3 miles, stays between Center View Drive and Pierson Run Road.

Unfortunately, the trails are poorly designed, poorly maintained, poorly mapped, and poorly blazed, if at all. For example, across the road from the log cabin is a sign for the Log House Trail, which doesn't appear on any park map. It's actually the western leg of the Carpenter Trail plus the eastern section of the Center Trail. Mountain bikes have widened and grooved trails intended for hikers, and many unofficial side trails have eroded and scarred the scene. Map-dependent hikers must feel frustrated. Park officials should enforce their rules and improve their trail routes.

The park also features slopes for downhill skiing, a wave pool, tennis courts, a playground, picnic areas, athletic fields, an archery range, and an activities center.

Geology. Bituminous coal tailings are still evident along trails east of Pierson Run Road. Mining stripped the surface vegetation to extract the combustible fossilized remains of vegetation that grew here 300 million years ago, during the Pennsylvanian Period.

Boyce Park straddles the summit of two watersheds. Pierson Run flows southeasterly into Abers Creek, Turtle Creek, and the Monongahela River. Water from the northern edge of the park drains into Plum Creek and the Allegheny River.

Wildlife. Nature is healing the place, and today there are forty-five species of trees and shrubs, over a hundred kinds of wildflowers, sixteen mammal species, and a growing roster of birds, with thirty-six species so far observed. Canopy trees include red, sugar, and silver maples; black cherry; shagbark hickory; white ash; sycamores; tulip tree; white, red, and pin oaks. Beneath these grow sassafras, chokecherry, black gum, mulberry, persimmon, hawthorns, hackberry, and river birch. Red osier dogwood, black locust, redbud, mapleleaf viburnum, and hobblebush represent some of the flowering trees and shrubs. Wildflower seekers can look for showy orchis, bluets, lady's thumb, red trillium, fire pink, yellow corydalis, Indian pipe, yellow wood sorrel, bloodroot, golden Alexander, celandine poppy, and common mullein.

Birding will improve as habitats develop. Right now, you may see the yellow-bellied sapsucker, red-breasted nuthatch, chipping sparrow, rufous-sided towhee, long-eared owl (PA rare), eastern phoebe, red-winged blackbird, and ruffed grouse. Mammals include the white-tailed deer, eastern flying squirrel, red fox, striped skunk, white-footed mouse, and star-nosed mole.

History. Carpenter Log House was the home of Jeremiah Murry Carpenter until his death in 1890. Descendents stayed there until 1958, when the property was sold to the parks department. The original two-story cabin was moved to Point State Park in 1958 for the bicentennial of Fort Pitt. The circa 1820 log cabin in Boyce Park was acquired in nearby Murrysville by the Allegheny Foothills Historical Society in 1981. Restoration was finished in 1988. The home is open on Sundays 1 to 4 P.M. from Memorial Day to late October, plus one weekend in December. William D. Boyce, the park's namesake, was a benefactor and supporter of area scouting.

12

Bradford Woods

B radford Woods's claim to fame is the meteorite that landed here more than a century ago. Aside from this, it serves as a big block of public woods for hikers, hunters, and wildlife watchers.

Ownership. Pennsylvania Game Commission (State Game Lands 203).

Size. 1,247 acres.

Physiographic Region. Pittsburgh Low Plateau.

Nearby Natural Attractions. North, Boyce, and Harrison Hills Parks; Beechwood Farms and Frick Woods Nature Reserves; Dead Man's Hollow and Barking Slopes Wildlife Preserves; and the Flower and Wildlife Preserve.

Features. Parking areas on Game Lands Road and Marksman Park Road provide access into the rectangular game land. Unmarked trails lead from these spots. You can also tramp on unimproved and unmaintained gravel roads traversing the property and a rifle range.

For more information, contact the Pennsylvania Game Commission, Southwest Regional Headquarters, P.O. Box A, 339 W. Main St., Ligonier, PA 15658. telephone (724) 238-9523.

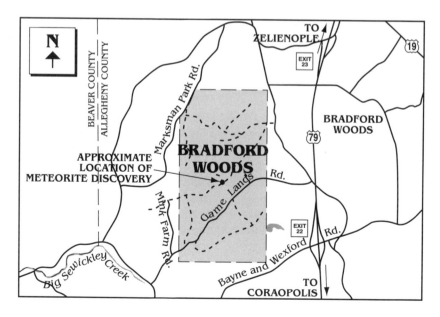

Geology and History. One day in September 1886, George Hillman was strolling back to a farmhouse for lunch when he heard an explosion, a loud hiss, and a thud. He kicked away loose dirt and weeds, and uncovered a dark, heavy stone about 3 inches long. Later, he read a local newspaper account of a meteor's appearance and deduced that the strange rock he had discovered was a meteorite. Hillman put the object in the cupboard, where it stayed for decades.

In 1946, a geology student took Hillman's curious stone to Dr. Henry Leighton, a geologist at the University of Pittsburgh. Leighton determined that it was indeed a meteorite. Here's Leighton's description of the item, as printed in the booklet *Meteorites Found in Pennsylvania,* published by the Pennsylvania Geological Survey: "It is shaped somewhat like an old fashioned pan biscuit with one smooth, curved surface like the biscuit top and three more square faces like the broken faces of a biscuit. The surface has the glazed, varnishlike, pitted surface characteristic of meteorites and is nearly black. It would seem that it is a part of a smooth, pebblelike, elliptic body which, as it reached the Earth's atmosphere, exploded, the broken surfaces becoming fused and pitted in the rush through the atmosphere."

The rock, dubbed the Bradford meteorite after the Allegheny County town where it landed, measured 55 by 65 by 85 millimeters and weighed 762 grams. The impact point was located just a little north of the rifle range.

Wildlife. As its name implies, Bradford Woods is largely forested, with some sections that had been cleared for farm plots and timber. The slope and uplands along the southern side of the East Branch of Big Sewickley Creek have mature groves that represent a recovering dry-mesic acidic central forest community, uncommon in the region.

13

Brady's Run County Park

This steeply angled, west-east valley remains luxuriantly cloaked by mature hardwoods for some 4 miles between two state highways. It's a favorite place for local bird fanciers as well as hikers with mountain goat tendencies.

Ownership. Beaver County Department of Parks and Recreation.

Size. 1,260.7 acres.

Physiographic Region. Pittsburgh Low Plateau.

Nearby Natural Attractions. Raccoon Creek State Park and Brush Creek and Economy County Parks.

Features. Six trails totaling 20 miles string along the steep, wooded ridges above Brady's Run. Most hikers convene at a parking

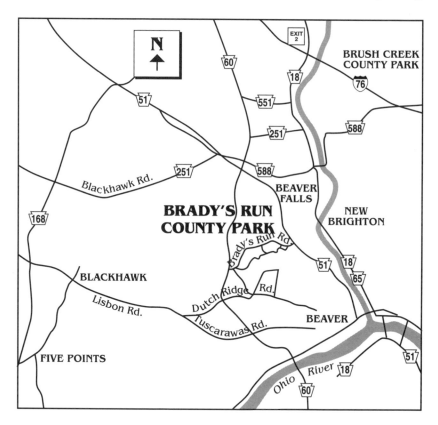

41

lot on the north side of Brady's Run Road, near the intersection with PA 51. Study the trail map sign before departing.

Brady's Run North Trail starts at the parking spot, and Brady's Run South Trail begins across the road by the parking lot for the ice rink. Heading west on either trail will bring you to the park lodge. The two can be combined for a round-trip. Shorter trails depart from the trailhead parking lot and from the Calland Arboretum (follow signs branching north off Brady's Run Road).

The bottomland along the South Branch of Brady's Run is largely open space for fishing, picnicking, and games. Here you will find a meeting lodge, a maple syrup sugar shack, playgrounds, a recycling center, a beach and bathhouse, a horse arena, tennis courts, and parking.

Geology. Topographically, the park resembles the wrinkled region it is a part of. The South Branch of Brady's Run has sliced a V-shaped ravine, exposing 300-million-year-old Homewood sandstone and shale of the Pennsylvanian Period. The stream merges with the north spur and empties into the Beaver River at Fallston.

Wildlife. The park's sugar maples yield enough syrup for an annual maple sugar festival. Along with these hardwoods grow stands of beeches, red and white oaks, shagbark and pignut hickories, American elm, white ash, black cherry, hemlocks, tulip tree, and planted red pines. Flowering shrubs include mountain laurel, juneberry, flowering dogwood, chokecherry, and great rhododendron.

Wildflowers at Calland Arboretum, where students from Geneva College conduct research, are arrow-leaved violet, sessile bellwort, and rattlesnake weed. On the middle and bottom sections of the ridge grow Solomon's seal, jack-in-the-pulpit, Indian pipe, rue anemone, mayapple, enchanter's nightshade, Carolina rose, and jewelweed. You'll also find interrupted, Christmas, and rattlesnake ferns.

Bird-watchers assemble here for spring warblers and for the annual Christmas bird survey. Dr. John Cruzan of nearby Geneva College, the Pennsylvania Game Commission's bird man for Beaver County, recently sighted twenty-five cerulean warblers, a good sign for this declining deep-forest species. Trained eyes and ears may find the American redstart and black-and-white, Kentucky, and hooded warblers. Golden-crowned kinglets often hang around Calland Arboretum, an area dedicated as a nature reserve. You also may find the yellow-throated vireo, brown creeper, wood thrush, eastern pewee, red-breasted nuthatch, great-crested flycatcher, and chickadee. The creek and lake attract the great blue heron (PA threatened), belted kingfisher, mallard and pintail ducks, and Canada goose. Cooper's hawks often patrol the valley.

White-tailed deer, striped skunks, foxes, raccoons, and flying squirrels are among the wildlife finding sanctuary, as well as the eastern garter and black rat snakes, and the dusky, two-lined, and redback salamanders.

History. The park's namesake, Capt. Samuel Brady, was a soldier, frontiersman, and scout on par with Daniel Boone and Simon Kenton. During Indian wars, Brady and his Rangers raided enemy settlements along the Beaver, Ohio, and Muskingum rivers, often from hiding places along the tributaries of those waters. On a hunting trip, Brady was captured by Indians and taken to a village a few miles above the mouth of the Beaver River. He escaped death by abducting a child, throwing it into a bonfire, and sprinting into a ravine, possibly the one carved by Brady's Run.

Land for the park was acquired between 1946 and 1970. The dam that created the lake was finished in 1948, and the park was dedicated in 1950. Brady's Run Lodge opened in 1988, partly to accommodate the large crowds attending the park's maple syrup festival. Calland Arboretum commemorates the park's first administrator, Edward Calland, director of the Beaver County Department of Public Works.

Brucker Great Blue Heron Sanctuary

The place celebrates great blue herons, which find nesting refuge in the sanctuary's tall trees. But you have to be here at the right time of year. The only heron I saw here on my visit in mid-June was winging over the rookery en route to a distant evening roost. A sign on a bulletin board in the observation deck noted that the herons and their young had flown the coop. So instead, I watched half a dozen bluebirds move across the meadow with their awkward youngsters, plus a squadron of acrobatic barn swallows diving at insects and a pair of scolding red-winged blackbirds. At sunset, a doe and her fawn crept into the field behind a cover of floating, ashen mist, and a barred owl softly sounded.

Ownership. Thiel College, Brucker Great Blue Heron Sanctuary.
Size. 45 acres.
Physiographic Region. Glaciated Plateau.
Nearby Natural Attractions. Pymatuning Wetlands, Conneaut Marsh, Tryon-Weber Woods, Wallace Woods, M. K. Goddard State Park, and Shenango River Lake.
Features. From the parking lot, a hundred-yard grass trail leads to an observation pavilion built in 1987 by the Mercer County Federation of Sportsmen. Beyond this, another short path enters the meadow and stops beneath a sprawling, shady oak, which offers a bench for wildlife watching.

To protect nesting herons, visitors are not permitted to walk in the acreage holding the nests and must stay within posted boundary signs from February through August. You can watch the birds from an observation deck. It's best to visit in March or April, before the tree leaves hide the herons' activity. During the remainder of the year, you are free to roam the grounds. Hunting is permitted during restricted periods.

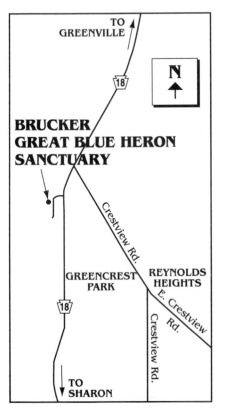

Geology. The preserve is a few miles west of the Shenango River Lake. Soils in this rolling terrain were developed from glacial till, sediments deposited by the Wisconsinan glacier about 12,000 years ago. The Shenango River likely flowed northerly, toward Lake Erie, until it was rerouted southward by the glacier.

Wildlife. Hundreds of noisy great blue herons arrive each spring to nest in this, their largest rookery in western Pennsylvania. Herons are especially sensitive to disturbances during their nesting time, but this rookery, flanked by a busy highway, industrial park, and active railroad, is anything but quiet. Nevertheless, they chose this site, probably because of the trees and their proximity to food. These graceful birds, listed as threatened in Pennsylvania, prefer the towering oaks, ashes, and hickories but also nest in sycamores and cottonwoods. Host trees often cradle five to ten nests, though one favorite in the sanctuary held seventeen. Males choose and contruct the nests, usually 70 to 90 feet off the ground. A nest typically measures 3 to 4 feet across, big enough for three or four bluish eggs, which parents take turns incubating for four weeks. The nests serve the birds year after year.

Food is plentiful in the area. Herons hunt for fish and frogs in nearby lakes and streams, notably the Shenango River Lake and its tributaries. Parents feed their nestlings for several months. Youngsters perch and hop on branches before becoming independent at four months.

History. Edward Brucker, a birder and angler from Masury, Ohio, had been enjoying this rookery since 1978. In April 1985 Brucker, now residing near Sharon, saw that logging for a gas company right-of-way within 200 feet of the colony caused the abandonment of seventeen nests. Brucker persuaded the company to postpone its work until nesting was completed. A year later, he briefly stopped a lumber company from clear-cutting the spot by getting the U.S. Fish and Wildlife Service to protect the birds as migratory species. The logging ban ended in August, but that gave Brucker and his allies (Mercer County Federation of Sportsmen, Greenville-Reynolds Development Corporation, Pennsylvania Game Commission, and the Audubon Society) time to prevail upon the landowners, local industries, to preserve the rookery. The herons hatched at the sanctuary today are the progeny of those saved by Edward Brucker when he stopped the logging company from removing the tall nesting trees, thereby perpetuating the colony.

Buttermilk Falls Natural Area

Water develops, defines, and decorates this pocket-size prize. In budding spring, Hires Run wears luxurious silver satin as it spills over 45-foot Buttermilk Falls. Lush greenery darkens and cools the lean lick in summer. By autumn, the falls shrink to a few strings of pearls dangling off the ledge.

Ownership. Indiana County Parks.

Size. 48 acres.

Physiographic Region. Allegheny Mountains.

Nearby Natural Attractions. Yellow Creek State Park, Black-lick Valley Natural Area, and Blue Spruce, Hemlock Lake, and Pine Ridge County Parks, and Conemaugh Gorge.

Features. From the parking lot at the end of Valley Brook Road, hike down the abandoned lane that switchbacks left to a gate. Walk around the gate and follow an unmarked path across the top of the falls to the northeast bank of Hires Run. You'll walk less than half a mile. Another short trail, across the road from the parking lot, visits the overgrown grounds of the former McFeely homestead. The Conemaugh Power Plant comes into view if you walk straight to a hill-crest on old Valley Brook Road.

The natural area is open daily from 8 A.M. to 8 P.M. For more information, contact Indiana County Parks, Blue Spruce Park Rd., Indiana, PA 15701, telephone (724) 463-8636.

Geology. Several miles from its junction with the Conemaugh River, Hires Run spills over a 45-foot cliff of 300-million-year-old bedrock, creating Buttermilk Falls. Late-winter thawing and spring rains enliven the run and conceal the alternating strata of shales and sandstones behind the draping cascade. The layers become exposed in late summer, when the run dwindles to a mere trickle. Thin plates of shale cap the falls, followed, in descending order, by a massive band of sandstone, then another layer of shale that's thicker than the cap, followed by more sandstone. Geologists put these specimens in the Pennsylvanian Period, Conemaugh Group, Casselman Formation.

An enormous sandstone boulder at the bottom of the falls was once attached to the cascade's brow. Weaker shale beneath the resist-

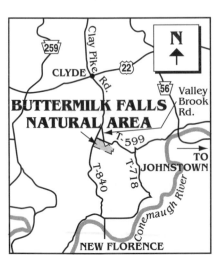

ant sandstone eroded faster, forming an ever-deepening recess behind the spill and below the sandstone, a process called undercutting. Eventually the overhanging nose, having lost the underlying support of shale, broke along a crack and crashed to the valley floor. Other slabs cluttering the streambed fell for the same reason.

Wildlife. Naturalists have counted forty-seven species of trees and shrubs and eighty-seven varieties of wildflowers. The steep-sloping 8 acres surrounding the falls boasts the biggest and noblest trees. Mature American beech, eastern hemlock, tulip tree, sugar maple, red maple, and white, red, and chestnut oaks top the canopy. Beneath these thrive basswood, white ash, black cherry, witch hazel, spicebush, and hornbeam. Elsewhere, reverting farmland supports thick clusters of young red maple, black cherry, black locust, white ash, sassafras, crab apple, tulip tree, Hercules' club, greenbrier, and blackberry.

Wildflowers include jack-in-the-pulpit, boneset, enchanter's nightshade, sweet cicely, mayapple, jewelweed, Indian cucumber root, and bird's-foot trefoil. The toxic water hemlock and poison hemlock, members of the parsley family and unrelated to the hemlock tree, grow in the meadows. The ground is decorated by seven kinds of ferns, notably cinnamon, sensitive, and hayscented, and three types of club moss.

History. Buttermilk Falls probably constituted the hunting grounds of the Shawnee and Lenni-Lenape tribes until they were vanquished in the mid-1700s. An 1871 property map indicates Mrs. L. Coldman as the owner of land by the cascade, noted simply as "fall 45 ft." on the map. Local legend has it that the name of the falls recalls buttermilk made by a neighbor, Mrs. Wilson.

Fred McFeely, a Latrobe industrialist, sensed the magic of the cascade when he bought the place from Henry Wesenberg in 1931 to build a summer home. McFeely's grandson, Fred Rogers, the "Mister Rogers" of TV fame, made many childhood visits to Buttermilk Falls. In 1956 the estate was purchased by Leo and Rita Nist. The Keystone-Conemaugh Group, a consortium of nine utilities that owned the nearby power plant, bought the place in 1972 and donated the site to Indiana County Parks in 1996.

16

Cedar Creek County Park

The park, which is populated by hemlocks and not cedars, features a deeply incised ravine covered with trees and wildflowers, as well as scenic frontage along a calm stretch of the Youghiogheny River.

Ownership. Westmoreland County Bureau of Parks and Recreation.

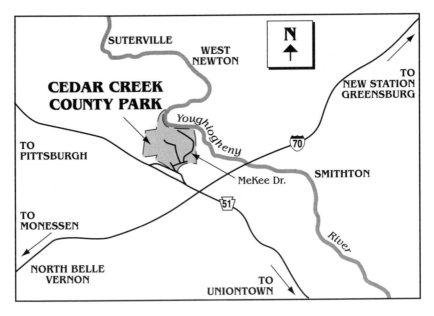

Size. 460 acres.

Physiographic Region. Pittsburgh Low Plateau.

Features. Cedar Creek Gorge Trail, a mile-long loop, begins at the north end of the park. To get to the trailhead, follow the main park road, McKee Drive, off Port Royal Road, to its end at the boat launch. Bridges at each end of the loop carry hikers over Cedar Creek. Benches are provided. The spot also serves as the trailhead of the Youghiogheny River Bike-Hike Trail, which goes northerly 18 miles to Boston and south 2 miles to Smithton.

The park also has picnic pavilions, an amphitheater, a group campground, a boat launch, bike rental, refreshments, a sand volleyball court, an ice-skating area, ballfields, and an airfield for model radio-controlled airplanes. Hunting is permitted in designated areas.

Nearby Natural Areas. Twin Lakes County Park, Nature Park, and Sewickley Creek Wetlands, all Westmoreland County parks; Laurel Ridge, Laurel Summit, Linn Run, Laurel Mountain, and Keystone State Parks; Powdermill Nature Center; Conemaugh Gorge, and Forbes State Forest.

Geology. Typical of this physiographic region, Cedar Creek cuts a deep gash in 300-million-year-old bedrock before dumping into the Youghiogheny River. Waterfalls from tributaries trickling over Pennsylvanian Period sandstones and shales decorate the 200-foot ravine.

Wildlife. Cedar Creek Gorge shelters sycamores, red maple, hemlocks, and grapevines close to the creek. Beeches, black cherry, and oaks thrive higher up the ravine slopes. Though red cedars supposedly once grew on the grounds, the creek was named by settlers who mistook hemlocks for cedars. Pines and spruces have been planted for shade, erosion control, and beauty.

A score of wild turkeys flushed from the gorge rim during my winter hike. Pheasants, owls, Canada geese, wrens, sparrows, and woodland warblers reside here. Some sixty bluebird boxes provide this attractive bird with shelter. The birds are joined by raccoons, foxes, skunks, groundhogs, and deer. Black rat, water, and garter snakes are found here, too. The Youghiogheny River, which washes the east border of the park, contains trout, bass, catfish, bluegills, and muskellunge.

History. The ruins of a gristmill stand near the mouth of Cedar Creek, a reminder of the valley's industrial past. Rostraver Township bought the former farmland in the 1960s, then later sold it to Westmoreland County.

Clear Creek State Park

Beartown Rocks
Kittaning State Forest

Wasteful logging and fires made this area virtually lifeless a century ago. Today these state-owned lands protect the watersheds of crystal-clear creeks that flow into national scenic rivers in northwestern Pennsylvania.

Ownership. Pennsylvania Department of Conservation and Natural Resources, Bureau of Forestry, and Bureau of State Parks.

Size. Clear Creek State Park, Jefferson County, encompasses 1,676 acres. Former Clear Creek State Forest, now Kittaning State Forest, comprises 13,266 acres over Jefferson, Venango, and Forest Counties. (Also see Allegheny Gorge.)

Physiographic Region. Tracts along the Clarion River are located in the Low Plateau; eastern and southern portions of the state forest are in the Allegheny High Plateau.

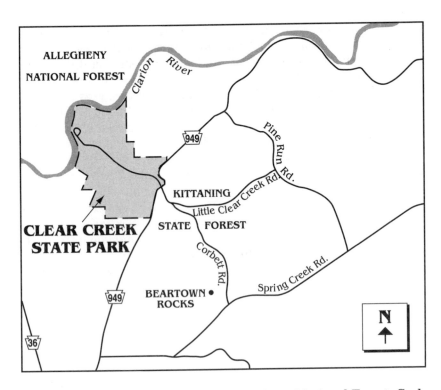

Nearby Natural Attractions. Allegheny National Forest, Cook Forest State Park, and State Game Lands 24, 28, 39, 44, 54, and 283.

Features. A good starting point is the nature center at Clear Creek State Park, which features exhibits on logging history and wildlife. The Ox Shoe Self-Guiding Historical Trail, an 0.8-mile loop, begins across the road from the nature center. Look for a guide at the trailhead. The trail name derives from the metal shoes loggers put on oxen to protect their cloven hooves. Beyond this, the park has 15 miles of hiking trails, the best being the 1.5-mile Clear Creek Trail, an old logging road running along the stream between the campground and swimming beach. The River and Irish Rock Trails, departing from the north loop of the campground, parallel the Clarion River. The park also has cabins, picnic areas and shelters, camping, a playground, Frisbee golf, and a canoe launch into the Clarion River, a national scenic river. Clear Creek is a favorite of trout anglers.

The Jefferson County section of Kittaning State Forest, abutting the state park, features the 2-mile Beartown Rocks Trail. The route starts on the east side of PA 949, a little south of the state park entrance. Park in the picnic area across the road. Clear Creek, a tributary of the Clarion River, will be on your left for half a mile. Ahead, it crosses Trap Run and finishes at Beartown Rocks Overlook. The vista also can be reached by car. From PA 949, across from the state park entrance, follow a gravel road called Little Clear Creek Road for a quarter mile, then bear right on Corbett Road. Another dirt road to the site branches from the right.

For more information, contact Kittaning State Forest, District Forest Office, 158 S. Second St., Clarion, PA 16214-1904, telephone (814) 226-1901, or Clear Creek State Park, R.R. 1, Box 82, Sigel, PA 15860-9502, telephone (814) 752-2368.

Geology. Hikers who walk from the Clarion River to Beartown Rocks vista, via Clear Creek and Bear Town Rocks Trails, cross from the Pittsburgh Low Plateau physiographic region to the Allegheny High Plateau. Beartown Rocks is a rock city of jumbled huge boulders, ledges, outcrops, and narrow passages. Rock cities occur when thick beds of bedrock, in this case Pottsville conglomerate, split along widely spaced joints after weaker underlying strata erodes. Further erosion, slumping, frost heave, tree roots, and vegetation enlarge cracks.

Wildlife. The fifty species of trees and shrubs include scarlet and white oaks, red pine, cucumber magnolia, mountain laurel, butternut, great rhododendron, hemlocks, white pine, sour gum, sassafras, and quaking aspen. The slopes of the state park and adjoining state forest are covered by mountain laurel, the state flower. Botanists have counted 177 wildflower species, including round-leaved orchis, bee balm, evening primrose, jewelweed, bird's-foot trefoil, yellow wood sorrel, bouncing bet, heal-all, and halberd-leaved violet. Walking, ebony spleenwort, lady, cinnamon, and interrupted ferns wave their fronds here. There also are fifty-one kinds of fungi and mushrooms, such as tapioca slime, dead man's fingers, stinkhorn, yellow fairy cups, and ringless honey mushroom.

Beartown Rocks is a good place to spot the northern goshawk (PA rare), bald eagle (PA endangered), wild turkey, and orange-crowned warbler. White-tailed deer, squirrels, gray foxes, and raccoons are common mammals, and river otters and minks might be seen by skilled observers. Black bears used to reside beneath a cliff off Corbett Road, hence the name Beartown Rocks.

History. Sawmills set up along rivers and creeks in the 1880s. Hemlocks and white pines were the first to fall. They were dragged to waterways, tied into rafts, and floated down the Clarion River to Pittsburgh. By 1900 the virgin forest on these tracts was gone. A fire ignited near Sigel and swept north, vaulted over the Clarion River, and burned as far as Loleta, where it was stopped only by prolonged rain. Later, deer ate everything rising from the ashes, but then disappeared themselves. By 1918 an imported blight had killed every standing American chestnut.

The healing process started in 1919, when the commonwealth purchased 3,200 acres. It continued to buy forest land until 1980. Clear Creek opened its first public campsites in 1922. The Civilian Conservation Corps in the 1930s was responsible for the state park's swimming beach, cabins, trails, roads, bridges, and buildings. In 1998 Clear Creek State Park administratively merged with nearby Cook Forest State Park.

18

Conemaugh Gorge

Two striking gorges have been carved through massive, parallel ridges of rock by a diminutive river called Conemaugh. For centuries, these river gaps served as convenient routes for small boats, canal barges, and railroad cars. Now we favor them for their beauty and outdoor challenges.

Ownership. The Laurel Highlands Trail runs through Laurel Ridge State Park, owned by the Pennsylvania Department of Conservation and Natural Resources, Bureau of State Parks. The Pennsylvania Game Commission takes care of State Game Lands 153.

Size. The described route goes through the northernmost section of Laurel Ridge State Park (13,625 acres total) and the northern segment of the 2,926-acre State Game Lands 153.

Physiographic Region. Allegheny Mountains.

Nearby Natural Attractions. Charles F. Lewis Natural Area, Pine Ridge Park, State Game Lands 276, Blacklick Valley and Buttermilk Falls Natural Areas, both Indiana County parks.

Features. The 70-mile Laurel Highlands Trail tracks through Conemaugh Gorge before reaching its northern terminus in Laurel Ridge State Park. Heading south on PA 56 from Seward, look for the right turn into the state park. Trailhead parking is located at the end of the park road.

Half a mile from the trailhead, the yellow-blazed path crosses a powerline, creating a view of the gorge and a clearing for rose-

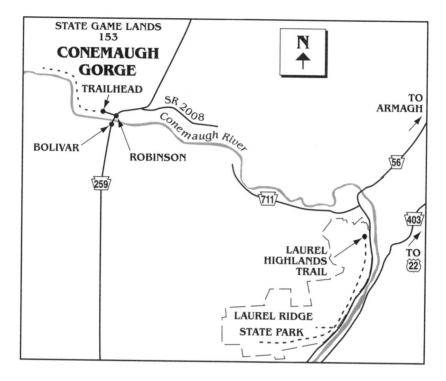

breasted grosbeaks, sparrows, and rabbits. Just before you reenter the woods, note the power plant to the right. You reach the edge of the gorge about a mile and a half from the start, but views are obscured by vegetation until milemarker 68, two miles from the trailhead. Decent views continue for another mile or so, then the trail turns away from the river to the crest of the ridge. Here you can backtrack, completing a 6-mile round-trip, or continue southbound on the Laurel Highlands Trail. Milemarkers are posted along this trail.

A riverside trail starting in the village of Robinson stays above the north bank of the Conemaugh River as it saws through Chestnut Ridge. The unblazed route passes through State Game Lands 153. The trailhead is at the end of Front Street, off PA 259, just before the bridge over the Conemaugh River. Park by the stone railroad bridge and head downstream. This braided path parallels railroad tracks before entering the game lands and climbing a bluff. You're going to have to feel your way on this adventure.

For more information, contact Laurel Ridge State Park, R.D. 3, Box 246, Rockwood, PA 15557, telephone (814) 455-3744, or Pennsylvania Game Commission, Southwest Region Headquarters, P.O. Box A, 339 W. Main St., Ligonier, PA 15658, telephone (412) 238-9523.

Geology. The Conemaugh River is one of only three watercourses that cuts through Laurel Ridge and Chestnut Ridge. The others are the Youghiogheny River (see Ohiopyle State Park) and Blacklick Creek (see Blacklick Valley Natural Area). The river starts a few miles east in Johnstown, below the confluence of Stonycreek River, Little Conemaugh River, and other streams.

It originated long ago, when water pooling east of Laurel Ridge spilled over a gap or through a fracture in the anticline. Thereafter, rapid downcutting erosion occurred at this tight squeeze, creating a precipitous, narrow gorge. The process was repeated downstream at Chestnut Ridge.

Bedrock of the Pennsylvanian Period (300 million years ago) and the Mississippian Period (340 million years ago) is exposed in the gorge. Pennsylvanian rock covers the summit and slopes of Laurel Ridge and Chestnut Ridge, but underneath the shell, where the river cross-sections the ridge, Mississippian rock appears.

Trained eyes might find the ruins of a sandstone quarry operation, roughly a mile along the Laurel Highlands Trail. The foundations of a cable car are becoming hard to discern due to vegetation.

Wildlife. Both gaps are luxuriantly covered with second- and third-growth hardwood forests. The highest elevations have chestnut and white oaks and mountain laurel. Slopes allow space for black cherry, black and yellow birches, hemlock (scattered), tulip tree, red oak, sugar and red maples, cucumber magnolia, black tupelo, and shagbark hickory. The understory includes sassafras, great rhododendron, striped maple, lowbush blueberry, witch hazel, spicebush, hornbeam, ironwood, wintergreen, and serviceberry. Wildflowers are abundant in spring, and there are acres of ferns, especially cinnamon fern.

The panoramas can be outposts for observing migratory birds, especially soaring ones taking advantage of updrafts off the ridges. Typical Pennsylvania woodland mammals live here. This is timber rattlesnake and copperhead country, so watch your step.

History. The name Conemaugh may derive from a Native American expression meaning "otter creek." The Pennsylvania Canal and Pennsylvania Railroad ran through the Conemaugh Gap in the nineteenth century. The canal is gone, but a railroad line still carries cargo. In 1952 an archaeological team from the Carnegie Museum of Natural History uncovered the ruins of an Indian village near Blairsville.

Conneaut Marsh

The Iroquois called it *konn knu yaut,* meaning "melted snow water lake," an appropriate name for a glacier-bred body of water. Europeans clipped it down to Conneaut, the name put on the nearby pool, the commonwealth's largest natural lake.

Lake water draining southward rinses wetlands ranging from open water to swamp forest, though a century ago, much of the mire was a meadow for pasturing milk cows. Waterbirds bulk up in these wet areas during their migrations.

Ownership. Pennsylvania Game Commission.

Size. State Game Lands 213 totals 5,619 acres.

Physiographic Region. Glaciated Plateau.

Nearby Natural Attractions. Pymatuning Wetlands, Woodcock Creek Lake, Erie National Wildlife Refuge, Tryon-Weber Woods, and Wallace Woods.

Features. The best way to experience the marsh is by navigating the main channel, Conneaut Outlet, in a canoe. Boat launches can be found at the intersection of Watson Run and Geneva Roads, Towpath Road (beneath I-79 pillars), and off PA 285, south of Geneva. Parking is abundant at the Towpath Road launch, spartan

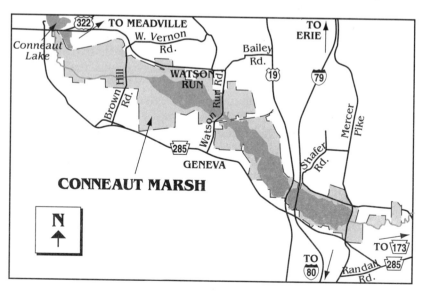

at Watson Run Road, skimpy at the other. Suggested routes are a round-trip from the Watson Run Road launch northwest to Brown Hill Road (Mud Pike bridge), the last half mile being a woodland stream, and from the launch south of Geneva to the Mercer Pike bridge. Paddlers will encounter obstacles, shallow sections, and portages.

Game commission parking areas on Mercer Road (southeast end of the marsh), Geneva, Lily Pond, Brown Hill, and Watson Run Roads, and PA 285 are good wildlife observation locations. Access to the upper marsh stems from a game commission road branching south from US 322 at the east edge of the town of Conneaut Lake. Don't use vantage points from active railroad beds and busy highways, US 19 and I-79. Hunting, trapping, and fishing are permitted in the game lands.

For more information, contact the Pennsylvania Game Commission, Northwest Regional Office, P.O. Box 31, 1509 Pittsburgh Rd., Franklin, PA 16323, telephone (814) 432-3187.

Geology. Nearby Conneaut Lake, the state's largest natural lake, was once a large kettlehole lake formed at the end of the ice age, about 12,000 years ago. It started as a huge slab of ice stretching for several miles that had calved from the face of the slowly retreating Wisconsinan glacier. This elongated ice slab broke in an existing valley. The enormous weight of the ice depressed the ground still further, then sediment-laden glacial meltwater built a high collar around it. When temperatures rose, the ice melted in this basin.

Conneaut Marsh, one the commonwealth's largest, was created during the same period when an ancient stream channel filled with glacial outwash. Since the ice age, sediments and plants have filled in much of the southeastern portion of the glacial lake. Conneaut Outlet drains the lake and flows through the marsh to French Creek.

On Ellion Road, a few miles east of the marsh, look for a gravel mound called a kame. Here the Wisconsinan glacier slowed its withdrawal, enabling gravel and cobble to pile up beneath the lip of a meltwater stream. Kames are usually dome-shaped, like sand in an hourglass, but this one stretches north-south for a mile and stands 100 feet. The prominent feature is on private property, but it can be examined from the road.

A side trip to Rock Creek Falls, at the end of Rock Creek Road, off Mercer Road (SR 2003) near Custards, shows a 20-foot hanging valley formed at the end of the ice age. The feature is not located on game commission land. Here Rock Creek, a tributary of Conneaut Outlet, slides over resistant caprock of Shenango sandstone bedded above less resistant Meadville shale. Both strata were formed during the Mississippian Period, 350 million years ago. During the ice age, the ancient channel now occupied by the marsh swelled to the elevation of the falls. When the flow of the main channel subsided, the mouths of feeder streams were left hanging. Since then, the creek has been downcutting and eroding upstream.

Wildlife. Conneaut Marsh, locally known as Geneva Marsh, is a mosaic of moist habitats. The 2.6-mile upper marsh, from Conneaut Lake to Brown Hill Road (Mud Pike), is largely a swamp forest, with Conneaut Outlet being the only open water. Wood ducks, pileated woodpeckers, barred owls, wood thrushes, vireos, and migrating warblers, notably the prothonotary warbler (PA rare), reside in this area.

The middle marsh, the 2.5-mile stretch between Brown Hill Road and Geneva Bridge (Watson Run Road), is characterized by emergent vegetation—cattails, spatterdock, smartweed, and water lilies—amid ponds and braided currents. You will see many varieties of ducks and occasional rarities like the peregrine falcon, bald eagle, short-eared owl (all PA endangered), sandhill crane, and yellow rail. Also look for American and least bitterns (both PA endangered), sora and Virginia rails, common moorhen, marsh wren, and American coot (all PA rare). Mudflats attract shorebirds such as the semipalmated plover, greater yellowlegs, least sandpiper, and dunlin.

The lower marsh from Geneva Bridge to Mercer Pike (SR 2003), narrows to a width of half a mile but still has patches of emergent vegetation, open pools, and fingers of swamp forest. Dabbling ducks like gadwall, northern pintail, American wigeon, northern shoveler, and green-winged teal hide in the vegetation. Open water harbors the common goldeneye, bufflehead, scaup, and other diving ducks. During migrations, the common loon, tundra swan, and scoter land here. Shrubby spots conceal the willow flycatcher, eastern kingbird, yellow warbler, swamp sparrow, and common yellowthroat. Forested areas may host the eastern pewee, great crested flycatcher, scarlet tanager, and various warblers. Red-headed woodpeckers occupy snags at the swamp edge.

Canoists cruise by muskrat and beaver lodges, basking turtles and snakes, stalking herons, squadrons of dragonflies and damselflies, and colonies of water lilies, arrowhead, buttonbush, and pickerelweed. In spring, the choral serenade of spring peepers crescendoes, and bullfrogs bellow at dusk. Toss a line into the water for northern pike, largemouth bass, and carp. Raccoons, opossums, bobcats (PA rare), and deer leave tracks on mud banks.

History. In 1868 the Pennsylvania legislature began funding swamp-siphoning projects to increase agricultural production. Within a few years, civil engineers had transformed a lazy, braided, serpentine current into a ditch 8 feet deep and 16 feet wide. Water could no longer linger in the marsh. The neatly angled trough, Conneaut Outlet, ran from the lake to within 2 miles of French Creek. Livestock grazed in pastures bordering the channel for the next half century.

Unlike so many stories about marshes, this one has a happier ending, thanks to the automobile. Another government project in the 1920s, this one being US 19, resulted in the construction of a causeway across the outlet. Additional transportation embankments, the abandonment of farms, and other land-use changes led to the rebirth of the swamp.

Preservation started with the Western Pennsylvania Conservancy's acquisition of 683 acres in 1976. The conservancy secured another 175 acres in 1981, and donated both parcels to the Pennsylvania Game Commission, which has purchased the bulk of the site.

◆ 20 ◆

Cook Forest State Park

This hallowed fairyland protects the largest, oldest, and tallest coniferous stalwarts of the original Penn's Woods. The celebrated trees here have been compared to their stolid kin in Germany's fabled Black Forest and California's Sequoia National Park and Muir Woods. Hollywood filmed a wilderness epic beneath these boughs, and a premier travel magazine ranks the park among the best the nation, largely because of the trees. The Clarion River, a national scenic river, adds its brushstroke to the scene.

Ownership. Pennsylvania Department of Conservation and Natural Resources, Bureau of State Parks.

Size. 6,668 acres (does not include Clear Creek State Park).

Physiographic Region. Pittsburgh Low Plateau.

Nearby Natural Attractions. Allegheny National Forest, Kittaning State Forest, Clear Creek State Park, State Game Lands 283 and 284, and the Clarion River, a national scenic waterway.

Features. The main attraction is the Cathedral Natural Area, a hundred-acre grove of the oldest and largest white pines and hemlocks in Pennsylvania. Specimens measure 200 feet high and have

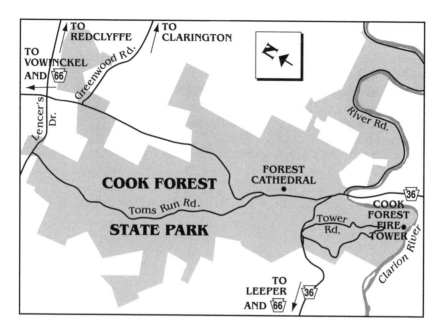

trunks of 3 to 5 five feet in diameter. To see these old-growth trees, park at the Log Cabin Inn Visitor Center and the main park road (SR 1015) and follow the Longfellow Trail, named in honor of poet Henry Wadsworth Longfellow. You cannot miss the masterpieces. In half a mile, at the junction with Indian Trail, look for a plaque commemorating the spot as a national natural landmark. To fully appreciate the giants, follow Indian Trail a few steps, then go right on Joyce Kilmer Trail, left on Rhododendron Trail, and left on Indian Trail back to Longfellow Trail. Short trails designated by the letters A, B, C, D, and E also go by the big trees. These trails branch from Longfellow Trail and the Indian and Rhododendron Trails, which depart from a loop road by the park office in Cooksburg (PA 36).

Smaller patches of virgin timber stand in the Swamp and Seneca Natural Areas. The Swamp Natural Area is in the northeast corner of the park, east of the Baker Trail, which runs the length of the park. Using the state park map, travel north from the Log Cabin Inn Visitor Center 3.2 miles and turn right on Greenwood Road (SR 1012). The trail is a hundred yards or so on the left. Park off the road. Hike north about half a mile. The giant hemlocks and scattered pines will be hiding in a wet depression to the right. Because they are harder to find, these venerable trees have few human visitors.

Seneca Natural Area protects a 70-acre thatch of virgin hemlock and pitch pine along the Seneca Trail. From the park office, cross PA 36 and hike the steep, difficult path about half a mile. The ancient groves and connecting trails are marked on the state park brochure map.

Beyond these sites, the park has 27 miles of trails (try the Liggett and Browns Run Trails, also overlapped by the North Country Scenic Trail), camping, a swimming pool, canoeing, cabins, bridle trails, an elderhostel, a craft center, a 200-seat theater, a nature center (Log Cabin Inn), picnicking, a fire tower, snowmobile and ski trails, fishing, and hunting. Additional outdoor recreation is available at Clear Creek State Park, which merged with Cook Forest in 1998 to form the state's third largest park. The commercial trappings of a resort destination surround the park.

For more information, contact Cook Forest State Park, P.O. Box 120, Cooksburg, PA 16217, telephone (814) 744-8407.

Geology. The bedrock beneath the ancient trees, mostly coarse sandstone, started as sediment on a seabed 300 million years ago during the Pennsylvanian Period. Later, tectonic collisions in the east created a dome-shaped bulge in the Earth's crust that raised the local elevation to 1,600 feet. The crest of this dome centered in McKean and Potter Counties. Cook Forest was located at a lower elevation on the south slope of the dome. During the ice age, glaciers could not surmount the dome, so they spread and probed to the east and west, thus sparing Cook Forest from direct glacial disturbance.

Nevertheless, glaciation changed the landscape significantly. Meltwater pouring off the ice flooded rivers, rerouted streams, eroded valleys, and wrinkled the big dome. The Clarion River is a glacial-bred river. Large blocks of sandstone on Seneca Point are the products of erosion.

Mineral springs containing concentrations of sulfur and iron once lured thousands of people here at the start of the twentieth century. Seneca Trail Springs, a quarter mile from Cooksburg, featured a boardwalk illuminated by natural gas extracted from the park. People drank the water and bathed in it, believing it restored youth and fought diseases such as arthritis.

Wildlife. The cooler climate during the ice age likely supported spruces, balsam fir, white birch, and arborvitae, species common today in northern Canada. Hemlocks and possibly white pines also established colonies at this time. As the ice retreated, plants from southern climes crept into the area, but here erosion by glacial meltwater had washed away soil suitable for hardwoods, so the conifers maintained their foothold.

The eastern white pines in the Cathedral Natural Area sprouted after a severe drought and fire in 1644 (the year of William Penn's birth) cleared the slopes, except for a few hardy or lucky survivors whose cones reseeded the forest. The pines grew quickly and straight in the open, and their shade and acidic needles kept the understory clear of hardwoods. Shade-tolerant hemlocks rose with the pines on cool, moist, north-facing slopes. The evergreens have basked in the sun ever since. The oldest standing white pines are known as cork pines because of their corklike, deeply furrowed bark.

Long ago, the virgin tracts were larger, but logging, disease, natural encroachment, storms and other calamities have whittled them down. Civilian Conservation Corps laborers fought white pine blister rust, a fungal disease, by removing gooseberries and currants that hosted the blight. Three hurricane-force storms in the 1950s and a tornado in 1976 flattened the equivalent of 2.1 million board-feet of lumber, some of it salvaged for park buildings.

Forty-five varieties of trees and shrubs grow in Cook Forest, including robust specimens of beeches, sugar maple, black birch, yellow birch, black cherry, red oak, red maple, and cucumber magnolia. Impenetrable thickets of great rhododendron growing along Toms Run have individuals more than a century old. Hikers will need field guides to identify the 152 kinds of wildflowers, such as jack-in-the-pulpit, partridgeberry, trailing arbutus, yellow wood sorrel, jewelweed, lily of the valley, bluets, fringed polygala, hoary mountain mint, and painted trillium. Fourteen species of ferns thrive, especially common woodfern and New York, sensitive, cinnamon, and interrupted ferns. Trained eyes might spot fifty types of fungi and mushrooms, notably scarlet waxy cap, destroying angel, chicken, panther, and black velvet bolete.

Thirty-nine mammal species include voles, mice, shrews, moles, bats, bobcats, porcupines, river otters, and coyotes. Spotted, dusky, slimy, and red-backed salamanders are among the thirteen kinds of amphibians found here. Ten reptile species range from the tame and common painted turtle to the timid but poisonous timber rattlesnake. Nineteen types of fish swim in park waters, notably brown, brook, and rainbow trout, darters, and mountain brook lamprey.

Eighty-two bird species have been seen in the park. Conifer-loving birds include the barred owl, yellow-bellied flycatcher, hermit thrush, pine grosbeak, pine siskin, dark-eyed junco, and red-breasted nuthatch. Also look for the northern saw-whet owl, yellow-billed cuckoo, blue grosbeak, bobwhite, and chestnut-sided, yellow, and black-throated blue warblers. Migrating bald eagles occasionally stop to feed in the Clarion River, and in April the gobbles of wild tom turkeys echo across the woods.

History. Native Americans left their mark by carving petroglyphs on sandstone boulders. Senecas lived here when Christian Frederick Post, diplomatic agent for the colonial assembly, arrived in 1757 to make sure that the Senecas remained allied to the English, like their Iroquois brethren, during the frontier war with France.

John Cook, the park's namesake, was the first permanent white settler. He came in 1826, commissioned by Pennsylvania's government to test the idea of building a canal along the Clarion River. Cook saw no potential for a canal but plenty for a sawmill. After buying 765 acres, Cook brought his wife and ten children to a cabin at the confluence of Toms Run and the Clarion River, a place now known as Cooksburg. The frontier entrepreneur logged the forest, built several water-powered sawmills, rafted logs to Pittsburgh, and constructed flatboats. His son, Anthony (a.k.a. Andrew), added a flour mill, other mills, an inn, and a store to the family holdings. Upon Anthony's death, A. Cook Sons Company managed the business.

Preservation of the big trees began with the formation of the Cook Forest Association in the 1920s. With endorsements by Gov. Gifford Pinchot, the group raised money toward the state purchase of 6,055 acres from A. Cook Sons Company in 1927. Seneca Point Fire Tower (Old #9) was erected in 1929 for fire protection. In the 1930s Civilian Conservation Corps workers constructed many of the park facilities used today.

The 171-acre Cathedral forest was made a national natural landmark on October 2, 1969, by the U.S. Department of the Interior. The Cathedral, Swamp, and Seneca groves became state park natural areas in the 1990s. In 1995 the park acquired 745 more acres from the Western Pennsylvania Conservancy. Clear Creek State Park merged with Cook Forest State Park in 1998.

21

Crooked Creek Lake

Maybe the dam built in 1949 calmed these flood-prone waters, but it didn't straighten Crooked Creek. From an airplane, the silver-blue streak across the green landscape looks like a lightning bolt, or perhaps one of those dragons depicted in medieval tapestries. This corps of engineers park, lush again after a half century of growth, falls into the out-of-the-way, best-kept-secret category. Bird-

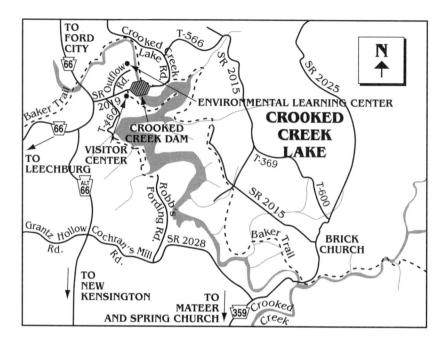

ers scan the shore during migrations for ospreys, bald eagles, and great blue herons.

Ownership. U.S. Army Corps of Engineers.

Size. 2,664 acres.

Physiographic Region. Pittsburgh Low Plateau.

Nearby Natural Attractions. Todd Sanctuary, in southeastern Butler County, and Mahoning Creek Lake, another U.S. Army Corps of Engineers project, in northeastern Armstrong County.

Features. Crooked Creek Lake boasts nearly 50 miles of hiking paths, ranging from half-mile connector trails to a 33-mile equestrian trail. Start with the 2-mile Laurel Point Trail, which begins above the boat ramp on T460 (follow park signs to the boat launch). Royal blue blazes mark this lasso-shaped path. Originally built by local Boy Scouts, the trail takes you through groves of oaks and mixed hardwoods, pine plantations, ravine crossings aided by wooden stairs, thickets of rhododendron and mountain laurel, and patches of meadow. The white-blazed bridle trail shares portions of this route and branches to other destinations in the park. Rest rooms are located near the trailhead at a nearby picnic area.

Two easy, interconnected interpretive trails begin at the end of Outflow Road, below the dam. Shrub Swamp Trail, a mile loop, journeys along Crooked Creek and through wetlands in its dense bottomlands. At Station 19 of this trail, a side path leads to higher ground and the mile-long Discovery Trail, which offers twenty-four interpretive spots and a wildlife observation blind. Informative brochures on these paths are available at the Environmental Learning Center off Outflow Road or at the project headquarters. A fishing platform, picnic area, and latrines are available at the trailhead.

The mile-long Songbird Trail, branching from Justice Picnic Area on Crooked Creek Lake Road, caters to birders. A nature guide for this easy trail can be picked up at headquarters.

Long-distance hikers trudge the more challenging, lonelier 10-mile segment of the Baker Trail, which winds in and out of the public property line on the northeastern side of the lake. The best trailheads are located at the horse riders' access on SR 2019, north of the dam, and at Cochran's Mill on SR 2025, south of the hamlet of Brick Church, near the confluence of Crooked Creek and Cherry Run. An overnight Adirondack-style shelter, a fancy lean-to, straddles Cherry Run near the Cochran's Mill trailhead. This American Youth Hostel trail runs 140 miles, from Allegheny National Forest to the merger of the Allegheny and Kiskiminetas Rivers in nearby Schenley. A proposed route from Crooked Creek Lake to Conemaugh Gorge would connect the Baker and Laurel Highlands hiking trails.

The Fort Armstrong Horseman's Trail, also open to hikers, traces the project's perimeter for most of its 33 miles, but in places it follows gravel backroads or abandoned lanes. Segments overlap with Baker, Shrub Swamp, and Laurel Point Trails. Start your journey at the horse park on SR 2019 (north of the dam), Outflow Road, Robb's Fording Access Area, or Baker Trail access on SR 2025. Pick up a map at the park office.

Trails are open daily from sunrise to sunset. The corps and local historians recently developed a twenty-seven-stop auto tour of historic sites around the lake. The park also offers camping, hunting, fishing, picnicking, ballfields, playgrounds, an ice-skating pond, sledding, boating (ramp fee), and swimming beach (fee). The park office is open daily 7:30 A.M. to 4 P.M. For more information, contact Resource Manager, Crooked Creek Lake, Box 323A, R.D. 3, Ford City, PA 16226, telephone (724) 763-3161.

Geology. Below the dam, fossil hunters found the imprint of a strange, fernlike plant in 300-million-year-old rock from the Pennsylvanian Period. The impression was from a lepidodendron, a huge lycopod or club moss, that had spiky bark resembling the rind of a pineapple or the bark of some palm trees. Lepidodendron was part of a swampy tropical forest when western Pennsylvania, part of the North American continental plate, stood near the equator. Although these fossils were discovered in dark, organically rich shale, the remains of the verdant, ancient rain forest formed the vast coal beds now being mined in the region. Coal had its origins in the tropical vegetation that accumulated in shallow swamps. Although vegetation has nearly hidden the black seams, exposed coal beds can still be found in several places above the lake, notably where the Laurel Point Trail crosses Coal Bank Hollow Run.

The watershed is polluted by a by-product of coal mining known as "yellow boy," which is iron oxide, or rust. You can usually find this pollutant flowing beneath the footbridge by the SR 2025 access to the Baker Trail. Curiously, water piped in from a spring above the coal deposit is available to thirsty hikers. Treat the water, just to be safe.

The road to the swimming beach rides atop a thin, fingerlike peninsula of hard, resistant Pennsylvanian rock capped by sandstone that breaks into blocks and thick plates. These dense, heavy sedimentary layers pressed the softer organic layers below into coal. Crooked Creek had to zigzag around them, finding the path of least resistance.

Wildlife. Crooked Creek's myriad habitats makes it ideal for nature study. Its location is significant enough for Audubon members to include it in annual bird counts. The lake attracts the osprey, bald eagle (both PA endangered), and great blue heron (PA threatened). Hiking the Shrub Swamp Trail before dusk, I flushed a great blue heron, whose squawk echoed through the Crooked Creek valley. Early the next morning, an unidentified owl silently floated away when I crested a ravine on the Laurel Point Trail.

The Songbird Trail has been developed to attract birds for hikers to observe. Varied habitats—shrubs, pond, evergreens, hardwoods, and meadows—bring different species. Look for wood ducks, green herons, and Canada geese at the pond, least flycatchers and eastern pewees in overgrown meadows, white-breasted nuthatches and ruby-crowned kinglets in pines, finches and warblers in shrub thickets, and red-winged and yellow-headed blackbirds in the swampy wetlands. You are likely to flush a ruffed grouse and to spot a red-tailed hawk hovering above. Other birds include the eastern bluebird, wild turkey, rough-legged hawk, and great horned and saw-whet owls. Birders have noted 110 species at Crooked Creek Lake.

An interpretive guide for this trail comes with a bird checklist. The park office also has interpretive guides for the Discovery, Shrub Swamp, and Songbird Trails that provide information on natural events, trailside flora, and resident fauna. Trees include red maple, flowering and osier dogwoods, red oak, sycamores, bigtooth aspen, sassafras, shagbark hickory, ironwood, black cherry, spicebrush, basswood, black locust, white ash, hawthorns, and American bladdernut, the last growing at the edge of its range. Keen eyes may also see the black birch, white pine (planted for reforestation decades ago), white oak, beeches, and a few white birch. Other plants include rhododendrons, mountain laurel, thickets of multiflora rose and blackberries, acres of club mosses, goldenrod, bluets, trout lily, red trillium, cutleaf toothwort, mayapple, and black snakeroot. You may also see maidenhair, evergreen wood, and Christmas ferns.

History. Archaeologists uncovered ninety-one flint chips and points during a 1986 excavation near the dam. The artifacts suggest that Native Americans established a hunting camp or small settlement by Crooked Creek. A frontier-style industrial revolution came to the valley in the early nineteenth century. George Painter started a flour mill in 1804, which was followed by the Crooked Creek Saltworks in 1820 and David Rearick's sawmill in 1830. The site is best known as Cochran's Mill after its last owner, Michael Cochran (1858). Robert Walker built a unique flour mill in 1836, near the present Tunnelville swimming beach. He excavated a diversion tunnel through the neck of a narrow river bend to power his paddle wheels. His mill indicates that farmers had success growing grain in the valley. The gristmill stone from his mill was recovered by the Galbraith family and fitted into the exterior stone wall of their homestead.

Severe flooding along the Allegheny River on St. Patrick's Day, 1936, prompted construction of the flood control dam, which the corps finished in 1940. The summer pool flattens at an elevation of 845 feet, but during Hurricane Agnes in 1972, the lake reached its high-water mark of 901 feet, just 19 feet shy of topping the dam.

Dead Man's Hollow
Wildlife Preserve

This scenic gash in southeastern Allegheny County has a colorful human history and a new owner. The deep hollow muffles the noise of nearby suburbia while amplifying the sweet sounds of songbirds and trickling water. In a decade or so, this tributary of the Youghiogheny will reclaim its former natural glory. The preserve adds a side show to the Youghiogheny River Trail.

Dead Man's Hollow Wildlife Preserve ————————— 67

Ownership. Allegheny Land Trust.
Size. 377 acres.
Physiographic Region. Pittsburgh Low Plateau.
Nearby Natural Attractions. Barking Slopes Wildlife Preserve, the Flower and Wildlife Preserve (Trillium Trail), Beechwood Farms and Frick Woods Nature Reserves, and several Allegheny County parks: Harrison Hills, and North, Deer Lakes.
Features. The best way to explore the preserve, technically called the Wildlife Preserve at Dead Man's Hollow, is to follow the Youghiogheny River Trail, a bike-and-hike rail-trail, from the town of Boston. Travelers crossing the PA 48 bridge from Versailles will find a four-way intersection at the Boston bridgehead. To reach the trailhead, take the sharpest right turn, onto West Smithfield Street, and the next immediate right. At the bottom of the hill, you will find parking, a latrine, fishing access, and ballfields.

Head northwest on the bike trail, with the Youghiogheny River on your right. In less than a mile, you'll reach the nature trail on the left. Bike racks are available at the trailhead in summer. The main nature trail goes half a mile upstream (west) into Dead Man's Run ravine, concluding with a loop shaped like the eye of a needle. A shorter trail stems northbound from the north leg of the main trail loop and ends at a trail access on Orchard Drive in Liberty. Newly constructed bridges span the brook, and there are plenty of benches for rest and wildlife watching. Trails are open daily from sunrise to sunset. Hunting is permitted from October through January.

For more information, contact Allegheny Land Trust, 425 Sixth Ave., Suite 800, Pittsburgh, PA 15219, telephone (412) 350-4666.

Geology. Mile-long Dead Man's Run slashes a deep ravine through 300-million year old sandstone and shale before unloading into the Youghiogheny River. Feeder streams tumble over small waterfalls. Springwater leaks from the rock walls along the bike trail and near the preserve's trailhead. Crossbedding, showing changes in currents during long-ago deposition, can be seen in sandstone outcrops at the trailhead.

Wildlife. The preserve is the largest privately protected conservation area in Allegheny County, according to the Allegheny Land Trust. This newly acquired preserve is rebounding from decades of mistreatment, including illegally dumped garbage (now removed), erosion caused by motorbikes, and invasion by non-native species.

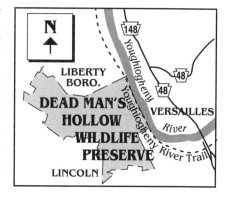

Flora and fauna inventories are under way to record the rich diversity at this site. Maturing deciduous hardwoods, such as American beech, black cherry, and red maple, form the canopy. The vitality of seedling hemlocks indicates that this boreal conifer is making a comeback. Sycamores and pines have been planted to restore the native stock. Wildflowers are spreading each year.

History. Legends about monstrous snakes, festering corpses, misty specters, gun-toting bootleggers, and encampments of hobos kept this place wild by scaring away respectable folks. The "dead man" of the hollow recalls shopkeeper Robert McClure, who was robbed, abducted, and killed in the ravine by bandits in 1881. A posse of thirty concerned citizens followed the murderer's wagon tracks and filled him full of lead, saving taxpayers the cost of a trial and scaffold. A dozen years later, newspapers reported that "a gentleman swooned" after encountering the equivalent of the Loch Ness Monster in Dead Man's Hollow. The slithering reptile measured "30 to 40 feet long and 2 feet in circumference." The "monster" never resurfaced.

Monster stories may have been concocted to keep authorities from stumbling onto hidden treasures or illicit activities. During Prohibition, bootleggers operated stills in the hollow. The ruins of a sewer pipe factory (perhaps the origin of the monster) became a shanty for homeless people (then called hobos) during the Depression.

In recent years, the ravine was considered a prime location for a landfill. In 1996 the Allegheny Land Trust purchased 260 acres from Cleveland Works, a pipe manufacturer interested in reviving the factory. The following year, the Scott Conservancy bought 117 more acres for the land trust. Trails were built in 1997, including a 29-foot bridge over Dead Man's Run. Volunteers removed an amazing thirteen tons of trash and planted trees in disturbed areas.

Enlow Fork Natural Area

This quiet natural area straddles flora boundaries and two counties. An abandoned country lane braids with a mountain brook on a journey through a sheltered valley wrapped in wildflowers and birdsong. Saved from the dam builders, it's now a place to go backward in time, forward in outlook.

Ownership. Pennsylvania Game Commission.

Size. Enlow Fork Natural Area, otherwise known as State Game Lands 302, comprises 1,000 acres along the Washington and Greene county line.

Physiographic Region. Pittsburgh Low Plateau.

Nearby Natural Attractions. Ryerson Station State Park in Greene County, and Cross Creek and Mingo Creek Parks in Washington County.

Features. An abandoned dirt road snaking along the stream serves as a trail. From the parking area, continue down the road alongside a tributary of Enlow Fork. Where this rill joins the creek, the lane curves left past the sandstone abutments of a washed-out bridge. Ahead, the path stays above a sprawling bottomland pasture where deer gather at dusk, then it crosses the first of three steel deck bridges encountered on the walk.

Admire the mammoth, three-tined sycamore on the left. Its configuration suggests that it might have been Indian "signal tree." Woodland tribesmen sometimes pruned large trees into odd shapes to mark trails, portages, boundaries, or settlements. The striking figure flags your attention to the regiment of "smokestack" sycamores crowding the bottomland.

Ahead, on the right, a gravel road leads to parking for four-wheel-drive vehicles and north out of the valley. Hikers continue straight on the creek road. Beyond this junction, a quarter mile or so, another road stems left, crosses the creek on a steel bridge, and leaves heading south. Ignore this road, too. Half a mile from here, a third rusty, cob-

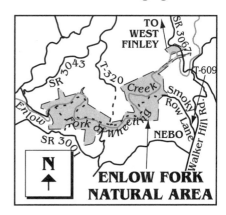

ENLOW FORK NATURAL AREA

webby, ivy-covered steel bridge spans the creek into Greene County. Backtrack from the next junction or at the state game land boundary for a walk of 6.5 to seven miles.

The road is maintained for use by game commission and gas company service vehicles and, judging from tracks, mountain bike riders. Encounters with vehicles are unlikely. This is an easy stroll down a remote country lane in a sheltered valley. The only sounds are those of birds, wind, the stream, and your footsteps.

Hunting and fishing are permitted. Wear bright orange, yellow, and blue if you hike during hunting season, and don't stray from the trail. For more information, contact the Pennsylvania Game Commission, Southwest Region, P.O. Box A, Ligonier, PA 15658, telephone (724) 238-9523.

Geology. Enlow Fork is a tributary of Wheeling Creek, which feeds into the Ohio River. It meanders westerly through a steep, isolated valley. Outcrops of Permian-era shale and sandstone close to 280 million years old can be seen from the trail. Some coal mining occurred here at the start of the century, but the seam proved too shallow for full-scale extraction.

Wildlife. Start with Enlow Fork, a cold, clear mountain stream that supports trout, rock bass, and smallmouth bass. Wading will usually scatter minnows, frogs, and crayfish. Beavers, mink, raccoons, great blue heron (PA threatened), and turkeys leave their tracks on beaches. Immense sycamores, some 5 feet in diameter, and hemlocks lean over the wide stream. Upland, trees common in southern and midwestern climes grow in this floristic crossroads. These include familiar members of Penn's Woods, such as the white, red, and chestnut oaks, as well as chinquapin oak, pawpaw, redbud, and Ohio buckeye, better known west and south.

Some smaller rarities occupy the spot, notably a forest snapdragon at the eastern extent of its range called blue-eyed Mary (PA rare), seen with Virgina bellflower in the bottomland, and Riddell's hedge nettle, a southern Appalachian species that blooms rose-purple in summer on moist rock ledges. These beauties may be missed among the display of large-flowered and red trillums, dame's rocket, dwarf larkspur, various violets, star-of-Bethlehem, twinleaf, blue phlox, Solomon's seal, celandine, trout lily, great blue lobelia, pink valerian, appendaged waterleaf, and wild columbine. Walking and bulblet ferns and liverworts daintily cling to wet, rocky slopes.

Birdsong echoes in this quiet, forested cut. Listen and look for the wood thrush, black-billed cuckoo, Baltimore oriole, blue-gray gnatcatcher, belted kingfisher, Acadian and least flycatchers, scarlet tanager, indigo bunting, downy woodpecker, red-eyed vireo, ruby-throated hummingbird, yellow-breasted chat, Carolina chickadee, and yellow-throated and yellow warblers.

At sunset, swallows and bats swarm over fields for insects, and owls hoot from treetop perches. Butterfies find a haven here, including the monarch, tiger and spicebush swallowtails, and several fritillaries. Deer are abundant, especially when winter drives nonresidents into this sheltered, peaceful valley.

History. A quarter century ago, the Western Pennsylvania Conservancy and Pennsylvania Game Commission saved this valley from being inundated by a large-scale flood control dam, citing the valley's unique habitats. Instead of a massive dam, a compromise floodgate was constructed at the West Virginia-Pennsylvania line. A system of sluices now controls water entering Wheeling Creek. So far, neither Wheeling Creek nor Enlow Fork has been flooded.

The game commission got the land in 1986 from the Western Pennsylvania Conservancy after U.S. Steel's plans for the valley, which included a dam, were scrapped. At the time of state acquisition, the lane along the creek was a state-maintained road serving several families. During the dam debate, archaeologists performing mandatory preconstruction digs found remnants of an Indian village thought to have been occupied by various bands hiding from marauding Iroquois.

Erie National Wildlife Refuge

More than a dozen imperiled creatures find sanctuary in this damp, undisturbed, and gently rolling land, including the olive-sided flycatcher, a bird once thought to have been extirpated from the commonwealth. The refuge is a natural mosaic of diverse habitats, a playground for 237 bird species, 47 mammals, and 37 amphibians.

Ownership. U.S. Department of the Interior, Fish and Wildlife Service.

Size. 8,750 acres.

Physiographic Region. Glaciated Plateau.

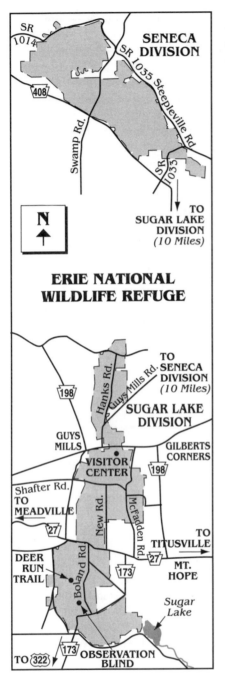

SENECA DIVISION

N ↑

ERIE NATIONAL WILDLIFE REFUGE

TO
SUGAR LAKE
DIVISION
(10 Miles)

TO
SENECA DIVISION
(10 Miles)

SUGAR LAKE DIVISION

GUYS MILLS

VISITOR CENTER

GILBERTS CORNERS

Shafter Rd.
TO
MEADVILLE

TO
TITUSVILLE

MT. HOPE

DEER RUN TRAIL

Sugar Lake

TO 322

OBSERVATION BLIND

Nearby Natural Attractions.
Woodcock Creek Lake, Pymatuning Wetlands, Wallace Woods, Tryon-Weber Woods, Conneaut Marsh, and State Game Lands 69.

Features. Ten miles separate the two divisions of the refuge. The visitors center is located in the 5,206-acre Sugar Lake Division on PA 198 in Guys Mills. Seneca Division, 4 miles southeast of Cambridge, is directly north, bordered by PA 408, French Creek, and Steepleville Road (SR 1035). To reach the 3,571-acre Seneca Division from the visitors center, go east on PA 198 about half a mile then left (north) on McFadden Road. In a mile turn right on Guys Mills–Townsville Road (SR 1018), then left on PA 408. A map in the refuge brochure shows other roads for car travel.

Tsuga Nature Trail, near the visitors center, is the most popular of the three hiking trails in the Sugar Lake Division. This 1.6-mile flat loop path allows the hiker to experience many of the refuge's diverse habitats, including grasslands, shrublands, croplands, man-made ponds, a beaver pond, mixed forest, and a grove of the trail's namesake, *Tsuga canadensis,* or eastern hemlock. An interpretive guide is available at the visitors center. The boardwalk bridging the beaver pond is an excellent viewing spot.

The longest and wildest track is the 3-mile Deer Run Trail, south of the visitors center on Boland Road. Look for a fishing deck and wildlife observation area across the road from the trailhead. The path crosses Fowler and Boland Roads and skirts along Pond 9. A mile south of here, near the intersection of Boland and Ritchie Roads, birders will find an observation blind beside Reitz's Pond on the west side of the road. West of Deer Run Trail, on Allen Road, try out Deer Run Overlook, which offers a view of a meadow favored by deer. Beaver Run Trail on Hanks Road (north of PA 198) consists of two half-mile paths—a loop and spur. Winterberry holly, or black alder, decorates the mile-long Muddy Creek–Holly Trail, located at the northern end of the Seneca Division on Johnstown Road (SR 1014).

Parking areas are located at each of the above landmarks. Other parking areas cater to bushwhackers and hunters. Trails are open daily from half an hour before sunrise to sunset unless otherwise posted. Visitors can view displays and obtain information at the visitors center, open Monday through Friday 8 A.M. to 4:30 P.M. Nature programs and slide talks are available to school classes and organized civic and professional groups. Hunting, fishing, and cross-country skiing are permitted in the refuge.

For more information, contact Erie National Wildlife Refuge, 11296 Wood Duck Lane, Guys Mills, PA 16327, telephone (814) 789-3585.

Geology. Before the ice age, all the water in the refuge drained north and west into French Creek. Woodcock Creek and Muddy Creek, both tributaries of French Creek, still adhere to the ancient north-tilting lay of the land. Geologists believe that meltwater from ice-age glaciers filled the watershed with more than 100 feet of sediment, along with huge blocks of ice. This glacial landscaping reversed the drainage of the southern end of the valley. South of PA 198, which acts as a divide, water goes south through a series of swamps and small lakes that constitute the Lake Creek watershed. Lake Creek trickles into Sugar Lake, which in turn discharges into Sugar Creek and French Creek above Franklin.

Wildlife. Naturalists have listed 102 wildflower species along the Tsuga, Deer Run, and Beaver Run Trails in the Sugar Lake Division. Marsh marigold, yellow rocket, trout lily, yellow pond lily, Canada mayflower, wild geranium, and violets are May bloomers. Wood sorrels, clovers, moneywort, heal-all, blue vervain, and Deptford pink arrive in June, followed by black-eyed Susan, evening primrose, enchanter's nightshade, butter-and-eggs, and stinking chamomile in July. Bladder campion, Indian tobacco, New York ironweed, boneset, jewelweed, and cardinal flower shine in August. One rarity, mouse-eared chickweed (PA endangered), thrives here. Fern plumes appear everywhere, among them, hay-scented, cinnamon, Christmas, sensitive, and royal.

Beavers are largely left in charge of managing the sluggish flows of Dead and Muddy Creeks in the northern Seneca Division. In the southern chunk, humans have planted grasses and forage crops, impounded brooks for glittering ponds, installed nesting boxes for bluebirds and wood ducks, and built observation decks and trails. Additionally, local farmers cultivate more than 700 acres of refuge land. After the farmers harvest their share, the rest is left standing in the fields for wildlife.

The beaver pond along the Tsuga Trail is a marsh created when beavers dammed a stream. Here, dead trees, called snags, provide homes for cavity-dwelling wood ducks and roosts for bald eagles, hawks, and ospreys. The mixed hardwood forest beyond the wetland contains second-growth oaks, beeches, hickories, walnuts, and black cherry. Elsewhere, you'll find aspen, hawthorns, maples, adlers, white and black birches, crab apples, planted pines, sumacs, hornbeams, witch hazel, willows, and a stand of mature eastern hemlocks.

Wildlife managers promise to make this a wetland paradise for waterfowl and other migratory birds. To that end, some 2,500 acres, nearly 30 percent of the refuge, consist of beaver floodings, marshes, swamps, man-made ponds, creeks, and soggy meadows. On peak days during spring and fall migrations, some 4,500 Canada geese and 2,500 ducks gather here, including wood ducks, mallards, hooded mergansers, pintails, scaups, American wigeons, golden-eyes, blue-winged teals, green-winged teals (PA threatened), buffleheads, and ring-necked ducks. Tundra swans and sandhill cranes (endangered) sometimes stop to forage.

The refuge provides nesting habitat for 113 species, notably the great blue heron (PA threatened) and bald eagle (PA endangered), as well as the red-tailed, sharp-shinned, broad-winged, and red-shouldered hawks; American kestrel; and great-horned, barred, and screech owls. Thirty-nine warbler species have been spotted here, including nesters such as the blue-winged, mourning, hooded, chestnut-sided, and magnolia. Prothonotary warblers (PA rare) visit from time to time.

Other imperiled or rare birds using the sanctuary are the osprey and peregrine falcon, American bittern, great egret, short-eared owl, and common tern (all PA endangered); upland sandpiper, sedge wren, and yellow-bellied flycatcher (all PA threatened); Swainson's thrush, marsh wren, northern goshawk, northern harrier, and pied-billed grebe (all PA rare or at risk); black-crowned night heron, northern bobwhite, and barn owl (PA rare); and long-eared and northern saw-whet owls (declining but not listed). The olive-sided flycatcher, listed as extirpated in the state, is a rare spring and summer visitor. Ruby-throated hummingbirds are abundant regulars arriving each spring from their wintering digs in Mexico and Central America.

These wetlands also support forty-seven species of mammals, ranging from tiny shrews, voles, and moles to predators such as the black bear, coyote, red fox, and mink. Other rodents include beavers, southern bog lemmings, porcupines, woodchucks, and squirrels. White-tailed deer are plentiful throughout the refuge.

Summer visitors have to steer clear of box turtles crossing the roads. This woodland reptile shares the refuge with its wetland kin, the snapping, midland painted, spotted, and eastern spiny softshell turtles. Snakes here are nonpoisonous, including the queen, northern redbelly, eastern milk, ringneck, and northern ribbon.

Wetlands are ideal amphibian habitats. Here you will find large, grotesque salamanders known as mud puppies and eastern hellbenders, along with the smaller spotted, redback, and slimy salamanders and green frogs, bullfrogs, northern spring peepers, and gray tree frogs. Refuge waters harbor warm-water fish species such as the black crappie, yellow perch, largemouth bass, bluegill, sunfish, and bullhead. Cold-water fish, trout and white sucker, swim in Woodcock Creek.

History. Duck and goose hunters paid for this refuge. Proceeds from the sale of migratory bird hunting and conservation stamps, better known as duck stamps, were used to establish this national wldlife area in 1959.

Flower and Wildlife Preserve

Late April through early May is the best time to visit this preserve. That's when thousands of large-flowered trilliums, the park's signature blossom, unfurl their three-petaled plumes.

Ownership. Borough of Fox Chapel.

Size. 35 acres.

Physiographic Region. Pittsburgh Low Plateau.

Nearby Natural Attractions. Beechwood Farms Nature Reserve, Dead Man's Hollow and Barking Slopes Wildlife Preserves, Frick Woods Nature Reserve, and Boyce, Harrison Hills, and North Parks, all Allegheny County parks.

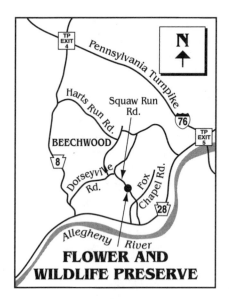

Features. The easy, half-mile Trillium Trail tracks above Stony Camp Run between two small parking lots on Squaw Run Road. Unofficial paths run parallel higher on the slope. Perpendicular routes straight up the slope lead to residential areas. Benches at the trailheads were provided by the Squaw Run Garden Club. For more information, contact the Borough of Fox Chapel, telephone (412) 963-1100.

Geology. Downcutting by Stony Camp Run has carved a steep-sided, V-shaped valley, a feature typical in Allegheny County. The run flows southeasterly into Squaw Run, a tributary of the Allegheny River. The bands of shale, siltstone, and sandstone bedrock that have elbowed to the surface, members of the Conemaugh Group, derive from deposits dating back to the Pennsylvanian Period, 300 million years ago.

Wildlife. Five kinds of trilliums explode like fireworks in late April to early May. The showiest and most abundant is the large-flowered trillium, *Trillium grandiflorum,* with its familiar trio of lily-like white petals. In good years, tens of thousands of these snowy trilliums brighten the ravine. They blush rose just before they wilt and wither. A greenish shade of this variety hides on the slopes, along with the malodorous purple trillium (*Trillium erectum*) and a yellowish associate, plus red trillium (*Trillium sessile*). There are other wildflowers as well, including perfoliate and large-flowered bellworts (related to trilliums), white clintonia, Dutchman's breeches, jack-in-the-pulpit, blue cohosh, wild geranium, spring beauty, trout lily, cut-leaved toothwort, round-lobed hepatica, mayapple, Virginia bluebell, skunk cabbage, false Solomon's seal, wild ginger, bloodroot, black snakeroot, and Virginia waterleaf. To a lesser extent, the floral fanfare continues downstream in Salamander Park, also owned by the Borough of Fox Chapel.

By summer the forest floor darkens, as towering, thick-trunked sugar maples, white and red oaks, tulip trees, basswoods, black cherries, sycamores, and birches leaf out. Hemlocks, some of them huge, and clusters of great rhododendrons guard the creek. Autumn is another splendid time to visit and admire the foliage.

This much-beloved park shows weariness from constant human usage and defoliation by deer. Suburban sprawl and a burgeoning herd have diminished this roaming herbivore's range and food choices, and preserves such as this one pay the price of development. Fenced-off areas called exclosures were erected in 1994 to keep out foraging deer as well as flower-picking humans. Two years must pass before trillium seeds germinate, then a few more before the plants flower. Picked flowers leave roots without surface food sources. It may take seven years for a picked flower to rebound.

History. In 1946 Richard Boyles, a local citizen who admired the wildflowers on the western slope of Stony Camp Run, bought the parcel just two hours before a land developer's final offer. The borough bought the place from Boyles three years later and turned it into parkland.

26

Forbes State Forest

Blue Hole and Cole Run Falls
Laurel Summit Bog (Spruce Flats Bog) and Wolf Rocks
Beam Rocks
Roaring Run Natural Area

Several richly forested sites in Forbes State Forest protect prime natural spots in the Laurel Highlands. Trails will please the easygoing traveler and hard-core hiker alike. The Laurel Highlands Trail snakes through state forest land and connects it to bordering state parks and game lands.

Ownership. Pennsylvania Department of Conservation and Natural Resources, Bureau of Forestry.

Size. The state forest comprises more than 50,000 acres. Roaring Run Natural Area totals 3,582 acres.

Physiographic Region. Allegheny Mountains.

Nearby Natural Attractions. Laurel Ridge, Laurel Hill, and Laurel Summit; Kooser, Ohiopyle, and Linn Run State Parks; and Powdermill Nature Reserve.

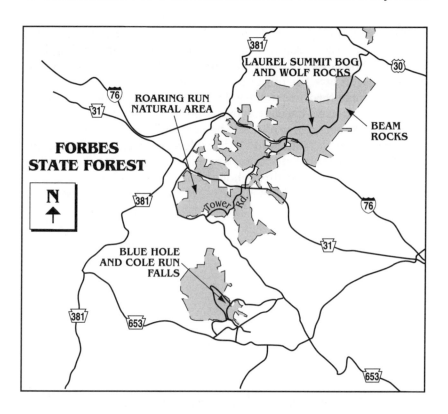

Features. The half-mile blue-blazed trail to *Beam Rocks* begins at a parking area on Laurel Summit Road and leads to the graffitti-stained rock formations and a striking view. Climb down the rocks carefully, and continue east a few hundred yards to reach the Laurel Highlands Trail, running through the valley.

The trails to *Laurel Summit Bog* (Spruce Flats Bog) and *Wolf Rocks* begin at Laurel Summit State Park, a 15-acre picnic area on Laurel Summit Road near its intersection with Linn Run Road. The trailheads are marked by wooden signs. The easy quarter-mile path to the bog ends at an observation platform constructed by the Youth Conservation Corps in 1993. A splendid view of Linn Run Valley and unusual rock outcrops punctuate the 2.2-mile (one-way) ramble to Wolf Rocks. Rest rooms, parking, and picnic tables are available at the trailheads.

Blue Hole refers to a mountain swimming hole below a small waterfall on the east side of Blue Hole Road, as well as to the creek. This local summer hangout in a Norman Rockwell setting is always cold and refreshing. Park in the pullover and remove your trash if you stop to picnic. Swim at your own risk and pleasure.

Cole Run Falls plunges 50 feet over several ledges in a rhododen-dron-rimmed ravine. You will find parking by the bridge on Cole Run Road, a tad northwest of its intersection with Gary Run Road. Follow the trail 50 yards to the cascade.

The nearly 3,600-acre *Roaring Run Natural Area* is a young, third-growth mixed-hardwood forest showing signs of restoration. The site is bordered by PA 31 on the north, Tower Road on the east and south, County Line Road (SR 1058) on the south, and PA 381/711 (Tannery Road) on the west. Seven hiking trails totaling nearly 20 miles wander through the natural area. Combinations of these trails provide six different loops for hikers. If you have time for just one walk, choose the middle loop composed of the Roaring Run and Painter Rock Trails. State forest trails are marked with fading blue blazes and generally follow old logging roads, skid trails, and railroad grades.

Northside trails—North Loop (2.7 miles), Painter Rock (3.9 miles) and McKenna (3 miles) Trails—via the steep Pike Run Trail (1 mile) are accessible from a small parking area on PA 31, 3 miles east of PA 381. Access to the South Loop (3.7 miles), Roaring Run (3.9 miles) and Birch Rock (0.6 mile) Trails in the southwestern corner is from an area on SR 1058 (County Line Road). Roaring Run Trail starts at a parking area on Fire Tower Road (T346) in the southeastern corner. Hikers will cross Roaring Run nearly thirty times on this route, so wet feet are inevitable. The eastern terminus of the McKenna Trail, in the northeastern corner, is on Tower Road near PA 31. This also provides access to Painter Rock Trail at Nedrow Cemetery, on a dirt road off Tower Road.

Long stretches of the 70-mile Laurel Highlands Trail pass through the state forest. The route appears as a dotted red line on the state forest public use map. All of the above landmarks are also shown on the map.

For more information, contact District Forester, Forbes State Forest, P.O. Box 519, Laughlintown, PA 15655, telephone (724) 238-9533.

Geology. All of these Forbes State Forest sites are on Laurel Ridge, one of a group of elongated, southwest-northeast rolls in the Allegheny Mountains. Like the Appalachian Mountains to the east, Laurel Ridge was formed during the great uplifting called the Alleghenian Orogeny, when Gondwana (Africa and South America) crashed into North America some 290 million years ago.

The Laurel Ridge summit is broad and flat. Bedrock consists of 300-million-year-old gray sandstone, conglomerate, and shales of the Pottsville Formation, from the Pennsylvanian Period, atop similar rocks of the 330-million-year-old Mauch Chunk Formation, from the Mississippian Period. The bands of small cliffs, or rock breaks, on Painter Rock in Roaring Run Natural Area belong to the Pottsville family.

Mountain water tumbling over resistant sandstone into Blue Hole looks blue-gray because it reflects the tint of the softer siltstone lining the pool. Cole Run Falls plunge over a 12-foot layer of Homewood Sandstone, a Pottsville member, then 8 feet over a similar strata.

Laurel Summit Bog looks like a muskeg in eastern Canada, though its origin cannot be traced to a continental glacier. Instead, it owes its existence to the lumberjacks who clear-cut this shallow ridgetop depression nearly a century ago. When loggers arrived in 1908, mature hemlocks had filled in a former bog. Their roots spread in moist, stable peat atop an impermeable layer of sandstone. The hemlocks thrived in the moist habitat and kept conditions in balance by transpiring excess water through their short needles. Clear-cutting and subsequent forest fires ruined the natural balance. Precipitation pooled in the basin again, creating bog conditions. Projects to regrow trees in the flats failed, and dynamiting the bedrock to drain the swamp didn't work either.

Roaring Run trickles from several springs near the summit of Laurel Ridge. It tumbles westward through a steep-sided, heavily forested ravine into Indian Creek, a tributary of the Youghiogheny River. It descends 1,220 feet over its 5-mile length.

Wolf Rocks and Beam Rocks show the powerful effects of mechanical weathering by frost wedging and, to a lesser extent, root growth. Water that froze in sandstone cracks acted as a wedge. Repeated freezing and thawing eventually broke up the bedrock into large chunks, boulders, and slabs. Erosion by precipitation and wind continues to widen and shape the overlooks. Both landmarks expose massive layers of crossbedded Pottsville sandstone.

Wildlife. Forests usually have a predominant species or two, such as the beech-maple community of northwestern Pennsylvania, oak-hickory east of the Allegheny Mountains, and beech-hemlock of the Allegheny National Forest. On Laurel Ridge, however, some two dozen species compete for supremacy, making these wooded lands diverse. Several centuries ago, a dense deciduous mixture of oaks, hickories, chestnuts, walnuts, sugar maples, and tulip tree held sway. Andre Michaux, a French botanist who collected samples here in 1785, noted the locale's mammoth white oaks. The original giants are gone, felled by loggers or disease, as in the case of the chestnut. The area seems to be at a crossroads of tree types migrating up river valleys or down mountain ridges from other regions. Repeated logging and other human developments have greatly influenced botanical events in the last century.

Laurel Summit Bog used to be called Spruce Flats Bog, even though spruce didn't grow here. Loggers initially misidentified local hemlocks as spruce, and the name stuck until a new generation of hemlocks reached maturity.

Technically, a bog is a wetland replenished by precipitation. Bog water stays trapped above an impermeable layer of bedrock or clay, leaving only by evaporation. Decaying vegetation and sediment accumulate, turning the bog's water dark brown and acidic. Consequently, a true bog supports flora capable of surviving in an acidic environment. Since bogs are rare, so are their residents. This is the domain of the large cranberry, a creeping shrub 6 inches high that colonizes pools. Look for its oval, alternating leaves with a reddish purple tint. Pink flowers in July are followed by half-inch red berries in November. Another late bloomer is cotton grass, which appears as individual clumps up to 10 inches tall, widely distributed throughout the mire. Its globular, cottony seedpod appears in late summer and often stays into midwinter.

Insectivorous plants find this place a paradise. Careful observers with binocular might see the diminutive, round-leaved sundew, whose cupped, hair-lined, closable leaves snare and devour insects. Victims fall for the tiny, scented dewdrops on the bristles of its paddle-shaped leaves. Look for vermilion-colored colonies near hummocks or on mats of sphagnum moss. Northern pitcher plants are easier to spot. In June search for bowing, pale yellow or pink flowers atop 18-inch stalks. Follow the stalk down to several greenish vases, the pitchers, which point skyward. Bugs falling into the tubes get trapped by sticky digestive juices and recurved hairs on the leaf edges. The pitcher plant was introduced to this reemergent bog by the Westmoreland County Botanical Society.

Various ferns spread on both sides of the short trail to the bog, and white and red pines, witch hazels, tamaracks, and some tulip trees rise among the hemlocks. Highbush blueberry, chokecherry, huckleberry, and dewberry are scattered around the edge. The snags poking above the water are from previous failed reforestation efforts.

The Audubon Society of Western Pennsylvania compiled a list of seventy-seven birds that rely on the swamp. Scan for the American kestrel, the continent's smallest falcon, as well as the scarlet tanager, dark-eyed junco, indigo bunting, cedar waxwing, hermit thrush, black-billed cuckoo, eastern phoebe, Acadian flycatcher, rose-breasted grosbeak, yellow-bellied sapsucker, and chestnut-sided, magnolia, golden-winged, blackpoll, black-throated blue, and yellow-rumped warblers. These birders found the first nest of the golden-crowned kinglet in western Pennsylvania. Mammals observed around the bog include black bears, which relish the berries, white-tailed deer, striped skunks, raccoons, and chipmunks.

The trail to Wolf Rocks is lined by ferns, mountain laurel, greenbrier, witch hazel, great rhododendron, red oak, black cherry, serviceberry, sugar maple, chestnut oak, mountain ash, and striped maple, named for its attractive white-striped, green bark. Wood from the striped maple was prized for the stocks of Pennsylvania long rifles. Close to the ground, look for trilliums, Indian pipe, and club mosses. Local storytellers claimed the rock outcrops were the last stronghold of timber wolves in the area, hence the name Wolf Rocks.

Because of repeated logging, the forests in Roaring Run Natural Area are in various stages of recovery. Fifty of the 120 tree species in Pennsylvania grow here. Slopes with drier southern exposures and broad western faces host species of the mixed oak community, notably white, red, and black oaks. North-facing slopes, valley bottoms, and sheltered coves protect trees associated with mixed mesophytic forests—tulip tree, sugar maple, white oak, and basswood, distingushed by its serrated, heart-shaped leaves. Areas recently logged have thickets of sassafras, black cherry, red maple, blackberry, and various shrubs. Great rhododendron thickets, best seen in late June, cover the rill and keep deep pools dark and cool for brook trout. Along hard-to-reach rock breaks, bands of old-growth chestnut oaks and black birches stand as reminders of prehuman forest life. Spring wildflowers include trout lily, hepatica, wild ginger, toothworts, jack-in-the-pulpit, halberd-leaved violet, bittercress, Dutchman's breeches, wild leeks, bluebell, mayapple, large-flowered trillium, wild geranium, and yellow violets on the hilltops.

Breeding birds in the natural area include the white-breasted nuthatch, Louisiana waterthrush, yellow-bellied sapsucker, great-crested flycatcher cedar waxwing, chimney swift, eastern pewee, wood thrush, common yellowthroat, and yellow-rumped and hooded warblers.

Beam Rocks overlooks a valley carved by Beam Run and Spruce Run, the latter again named by woodcutters who mistook hemlock for spruce, which is absent. The cool water of Spruce Run creates an ideal microhabitat for hemlock, mountain laurel, and rhododendron. Canopy trees include white oak, red maple, black cherry, pignut hickory, tulip tree, white ash, black gum, and cucumber magnolia. Hop hornbeam, ironwood, witch hazel, serviceberry, striped maple, dogwoods, hawthorns, and Hercules' club occupy the understory. Here you're likely to flush a ruffed grouse, which enjoys hemlock seeds. The boulder-riddled trail to the overlook goes through an oak woods, highlighted by trailing arbutus, mountain laurel, blueberry, and rhododendron.

Forbes State Forest is a sanctuary for the Allegheny wood rat (PA threatened); Allegheny cave amphipod, a rare invertebrate; mountain bugbane, a threatened wildflower at the northern extent of its range; and Keen myotis, a bat becoming a rarity.

History. The state forest commemorates Brig. Gen. John Forbes, who commanded a British force that blazed a military road from Raystown across Laurel Hill and Chestnut Ridge to attack Fort Duquesne (now Pittsburgh) in 1757. The French withdrew from the fort before Forbes laid siege. US 30 roughly follows the Forbes Road, and all but two small tracts of state forest land are south of that famous wilderness route. The headquarters in Laughlintown straddles the old road.

The Blue Hole Division of the state forest was purchased from United Lumber of West Virginia in September 1931. The area was the site of a Civilian Conservation Corps camp in the 1930s. CCC laborers operated a sawmill below Cole Run Falls and built trails in the forest.

Remnants of the Pittsburgh, Westmoreland, and Somerset grade, a logging rail line running parallel to Linn Run Road (along Fish Run Trail), may still be seen. The Laurel Highlands Trail crosses the rail grade southeast of Laurel Summit Road, across from Laurel Summit State Park. Just down this road, near Beam Rocks, is the Airglow Observatory, used by University of Pittsburgh astronomers.

In the early 1900s, after the construction of a railroad along Indian Creek to Kregar, the forest flanking Roaring Run was destroyed. The slopes were completely shaved, then etched by railroads, a logging road, and skid trails. The hiking trail along Roaring Run follows a tram road built by the Blair Lumber Company. Loggers clear-cut most of Painter Rock Hill in the 1960s. The area then was purchased by the Western Pennsylvania Conservancy, which turned it over to the Bureau of Forestry in 1975.

Fort Necessity
National Battlefield

The day was July 3, 1998. I watched a ceremony from heights above a circular wooden barricade. A bagpipe wailed, a drum tapped solemn marching beats, and blue musket smoke drifted across the field. Acres of the red-berried elder surrounded me, their fruit the color of blood spilled by 110 men 244 years earlier.

Ownership. U.S. Department of the Interior, National Park Service.

Size. 901 acres.

Physiographic Region. Allegheny Mountains.

Nearby Natural Attractions. Ohiopyle State Park, Bear Run Nature Reserve, Friendship Hill National Historic Site, Laurel Caverns, and Quebec Run Wild Area.

Features. First, get your historical bearings at the visitors center via a twenty-minute audio-slide show. Hiking trail maps, a bird checklist, exhibits, rest rooms, drinking water, and a gift shop are also found here.

The park is open daily from 8 A.M. to sunset. Visitors center hours are 8:30 A.M. to 5 P.M. Closed on Christmas. Admission is $2 for adults; children sixteen years and under get in free. Picnic tables and shelters are located at the end of Braddock Road. A memorial program is held on July 3, the anniversary of the battle.

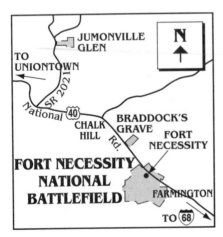

Follow the path from the visitors center to the stockade, reconstructed in 1954 to mark the bicentennial of the battle. After exploring the fort, head for the meadows along paths on the trail guide. Portions of trails trace Braddock Road, blazed in 1755 for Gen. Edward Braddock's ill-fated expedition to Fort Duquesne, as well as old farm lanes and the steps used by soldiers. A perimeter route covers about 2 miles, most of it through meadows and shrubland.

An uphill trail leads north from the visitors center to Mount Washington Tavern on US 40. The 170-year-old inn, now a park landmark, served travelers on the old National Road, but it no longer offers refreshments and lodging. General Braddock's grave is a mile west of Fort Necessity. Soldiers buried him in the middle of Braddock Road, then marched over the grave to disguise its location from pursuers.

Five weeks before the future president's surrender at Fort Necessity, scouts of Seneca chief Tanacharison led George Washington and his outfit to a small ravine 7 miles west of Fort Necessity. There they surprised and defeated French regulars camped beneath a ledge. As the park brochure accurately reports, "More than any other site in the park, Jumonville Glen evokes the isolated feeling of wilderness that characterized the Fort Necessity area in the 1750s." To get there, go west on US 40 toward Uniontown, then turn right at signs for the landmark. A short trail leads to the spot of the skirmish.

For more information, contact Superintendent, Fort Necessity National Battlefield, 1 Washington Parkway, Farmington, PA 15437, telephone (724) 329-5512.

Geology. Young George Washington built Fort Necessity in a clearing called the Great Meadows, located in a valley between Chestnut and Laurel Ridges, on the divide between two rivers. Water draining from the southwestern edge of the site goes into Big Sandy Creek, a branch of the Cheat River in West Virginia. A few hundred yards northeast of the fort, water moves north into Meadow Run, which empties into the Youghiogheny River at Ohiopyle State Park.

At Jumonville Glen on the summit of Chestnut Ridge, Washington deployed his troops atop ledges of Pottsville sandstone, the same 300-million-year-old bedrock that floors the falls at Ohiopyle.

Wildlife. The original Great Meadow was enlarged many times for farming, which continued until the 1930s. The vast woods that once surrounded the fort has been reduced to a few acres. Much of the battlefield is in various stages of succession, from grassland to young forest. Jumonville Glen is wooded with second-growth black cherry, oaks, and maples.

The edible purple-black fruit of elderberry ripens in late August to late September. The fruit of the American red-berried elder is bitter to humans but tasty to many birds and animals. Wildflowers include daisies, butterfly weed, Queen Anne's lace, and black-eyed Susan.

A recently developed checklist reveals that 165 bird species have been observed in the Great Meadow, including the Acadian flycatcher, eastern pewee, ruby-throated hummingbird, chimney swift, eastern phoebe, barn swallow, wood thrush, American goldfinch, rose-breasted grosbeak, and solitary vireo. Thirty-five wood warblers have been seen, including the northern paraula, American redstart, and yellow-rumped, prairie, hooded, bay-breasted, and black-throated green warblers. On my visit, I saw lots of fritillaries and checkerspot butterflies.

History. George Washington thought that the swampy forest clearing he called the Great Meadow was "a charming field for an encounter." Charming for the French and their Indian allies, it turned out. Military strategy and common sense suggested fortifying high ground, but the naive Virginia aristocrat instead chose open, low ground in a wet, shallow basin. Worse yet, an oak wilderness encircled the tiny stronghold, dubbed Fort Necessity. An enemy could creep within easy musket range and be protected behind trees.

Washington and his 392 men busied themselves improving a military road to Fort Duquesne, ambushing recumbent French soldiers, and digging trenches to repel an approaching French force. But on a rainy July 3, 1754, using the forest for cover and the heights to their advantage, 600 French and 100 Indians forced Washington's surrender.

Washington journeyed to this region five times before the American Revolution. He first came through here on a diplomatic mission in 1753, along an Indian path blazed in 1750 by Nemacolin, a Lenni-Lenape warrior. Virginia governor Robert Dinwiddie had sent Washington to Fort LeBoeuf, near Erie, to warn the French to withdraw from the forks of the Ohio. The French answered by occupying the forks and erecting Fort Duquesne. Washington's second visit resulted in the construction of Fort Necessity and his defeat there in July 1754. The French had the good sense to torch the stockade.

On June 25, 1755, Washington rode by the ruins of Fort Necessity with the 2,400-man army of Gen. Edwin Braddock, whose name became associated with the overland trail between Fort Cumberland (Will's Creek) and the forks of the Ohio (Pittsburgh). Braddock suffered an ignominious defeat approaching Fort Duquesne two weeks later. Washington miraculously survived the surprise attack and attended Braddock's burial a mile northwest of Fort Necessity.

Washington led the Virginia regiments in 1758, when Gen. John Forbes occupied an evacuated Fort Duquesne. Though Forbes blazed a new route to the fort, the Forbes Road, Washington returned to Virginia via the Braddock Road after the campaign.

He returned in 1770 to stake out land that he hoped would be given him for earlier military service. Washington chose the Great Meadow, though not for sentimental reasons. The tract promised profit because it straddled the Braddock Road, the main means of east-west travel until the National Road opened in 1818. In 1827 and 1828 Judge Nathaniel Ewing, then owner of the historic property, built the small mansion that became Mount Washington Tavern.

The National Park Service reconstructed Fort Necessity for its bicentennial program in 1954. The circular visitors center matches the dimensions of the palisade—53 feet in diameter, and 168 feet circumference.

Frick Woods Nature Reserve

To migrating birds, especially warblers, Frick Woods is a green oasis in Pittsburgh. To inner-city schoolkids, Frick Woods may mean their first experience with the natural world. To others, it's a rich repository of wildlife diversity.

Ownership. City of Pittsburgh.

Size. Frick Woods Nature Reserve is a 150-acre urban wildlife reserve in 627-acre Frick Park.

Physiographic Region. Low Plateau.

Nearby Natural Attractions. Beechwood Farms Nature Reserve, the Flower and Wildlife Preserve, Dead Man's Hollow and Barking Slopes Wildlife Preserves, Bradford Woods, and Harrison Hills, Boyce, and North Parks, all in Allegheny County.

Features. The reserve's trail system starts at the Frick Environmental Center, a three-level facility housing the visitor information center, library, staff offices, exhibits, classrooms, kitchen, and rest rooms. Educational programs on natural history and the environment are held here. A self-tracking, 6,000-watt photovoltaic system on the roof produces some of the electricity for the center, which is open weekdays 8 A.M. to 4 P.M. Interpretive guides and a trail map are available here.

Five interlocking trails measuring 2.5 miles wind through the reserve. The level North and South Clayton Trails go their separate ways from the parking lot and merge at the eastern end of the reserve, where there is a smaller gateway into the reserve. Woodland Trail is a quarter-mile paved interpretive path behind the center, a good choice for small children. The quarter-mile Nature Trail traces

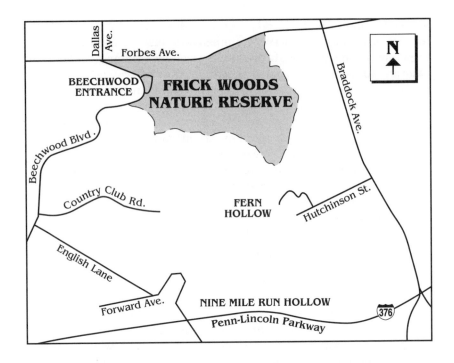

the north edge of a hollow and leads to the Falls Ravine Trail, which plunges into a 200-foot-deep gorge decked with waterfalls, ancient oaks, towering tulip trees, rock outcrops, and spring wildflowers. This path—the best in the reserve—intersects with trails that venture into Fern Hollow, Nine Mile Run Hollow, and other places in greater Frick Park. These former carriage lanes are wide, smooth, and easy to follow. Unfortunately, patrons ignore prohibitions against mountain bikes and unleashed dogs. Even storm-felled trees across the half-mile North Clayton Trail did not deter bicyclists.

Outside the nature reserve, Frick Park has picnic areas, athletic fields, tennis courts, a bowling green, and more walking paths. For more information, contact Frick Environmental Center, 2005 Beechwood Blvd., Pittsburgh, PA 15217, telephone (412) 422-6538.

Geology. The terrain resembles the rest of Allegheny County, a plateau deeply cut by streams, here Nine Mile and Falls Runs. Bedrock exposed by these currents—sandstone and shale mostly, with bands of limestone and coal—dates back 300 million years to the Pennsylvanian Period. Nine Mile Run enters the Monongahela River 9 miles above its merger with the Allegheny River.

Wildlife. One weekend in May 1998, during an event called BioBlitz, a crew of scientists and naturalists identified 1,471 species of life in Frick Park. The inventory included 974 species of insects,

344 kinds of plants, 83 birds, 38 fungi, 15 amphibians and reptiles, and 15 mammals. The crew found beavers busy on Nine Mile Run, the creek running through the southern part of the park. The team also recorded the park's first sighting of a surf scoter, an Atlantic coast shorebird, and it identified a ravine salamander, an amphibian usually found in extreme southwestern Pennsylvania.

The reserve's deciduous forest is primarily composed of red and white oaks, beeches, and sugar maple, with smatterings of shagbark and mockernut hickories, tulip tree, hemlocks, black willow, black locust, ashes, slippery elm, sycamores, and black cherry. Mountain laurel, hawthorns, staghorn sumac, silky dogwood, Hercules' club, rhododendrons, red chokeberry, highbush cranberry, witch hazel, iron-wood, hackberry, and spicebush grow in the understory. Spring wild-flowers include mayapple, jack-in-the-pulpit, cut-leaved toothwort, wild geranium, false Solomon's seal, and spring beauty, followed by jewelweed, joe-pye weed, milkweed, purple coneflower, and burdock in summer, and goldenrods and asters in early autumn. A wet meadow along Nine Mile Run east of Commercial Road contains cattails, swamp milkweed, bulrush, marsh Saint-John's-wort, and sedges.

Birdwatchers have sighted 169 species in the park and adjacent Homewood Cemetery. Woodland activity gets hectic when warblers arrive in spring. Check out Falls Ravine and Fern Hollow for Ameri-can redstarts, pine, black-and-white, yellow-rumped, Nashville, Tennessee, magnolia, black-throated green, cerulean, hooded, chest-nut-sided, Blackburnian, bay-breasted, worm-eating, Connecticut, blackpoll, and mourning warblers. Other birds include the yellow-bel-lied sapsucker, golden-crowned kinglet, common nighthawk, chimney swift, cedar waxwing, Carolina chickadee, red-bellied woodpecker, great horned owl, eastern phoebe, hermit thrush, and summer tan-ager (PA rare).

Resident animals include white-tailed deer, chipmunks, rabbits, gray squirrels, raccoons, shrews, brown bats, eastern box turtles, black rat and eastern garter snakes, spring peepers, and American toads.

History. Industrialist Henry Clay Frick donated these 150 wooded acres to the city of Pittsburgh in 1919, along with a $2 million trust fund for maintenance. The parcel became the cornerstone of a nature reserve bearing his name. When the park opened in 1927, the city car-ried out Frick's intentions that the place be kept in its natural state. By 1936 the park had increased to 476 acres, including a golf course and nature center.

The existing environmental education center opened in 1979. Frick's original acreage was rededicated Frick Woods Nature Reserve on Earth Day 1991. In 1996 the city purchased 111 more acres, enlarg-ing park to 627 acres.

Friendship Hill
National Historic Site

A lbert Gallatin came here when the nation was new, when wilderness beyond a fecund valley was the view. Today's outlook on the Monongahela River from Gallatin's bluff hardly merits a line. Come instead for the wildflowers and birds in the bush—and for an unhurried stroll for body and soul.

Ownership. U.S. Department of the Interior, National Park Service.

Size. 662 acres.

Physiographic Region. Pittsburgh Low Plateau.

Nearby Natural Attractions. Fort Necessity National Battlefield, Laurel Caverns, Bear Run Nature Reserve, Ohiopyle State Park, and Quebec Run Wild Area.

Features. The 3.8-mile Main Loop, designated a national recreation trail, journeys through conifer and hardwood forests, meadows, and shaded glens; across a bluff above the Monongahela River; along the river; and past waterfalls, pioneer graves, and ponds. A trail map is available at the visitors center in the Gallatin Mansion.

One recommended trail continues south between the mansion and a gazebo overlooking the river. Follow signs to Sophia's grave and green blazes thereafter. The toughest part of the route is a 200-foot descent from the bluff to river. Routes can be shortened or lengthened by following branch trails marked with red or yellow blazes. Park rangers estimate that there are 8 miles of track.

For more information, contact Friendship Hill National Historic Site, R.D. 2, Box 528, Farmington, PA 15347, telephone (724) 329-5512.

Geology. The landscape, typical of southwestern Pennsylvania, consists of a plateau incised by rivers and streams. The northbound Monongahela River flows more than 200 feet below the bluff behind Gallatin's home. The intermittent South, Dublin, and Ice Pond Runs empty into the Monongahela after draining the estate. These rills have carved seven small waterfalls in 300-million-year-old bedrock from the Pennsylvanian Period.

Wildlife. When Albert Gallatin arrived in 1785, the Monongahela River was just a pace or two behind the western frontier, then drawn at the Ohio River. From his bluff, he watched flatboats heading west and pioneers felling trees for riverside cabins. The forest seemed endless, and so did the human tide.

Agriculture, logging, transportation routes, and mining all adversely affected this land. Except for shade trees by the mansion and some oaks in hard-to-log ravines, the trees on this property have been cut down two or three times since Gallatin's day. One-third to half of the grounds remains unforested, though much of this open area consists of uncut meadows.

Today sixty-one kinds of trees and thirty-six shrubs thrive on the estate. Some are stalwart natives—red oak, beeches, ashes, sycamores, hemlocks, basswood, shagbark hickory, and white oak. Others are alien imports, such as Douglas fir, Osage orange, blue spruce, larch, ailanthus, and saucer magnolia. Understory trees and shrubs that brighten springtime include flowering dogwood, shadbush, redbud, crab apple, great rhododendron, and lilac.

Friendship Hill is a little-known wildflower treasure, with hundreds of varieties. From March to June, sixty-six species show their colors, including dwarf larkspur, Dutchman's breeches, bluets, squawroot, wild phlox, trout lily, and three kinds of trilliums. Oxeye daisy, boneset, wild bergamot, enchanter's nightshade, Saint-John's-wort, pokeweed, Queen Anne's lace, and arrowhead are some of the summer bloomers. Autumn brings asters, great lobelia, wintergreen, virgin's bower, beechdrops, and sneezeweed to the forefront.

A checklist of 152 species has been prepared for birders. The diversity of habitats—forests, fields, wetlands treating mine runoff, and creeks—accounts for the variety. Commonly seen on the property are the ring-necked pheasant, common nighthawk, screech owl, broad-winged hawk, American kestrel, eastern pewee, black-and-white and chestnut-sided warblers, ovenbird, red-eyed vireo, American goldfinch, dark-eyed junco, and scarlet tanager. Migrating waterfowl and birds of prey, notably ospreys, are sighted during their autumn and spring flights. State-imperiled birds including Bewick's wren, the pied-billed grebe, great blue heron, northern saw-whet owl, northern harrier, and summer tanager appear from time to time.

History. Abraham Alfonse Albert Gallatin (1761–1849) came to America from Switzerland in 1780. With the profits from business and teaching, he purchased this parcel in 1785 and built the home a few years later. Gallatin intended to become a wealthy western land speculator and gentleman farmer, but public service called him from Friendship Hill for long stretches of time. During a political career that spanned thirty-seven years, he served as a state legislator, congressman, U.S. treasury secretary for Jefferson and Madison, diplomat, and foreign minister to England and France. In the last twenty years of his life he resided in New York City, where he was president of a bank, founder of the American Ethnological Society, and president of the New York Historical Society. Gallatin's first wife, Sophia, is buried on the property. The historic site also encompasses some land owned by Gallatin's friend and neighbor, Thomas Clare, who called his estate Dublin. The Main Loop path also passes the Clare family plot. The historic site was established in 1978.

Fringed Gentian Fen

There's only one time to come here—a sunny day in early September—and only one reason: to see a rare, fussy wildflower beloved by poets. The shy fringed gentian, an endangered species, is the gem in this botanical jewel box. Don't drive across the state to see this place, though, unless you're hopelessly hooked on botany—or poetry.

Ownership. Western Pennsylvania Conservancy.

Size. 0.8 acre.

Physiographic Region. Glaciated Plateau.

Nearby Natural Attractions. McConnells Mill and Moraine State Parks, Miller Esker, and Jennings Environmental Education Center.

Features. Four-tenths of a mile down Frew Mill Road (SR 1012) from PA 388, look for orange telephone cable post 106, marking the start of the fen. You won't find signs or even the simplest accommodations. Good luck finding roadside parking. Sometimes a path is cleared from the road into the heart of the fen. Rubber boots and wild-flower field guides are recommended. And maybe a blank pad and pen in case inspiration strikes.

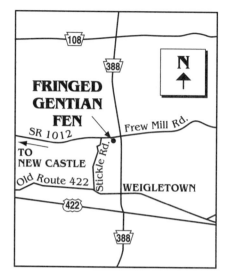

Geology. Though it resembles a regular cattail swamp, this wetland is a fen replenished by slow-moving spring and surface water that usu-ally exits into a stream. A bog, on the other hand, gets water only from pre-cipitation and has no outlet. Whereas a bog accumulates, a fen flushes. The outlet in this instance is Big Run, a tributary of the Shenango River.

Here, groundwater seeps through alkaline soil deposited by the Wiscon-sinan glacier around 12,000 years ago. Consequently, water percolat-ing through the fen distributes calcium, magnesium, and other elements favored by plants that thrive in cool, neutral to alkaline soils, like the fringed gentian.

Wildlife. The Mediterranean blue of the fringed gentian stirred the nineteenth-century hearts and pens of William Cullen Bryant, Emily Dickinson, and Henry David Thoreau. In his ode "To the Fringed Gentian," Bryant, the naturalist and poet, accurately described a petal with "heaven's own blue" that blossoms when "frosts and shortening days portend/the aged year is near his end." The flower's striking col-oration was "such a dark blue" to Thoreau. Dickinson called it a "purple creature that ravished all the hill," telling us of the bloom's abundance in her day.

The fringed gentian's decline stems largely from the loss of wet-lands, and partly from its peculiar ways. It requires hard-to-find wet soil fortified in magnesium with a neutral pH of 7. Being a biennial, it takes two years to unfurl its colors and fall to seed, so a patch cut down in its first year won't blossom the next. In spite of its cerulean beauty, it can be hidden by taller and pushier swamp growth. The stem grows only a foot to hold a 2-inch flower composed of four fringed petals. As Bryant observed, this jewel "look[s] through its fringes to the sky." Like its kin, it folds its wings at night or when a cloud starves it of light.

Ironweed, bur-marigold, spotted joe-pye weed, and various gold-enrods crowd the fen. Pick through the grasses to find white beauties called nodding ladies' tresses and turtlehead. Plant lore says that the turtlehead flower will open wider if the base of its blossom is pinched, though this has never worked for me. Look for the distinctive arrow-shaped leaf of arrowhead and for grass of Parnassus, whose white bloom sports green veins. A colony of great lobelia struggles by the brook.

31

Glade Dam Lake

Birdwatchers call this place the Glades, a sweet-sounding name for an artificial lake and surrounding land recovering from surface coal mining. Myriad microhabitats attract 200 species of birds to the site, and they, in turn, bring binocular-toting birders. Bald eagles, which began nesting here in the early 1990s, have become the star attraction. Many miles of unmarked trails are a bonus for hikers who enjoy wandering.

Ownership. The Pennsylvania Game Commission owns the property and calls it State Game Lands 95. Don't confuse this impoundment with Glade Lake in southern Butler County.

Size. Glade Dam Lake totals 400 acres. The multiparcel game lands comprise 9,268 acres.

Physiographic Region. Pittsburgh Low Plateau.

Nearby Natural Attractions. Moraine State Park, Jennings Environmental Educational Center, Miller Esker, Wolf Creek Narrows Natural Area, and Todd Sanctuary.

Features. In spring the northwestern three-quarters of the lake and the land flanking it, from Tinker and Christie Roads to the spillway, are a wildlife propagation area off-limits to people, as the bald eagles nesting there don't like human intruders. Consequently, local birdwatchers make their viewing rounds in cars and watch the eagles from a distance.

Glade Dam Lake's size changes dramatically during the year. The game commission lets the impoundment swell south to Calico Road, and sometimes to PA 138, for autumn migrations and through

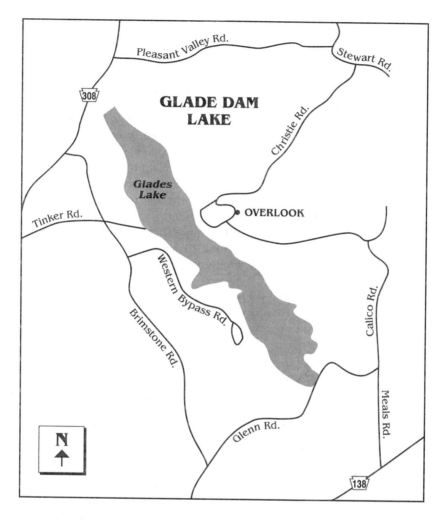

winter. Come spring and summer, open water is shrunk in half so that shoreline vegetation and its inhabitants can prosper. There are plenty of paths for walkers.

A route recommended by the Audubon Society of Western Pennsylvania starts at the spillway dam off PA 308, north of Moniteau High School, then goes to a number of locations that offer good birding, as detailed under Wildlife, below. Hikers will find a network of trails stemming from several of the locations. One overlook offers a sheltered bench. For birdwatching, take along binoculars or a spotting scope, if you have one. Boaters can launch small craft from a ramp at the end of Christie Road on the east shore. Pleasant Valley, Calico, and Christie Roads are not maintained in winter.

For more information, contact Pennsylvania Game Commission, P.O. Box 31, 1509 Pittsburgh Rd., Franklin, PA 16323, telephone (814) 432-3187. The map for this game lands does not show all the roads or all the trails on the site.

Geology. The 2.5-mile lake was formed by plugging the South Branch of Slippery Rock Creek, a tributary of the Beaver River. Glade Dam Lake is shallow, so it freezes earlier and thaws later than larger and deeper lakes nearby. When Lake Arthur, in Moraine State Park, loses its ice, you can still count on Glade Dam Lake to have some.

Much of the land surrounding the impoundment has been strip-mined for coal, a clue indicating that the bedrock beneath the lake dates back 300 million years to the Pennsylvanian Period. Oil and gas wells dot the landscape.

Wildlife. Some 200 species of birds are widely scattered among the site's many habitats, which include open water; snag-filled marshes; mudflats; swamp forests; dry and wet meadows; thickets of crab apple, multiflora rose, autumn olive, and shrubs; hardwood forests; red pine groves; cornfields; old orchards; hedgerows; and strip mines reclaimed by aspens, red maples, and conifers.

At the spillway overlook, the first stop on the birders' tour, look for cormorants, herons, swallows, waterfowl, eastern bluebirds, and belted kingfishers. Also look for a stone memorial to Woodrow E. Portzline, a game protector from 1948 to 1978, for his work in establishing this waterfowl area. The dam often attracts nesting cliff swallows. Ahead, a man-made wetland created in 1994 is beginning to bring in moorhens, rails, and bitterns. Park beyond the bridge.

A game commission road off Pleasant Valley Road leads to a swamp that supports rails, flycatchers, bitterns, and warblers in spring and rusty blackbirds in autumn. Several unmarked but easy-to-follow trails branch from the parking lot at the end of this road. Here you might find Baltimore orioles, grosbeaks, tanagers, chats, and blue-winged and golden-winged warblers.

Canada geese and killdeer usually lounge at a private pond on the south side of Pleasant Valley Road. Heading back to the lake on Christie Road, look for horned larks, grasshopper and field sparrows, yellow-breasted chats, and prairie warblers in fields. Turkey vultures once roosted in heights on Christie Road. The game lands parking area at the end of Christie Road offers a surface-level panoramic view of the lake. Continuing along the lakeshore, take the next left to the Vista Trail, parking at side of the road. The short path lead to a sheltered bench and the best view to watch bald eagles, ospreys, double-crested cormorants, gulls, terns, and waterfowl. Finely tuned eyes and ears might recognize an alder flycatcher. Finish the loop and continue east on Christie Road, past some cottages, to a gated dirt lane on the right. Stop at the lily pond on the right and look for a king rail, wood duck, coot (PA at risk), green heron, or sora. Midway down this path scan the opposite lakeshore for bald eagles (PA endangered). In the swamps and fields at the end of the trail, you may sight red-headed woodpeckers, merlins, long-eared owls, black-crowned night herons (PA rare), and least bitterns (PA threatened).

American kestrels and eastern meadowlarks are sure bets before arriving at wetlands, the next stop on the birders' tour. Kingbirds and cedar waxwings have been seen here, along with other wetland birds. Ponds and marshy areas on Calico Road are good for dabbling and diving ducks, and Harbor Acres Lake attracts buffleheads, mergansers, and other ducks, as well as ospreys (PA endangered). Encircling fields host bobolinks, bluebirds, and blackbirds. Common snipes, eastern phoebes, American pipits, swamp sparrows, and shorebirds gather at the southern end of the lake. Here you might glimpse a northern harrier (PA rare) or a short-eared owl (PA endangered), a winter guest. Herons and kingfishers hunt the abundant population of wood frogs.

Ahead, turn north on Brimstone Road (T464). Hunters know that wild turkeys, ruffed grouse, and pheasants hang out in the reclaimed strip mines. Parking areas on the right allow you to explore this area. Turn right on Western Bypass Road (a.k.a. Swope Road), and park at the overlook just beyond a right turn, another good location to observe waterfowl, hawks, and ospreys. Check out the ponds for ducks and geese. This road ends at a turnaround parking lot and an eastbound trail to Calico Road. The final stop is a former boat launch at the end of Tinker Road, where herons, gulls, waterfowl, and flycatchers have been seen. This spot is at the edge of the wildlife propagation area. Wear blaze orange during the autumn and spring (turkey) hunting seasons.

The game commission started a bald eagle nesting project in 1989, but the eggs did not hatch that year or in 1990. A second nest built in a more secluded spot in 1991 has fledged a dozen or so eaglets. Birders seeking a glimpse of the eagles should be quiet, slow-moving, and inconspicuous, and shouldn't prolong the visit. This mighty bird of prey gets ruffled by human intruders and may abandon its nest after only a few disturbances.

History. Glade Dam Lake was established in the mid-1970s in a region of reclaimed strip mines. Since then, the game commission has done salvage logging and created ponds, parking areas, and a boat launch. Other sections of State Game Lands 95 are located a few miles north and east of the lake.

32

Harrison Hills Park

Two long-distance trails bring hikers to this park's memorable panorama above the Allegheny River. Diverse habitats, a river corridor, and tall cliffs make this park a mecca for area birders.

Ownership. Allegheny County Department of Parks, Recreation and Conservation.

Size. 500 acres.

Physiographic Region. Pittsburgh Low Plateau.

Nearby Natural Attractions. Todd Sanctuary, Crooked Creek Lake, Beechwood Farms Nature Reserve, and North Park.

Features. Yellow blazes mark the cliff-edged Rachel Carson Trail, a 33-mile hike between Harrison Hills and North Park. This route, honoring the celebrated environmentalist Rachel Carson, connects with the Baker Trail, which concludes its 140-mile journey here. Both trails were blazed by the Pittsburgh Council of the American Youth Hostels. Baker Trail commemorates Horace Forbes Baker, the council's founder. The park, open 8 A.M. to dusk, provides picnic tables, rest rooms, a basketball court, and open play areas.

For more information, contact Allegheny County Department of Parks, Recreation and Conservation, Penn-Liberty Plaza, 1520 Penn Ave., Pittsburgh, PA 15222, telephone (412) 350-PARKS.

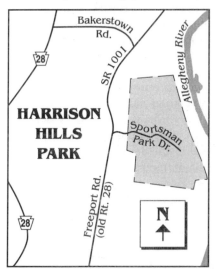

Geology. The park's riverside bluffs are evidence of the Allegheny River's ancient erosive power. Over many millenia, the current has cut through several hundred feet of bedrock, most of it formed during the Pennsylvanian Period, some 300 million years ago. The cliffside trail leads to side-cut waterfalls spilling over sandstone and shale. These suspended streams, or hanging valleys, have not cut through the bedrock as fast as the mightier main flow.

Wildlife. The forested slope and upland woods contains second-growth basswood, tulip tree, black birch, red and sugar maples, bitternut and

98

shagbark hickories, sassafras, serviceberry, and red, black, and white oaks. Ferns, lichens, and mosses thicken rock outcrops, fallen trees, and the forest floor.

The park's myriad niches attract 160 bird species. Birders should begin by going to the Michael Watts Memorial Overlook and begin scanning the sky. Updrafts rising more than 200 feet from the river often hold soaring turkey vultures; sharp-shinned, Cooper's, and red-tailed hawks; northern goshawks; merlins; and an occasional osprey. During the spring and autumn migrations, flocks of warblers arrive with waves of flycatchers, thrushes, sparrows, finches and vireos. The cliff edge is good for seeing treetop birds, like the cerulean, hooded, and black-and-white warblers. Experts have spotted the loggerhead shrike and white-winged crossbill on the property.

Nesters include the Acadian flycatcher, American redstart, Kentucky warbler, yellow-throated vireo, blue-gray gnatcatcher, broad-winged hawk, and great-crested flycatcher. Unkempt fields and meadow thickets protect the American woodcock, yellow-breasted chat, white-eyed vireo, eastern bluebird, eastern kingbird, willow and alder flycatchers, tree swallow, and prairie and blue-winged warblers.

A pond on the east side of the park, accessible via a trail at the end of Woodchuck Drive, attracts ducks, shorebirds, occasional herons, and swallows. Snapping turtles and muskrats also live in the pond. Rabbits, woodchucks, and crows venture to the roadsides.

History. Harrison Hills was dedicated a park in 1986. Michael Watts, honored at the overlook, was a local conservationist and clean water advocate.

33

Jennings Environmental Education Center

While poking around here one summer day nearly a century ago, botanist Otto E. Jennings stumbled onto magenta-hued patches of blazing star, a common prairie flower in the Great Plains but an anomaly in Pennsylvania. Nearby, he found clumps of other prairie petals struggling among shrubs and hardwood trees. Jennings had discovered a botanical shipwreck, a tiny relict of a prairie peninsula that poked into western Pennsylvania some 4,000 years ago.

Ownership. Pennsylvania Department of Conservation and Natural Resources, Bureau of State Parks.

Size. 295 acres.

Physiographic Region. Pittsburgh Low Plateau and border of Glaciated Plateau.

Nearby Natural Attractions. Moraine State Park (borders the center), Miller Esker, McConnells Mill State Park, Wolf Creek Narrows Natural Area, and Fringed Gentian Fen.

Features. The relict prairie encompasses about 30 acres of the grounds. The remaining 265 acres is a mixed hardwood forest typical of the region. Ten miles of trails wander through the site. To visit the prairie, take the Blazing Star, Prairie Loop, and Massasauga Trails, on the north side of PA 528. The flowers bloom from mid-July to Labor Day, with the star of the show—blazing star—peaking in early August. Take woodland strolls along the Deer, Oakwoods, Hepatica, and Glacier Ridge Trails, south of the prairie (2.5 miles), and behind the education center via the Black Cherry and Ridge Trails (1.5 miles).

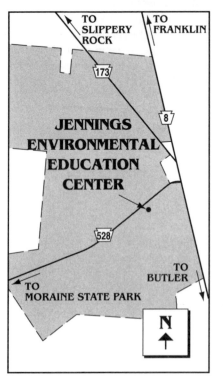

The Ridge Trail tracks across a terminal moraine that marks the stopping point of the Wisconsinan Glacier. Follow Glacier Ridge Trail, which branches from the south side of PA 528 west of the entrance, to hike into Moraine State Park.

The visitors center has exhibits and hosts nature programs year-round. School buses are a common sight in the parking lot. Picnic areas, shelters, and rest rooms are available. The center is open Monday through Friday from 8 A.M. to 4 P.M., and for weekend and evening programs. The trails are open every day from 8 A.M. to sunset. Naturalists conduct programs regularly, including prairie walks in summer.

For more information and a schedule of programs, contact Jennings Environmental Education

Center, R.D. 1, Box 281, Slippery Rock, PA 16057, telephone (412) 794-6011.

Geology. The prairie owes its slender existence to geological events that occurred here 14,000 years ago. Back then, this spot was covered by Lake Edmund, a freshwater impoundment created when the Wisconsinan glacier blocked the flow of Slippery Rock Creek. Fine sediments of silt, clay, and sand washed off the glacier and settled in layers on the lake bottom. When the glacier retreated, Lake Edmund drained, exposing the impervious sediments. About 6 inches of glacial till spread over the former lakebed, but this topping was thin and less fertile than surrounding areas. Consequently, trees have struggled to gain a foothold here. The other elements needed for a successful prairie—prolonged warmth and the plants themselves—came later.

Wildlife. About 7,000 years ago, a warmer and drier global climate enabled prairie flora from the Great Plains to spread eastward across Illinois, Indiana, Ohio, and western Pennsylvania. This "prairie peninsula" peaked about 4,000 years ago. When cooler and moister weather returned, the hardwood forest supplanted most of the prairie, which at the time of European settlement had shrunk to a few small, isolated pockets. Jennings saved this one from extirpation. It is the only state-protected prairie in the commonwealth.

There are only a handful of blazing star colonies in the state. Elsewhere, it's called gayfeather, liatris, or prairie pine. Blazing star (*Liatris spicata*) rises spikelike 3 to 6 feet before blossoming in bushy, thistlelike, purplish clusters. Oddly, it opens from the top downward. You'll have to look closely to see the star-shaped petal tube that gives the plant its common name.

Jennings also has Pennsylvania's most significant population of the state-endangered American columbo. The plant spends several years as a rosette, then launches a stalk 8 feet or more in a month. It blooms once and perishes, making it a monocarpic plant. Other state-imperiled plants are the cuckoo flower, Mead's sedge, tall tick clover, golden seal, hairy honeysuckle, Cary's knotweed, yellow water-crowfoot, and spikerush, once thought to have been extirpated.

All totaled, naturalists have counted 366 species of plants. Other prairie flowers growing in the wet meadows here include coneflowers, joe-pye weed, blue vervain, tall coreopsis, whorled rosinweed, and boneset. Also look for sweet william, ironweed, hawkweed, Bowman's root, steeplebush, yarrow, thistles, virgin's bower, meadowsweet, purple fringed orchid, tall meadow rue, blue skullcap, purple milkwort, hepatica, and Culver's root.

Prairies contain grasses too, and fourteen varieties enrich these patches, including bearded shorthusk, poverty oats, and wild chess grasses. Explore all niches for ferns, twenty-seven types in all. Take along a field guide to identify Boott's woodfern, marginal shield, Goldie's, filmy, New York, and crested ferns.

Hikers are apt to see fire-charred acres. Every year, a portion of the prairie is burned to clear out invasive shrubs and trees. The flames don't harm the prairie flowers and forbs, because their roots are deep in the ground. Fire is a necessary element of a prairie ecosystem and stimulates the plants' growth.

Seventy-five percent of the park is forested by forty-one kinds of trees and shrubs. Smooth alder, shagbark hickory, four types of dogwoods, hawthorns, serviceberry, American hazelnut, and shrubby Saint-John's-wort represent woody species characteristic of a prairie. Various oaks, sugar maple, American beech, hickories, black cherry, and white ash constitute much of the woods. Yellow birch and basswood cluster in rich, moist areas like Big Run Valley. Smooth blackhaw, staghorn sumac, fire cherry, and slippery elm also thrive here.

Jennings Center protects the venomous massasauga rattlesnake, an endangered species living here at the eastern edge of its range. Massasaugas are small, shy reptiles that live symbiotically with white crayfish. The snake snuggles into a crayfish hole but does not eat its host. Instead, it attacks meadow voles, the main predator of the crayfish, as well as mice, frogs, and birds. This system keeps the populations of crayfish, rattlesnakes, and voles in balance.

A bird checklist available at the visitors center lists 145 species in the park. Goldfinches swarm around the prairie in August. Unlike most birds, which nest in spring, these yellow puffs hatch their chicks when thistles and other meadow plants are producing seeds. Other nesters include the pileated woodpecker, barred owl, great-crested flycatcher, rose-breasted grosbeak, wood duck, and sharp-shinned, Cooper's, red-tailed, broad-winged, and red-shouldered hawks. Another prairie regular is the blue-winged warbler, with drab blue-gray wings and greenish back offset by a bright yellow chest. Thirty-five other kinds of warblers arrive in spring, notably the Tennessee, Nashville, bay-breasted, chestnut-sided, prairie, black-and-white, Kentucky, hooded, Cape May, black-throated green, yellow, and American redstart. Winter residents include kinglets, red-breasted nuthatch, evening grosbeak, and brown creeper.

History. The educational center is appropriately named after Otto E. Jennings, a botanist at the Carnegie Museum of Natural History in Pittsburgh who persuaded the Western Pennsylvania Conservancy to acquire the tract in 1950. The conservancy leased the site to Slippery Rock State College in the 1970s, but limited funding and lack of permanent staffing required its transferral to the Pennsylvania Department of Conservation and Natural Resources, Bureau of State Parks. Jennings Center became a state park in 1981.

34

Laurel Caverns

Pennsylvania's largest cave system continues to eat through the bowels of Chestnut Ridge. Most people explore only the lighted, blazed, and groomed portion of the underground maze. The other half of the cave stays dark and silent, except during special hard-hat and flashlight tours for the geologically inclined. New passages were discovered in 1995, and spelunkers figure that more catacombs remain to be seen. Meanwhile, gravity-driven groundwater continues to grind away the limestone that floored an ocean 300 million years ago.

Ownership. Privately owned by the Cale family.

Size. The grounds encompass 430 acres. Cave passages wander for 2.3 miles.

Physiographic Region. The caverns snake beneath the western slope of Chestnut Ridge in the Allegheny Mountains, near the eastern border of the Pittsburgh Low Plateau.

Nearby Natural Attractions. Fort Necessity National Battlefield, Quebec Run Wild Area, Friendship Hill National Historic Site, Ohiopyle State Park, and Bear Run Nature Reserve.

Features. Although Laurel Caverns lacks the intricate, colorful, and delicate rock formations, such as stalactites and stalagmites, found in other caves, the place has singularity, a maze of passages, and eager, well-informed guides. As owner David Cale writes, "The real beauty of Laurel Caverns is not to be found in its lighting effects or scenic passage vistas. Rather, it is to be found in an appreciation of the caverns as a time exposure of events which took place around it, events which commenced long before the thunder of the first dinosaur rumbled across the Earth."

Ninety percent of all visitors take the hour-long guided tour through the lighted, maintained portion of the cavern. Groups leave every twenty minutes with knowledgeable guides, who explain the geological history and the names of formations, such as the Grand Canyon, Pillars of Hercules, Dining Room, and Hall of the Mountain King, and tell some cave lore. Music from George Frideric Handel's "Messiah" accompanies a colorful light show in one tunnel. Another narrow passage is illuminated by sound-activated flashing lights.

Adventurous souls toting flashlights can journey into the stygian obscurity of the undeveloped caves on Saturdays, March through November. Guided tours leave at 10 A.M. and 2 P.M. Groups of six or more can reserve guided tours at other times and on other days. Although the trail is clear and easy enough for sure-footed hikers, it has more obstacles and rocky challenges than the lighted path. Dress in old jeans, sweatshirt, and hiking boots. Two flashlights with D size batteries are required. In these natural dark depths, hikers will see small waterfalls, a pair of streams, bat chambers, and rock features called the Post Office and Sleepy Rock.

Laurel Caverns offers programs for scouts earning merit badges in geology, climbing, ecology, and orienteering. An underground climbing wall and rappelling cliff add to these adventures. Schoolchildren can learn about trilobites and brachiopods in staff-directed fossil hunts. Call for program fees. The Norman E. Cale Visitors Center has a gift shop, rest rooms, a classroom, and an observation deck with a striking view. The site is open daily from 9 A.M. to 5 P.M. (last tour) May through October, and Saturdays and Sundays in March, April, and November. There is an admission charge. The Cale family operates a thirty-site campground next door.

Geology. During the Pennsylvanian Era, some 300 million years ago, parts of southwestern Pennsylvania slept beneath a shallow sea packed with creatures called corals, crinoids, bryozoans, brachiopods, cephalopods, trilobites, eurypterids, and microscopic diatoms. These ancient animals resided in shells primarily composed of calcium. When they perished, their calcium-rich remains mixed with sand on the ocean floor, the makings of limestone. Eventually the sea retreated, and the limey puddles were covered by layers of shale, sandstone, and coal. The Loyalhanna limestone forming Laurel Caverns was probably a flat stratum a mile underground by the time of the dinosaurs.

Other geological events are required for cave formation, however. Caves begin on the surface when carbon dioxide in the air dissolves in precipitation or groundwater to form a weak carbonic acid. As the acidic groundwater seeps down through hairline cracks and seams, it dissolves and removes crystalline calcium, known as calcite, from the limestone. The crack widens about $1/32$ inch per year. Over millions of years, the gash develops into a cave.

The sand grains in limestone stay packed in the hollow unless water flushes them away. Once a passage forms, the sand falls to the cave floor or clings loosely to the rock surface. You are likely to pick up some Paleozoic sand on your clothes if you brush against a rock wall during a cave walk. The calcite, meanwhile, continues its water-borne journey as calcium bicarbonate. When the trickle slows to a drip, some water evaporates and the calcium is redeposited as hollow stalactites, which hang from the cave's ceiling, stalagmites, cones that rise from the floor of the cave, and other stunning formations. There are few stalactites or stalagmites in Laurel Caverns, however, because of the high percentage of sand in the Loyalhanna limestone. Passages here are choked with sand, on which stalactites and stalagmites cannot grow. The cave-sculpting process occurs either when precipitation percolates through rock or as the underground water table seasonally fluctuates, first flooding then sinking.

Two events—tectonic activity and erosion—readied the deeply bedded Loyalhanna limestone for cave formation. The Alleghenian Orogeny, the collision of continental plates that formed the Appalachian Mountains to the east 250 million to 290 million years ago, had a rippling and uplifting effect to the west. Chestnut Ridge is technically considered part of the eroded Allegheny Plateau because its sedimentary bedrock, though arched and slanted, essentially remained unchanged in its horizontal bed. It also is a 100-mile anticline, or elongated ridge, the westernmost wrinkle of the last mountain-building episode. Erosion during the last 200 million years removed overlying strata and again exposed the limestone. Water then started its underground excavation.

A slab of Loyalhanna limestone 1 mile wide, 2 miles deep, and 50 feet high slants downward into the western slope of Chestnut Ridge. The slab is etched like a city street map, with crisscrossing lines representing hairline joints and the avenues for erosion. The cave entrance is 450 feet, or forty-five stories, above the lowest point in the cave.

Scientists have mapped more than a dozen miles of passages they believe are blocked by sand and boulders. Because of Laurel Caverns' location on a mountain summit, the cave remains dry, except after heavy rain. Consequently, water flushes sand very slowly. High-pressure water pumps have opened some predicted tunnels, but more suctioning is cost prohibitive.

Wildlife. Most of the life in Laurel Caverns is locked in the rock, or clinging to it. Bats—mostly eastern pipistrelles and large brown bats—roost year-round in a secluded chamber in the unlighted cave. All but a handful avoid the human-disturbed lighted portion until the place closes for the winter. Then colonies occupy nooks for hibernation.

Fossilized skeletons of 300-million-year-old marine life appear in the limestone. These include clam-shaped brachiopods, snail-like gastropods, extinct beetlelike trilobites, and crinoids, floral-looking coral divided into disklike segments.

History. The cave temperature is a constant 52 degrees F and provided humans with protection from winter cold and summer heat. Projectile points discovered in the cave suggest that Native Americans found shelter here. Nobody knows when humans of European descent entered the grotto, though it likely occurred in the latter half of the eighteenth century. Miners working in James Downard's nearby limestone quarry in 1776 probably ventured into it.

Richard Freeman, who acquired 400 acres next to Downard in 1794, was the first known owner of the cave, then known as Laurel Hills Cave. Back then, it was a notorious, fearsome place. Two local men named Crain and Simmons wandered in the labyrinth for three days before they were rescued. To stop intruders, Freeman sealed the entrance.

In 1814 John Delaney bought 36 acres around the cave entrance from Freeman. By 1816 Delaney had reopened the cave for geological exploration, mapping, and cavers. Though well known locally, Delaney's Cave could not be considered a tourist attraction. The cavern passed through several owners after Delaney's death in 1823. William Humbert bought the place in 1851 for $350, and he and his sons farmed the land for seventy-five years. During that period, local resort owners promoted the cave as a natural wonder.

Humbert's heirs decided to sell the property in 1926. Limestone companies had their eye on it, but Norman and Roy Cale saved the spot. By 1937 they had bought 1,030 acres. Ralph "Buzz" Bossart, a civil engineer and caver, mapped the maze in 1933 and noted that it had 1,720 visitors that summer. In 1961 Norman Cale and his grandson, David, decided to develop Delaney's Cave as an attraction. The first guided tour was led on July 1, 1964.

The elder Cale sold the property in October 1964 to Greensburg attorneys Emmett C. Boyle, Jr., and Ned J. Nakles. A new visitors center opened in 1970. Donald Shoemaker bought the place in 1972. David Cale bought out Shoemaker in 1986. Fortunately, none of the cave's many owners subdivided the surface for building lots or quarried the grotto for its limestone.

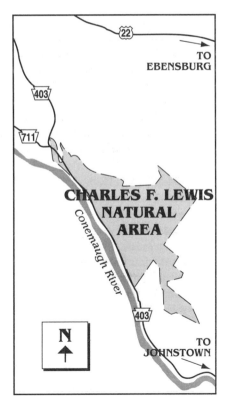

Charles F. Lewis Natural Area

Standing at the gateway to the Conemaugh Gorge, the Charles F. Lewis Natural Area shows different faces: a dark evergreen slit parallel to Clarks Run, festooned by hemlocks, ferns, rhododendron, and mounds of soft moss, as well as brighter bouldery hardwood ridges sugared in autumn by acorns and golden oak flakes. Rocky outbursts that shelter venomous snakes and bears offer views of river valleys and rugged mountains.

Ownership. The natural area is part of Gallitzin State Forest, owned by the Pennsylvania Department of Conservation and Natural Resources, Bureau of Forestry.

Size. 384 acres.

Physiographic Region. Allegheny Mountains.

Nearby Natural Attractions. Conemaugh Gorge, Laurel Ridge State Park, Blacklick Valley Natural Area, and Buttermilk Falls Natural Area.

Features. A large parking lot for the natural area is located on the east side of PA 403, 5 miles south of US 22 and 6.5 miles north of Johnstown. Walk through the arch at the back of the picnic area and follow the yellow-blazed Clarks Run Trail, a 2.8-mile loop. Go right at a T intersection. Hikers encounter steep climbs at the beginning and end of the circuit. A rarely trekked outer 5-mile loop, the Rager Mountain Trail, branches right, roughly 0.75 mile up the Clarks Run Trail. This trail leads to an excellent view of the Conemaugh Gorge. It rejoins the main route just before its descent to the parking lot.

Clarks Run Trail showcases a series of tiny but enchanting waterfalls. The last mile passes through a

107

bouldery forest near the crest of a rocky ledge, an ankle-twisting, rock-hopping passage through timber rattlesnake and black bear country. Explore the "rock city," but watch your step. Loose stones and roots become obstacles on the steep climb down. Sturdy hiking boots and a walking stick for balance and probing are recommended for this somewhat strenuous walk.

For more information, contact Gallitzin State Forest, P.O. Box 506, 155 Hillcrest Dr., Ebensburg, PA 15931, telephone (814) 472-1862.

Geology. The natural area is situated on the west slope of Laurel Ridge, adjacent to the water gap of the Conemaugh River. It protects the entire watershed of tiny Clarks Run, which starts on Laurel Ridge at an elevation of 2,120 feet and tumbles over a succession of cascades for 2 miles to its conclusion at the Conemaugh River at elevation 1,100 feet. For most of its short journey, Clarks Run tracks northwesterly like the river. This orientation tends to dump more precipitation in the ravine.

Clarks Run's downcutting has exposed 330-million-year-old sandstone, shale, and limestone of the Mauch Chunk and Pocono Formations (Mississippian Period) and sandstone and conglomerate representing the 300-million-year-old Pottsville Group of the Pennsylvanian Period. At lower elevations, the Conemaugh River has cut into 360-million-year-old Devonian bedrock of the Oswaya and Catskill Formations.

Repeated freezing and thawing in bedrock cracks, a weathering process called frost heave, produced the maze of rocky rubble and quirky-shaped boulders on ridgetops.

Wildlife. During my early-autumn hike, tons of acorns rained from chestnut and red oaks and had nearly filled the crevices and pockets on the boulder-strewn summit of Laurel Ridge, providing winter food for many animals. This elevated area also hosts sassafras, mountain laurel, and blueberry bushes, a flavorful attraction for bears. In contrast, hemlocks and rhododendrons, inhabitants of shady, moist spots, grow above the shoulders of Clarks Run. The slopes also are populated by American beech, black cherry, yellow birch, basswood, sugar maple, and tulip tree, the last three representing a hardwood cove community.

Spring unfurls mayapples, Canada mayflower, blue cohosh, wild ginger, trout lily, spring beauty, cut-leaved toothworts, violets, and white, red, and purple trilliums. A colony of Japanese bamboo by a footbridge across Clarks Run shows that even a remote ravine can become a sanctuary for exotic intruders.

Bring binoculars to look for the indigo bunting; yellow-breasted chat; gray catbird; Acadian flycatcher; blue-gray gnatcatcher; northern (yellow-shafted) flicker; pileated woodpecker; pine, blue (rare), evening, and rose-breasted grosbeaks; bank, tree, barn, and rough-winged swallows; Blackburnian, blackpoll, black-and-white, black-throated blue, and black-throated green warblers; barred, screech, and great-horned owls; and whippoorwill. You may observe hawks and bald eagles from the overlooks.

Reptiles and amphibians are fully protected here, even the poisonous timber rattlesnake and copperhead. Other snakes include the mountain earth, eastern worm, and northern redbelly snakes. In winter rattlers may hibernate with copperheads and other snakes in dens by south-facing rock ledges. Hundreds of vipers have been found in these dens. The snakes scatter in the spring.

History. The natural area is a fitting tribute to Dr. Charles Fletcher Lewis, a journalist, conservationist, and first president of the Western Pennsylvania Conservancy. These slopes were timbered at various times from the mid-1800s to the mid-1930s. Fires ravaged some of the slopes, as evidenced by the occasional charred snag.

36

McConnells Mill State Park

People come here to see the lush Slippery Rock Creek Gorge and to tour the restored gristmill that gave the park its name. The gorge is a giant gash carved by a boulder-laden glacier stream. Today, Slippery Rock Creek is an ethereal place of magic, mystery, and awe. Hemlocks, ferns, and moss-covered turf keep the misty chasm green and calm, while the gleaming, frothy, turbulent, trout-filled Slippery Rock Creek keeps scratching through 300-million-year-old sandstone.

Ownership. Pennsylvania Department of Conservation and Natural Resources, Bureau of State Parks.

Size. 2,529 acres.

Physiographic Region. Border of Glaciated Plateau and Pittsburgh Low Plateau.

Nearby Natural Attractions. Moraine State Park, Jennings Environmental Education Center, Miller Esker, Fringed Gentian Fen, Wolf Creek Narrows Natural Area, and Schollard's Run Wetlands.

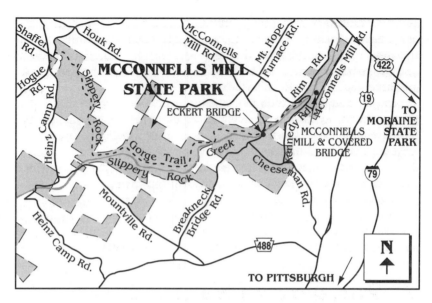

Features. Eleven miles of trails provide plenty of hiking opportunities in the gorge and along a tributary decorated in spring by wildflowers. The main drag is the Kildoo Trail, a self-guided nature trail running on both sides of the creek from the historic sites of the restored McConnells Mill and covered bridge to Eckert Bridge. A portion is paved, and a trail brochure is available. Most hikers start at a parking lot atop the gorge on McConnells Mill Road. (Parking at the mill is reserved for seniors and disabled visitors). A staircased path leads to the creek and mill. Round-trip is 1.8 miles. Alpha Pass Trail goes north from the mill half a mile to Alpha Falls on the east bank.

The longest, loneliest, toughest, and most rewarding route is the 6-mile (one-way) Slippery Rock Gorge Trail. It heads downstream from Eckert Bridge on the west bank, then turns west at Hell's Run and stays on the feeder's north side to a parking lot on Shaffer Road. This trail joins the Kildoo Trail at Eckert Bridge. Combined, these two paths form a 7-mile section of the North Country National Scenic Trail.

Hell's Hollow Trail branches from Slippery Rock Gorge Trail a few hundred feet from Shaffer Road and traces the south bank to Hell's Hollow Falls. This path, known for its wildflowers, was a hauling road to Lawrence Furnace, also located at the cascade.

Hikers beware: Rocks and boulders in the gorge are very slippery, and the current is deeper and more powerful than it appears. Swimming is not permitted.

The whitewater in the gorge thrills experienced kayakers, rafters, and canoists, who must follow safety guidelines spelled out in the park guide and be ready to portage around three dams. Experienced and outfitted climbers can rappel and climb in designated areas off Rim Road and near Breakneck Bridge. Novices in these sports should not climb here.

Hunting and fishing are allowed. All state regulations apply. Hunting is permitted in designated areas only. A special year-round fly-fishing spot is available at Armstrong Bridge. Picnic areas with rest rooms are located on McConnells Mill Road, above the gorge. Campers have to go to adjacent Moraine State Park.

Free tours of the gristmill are conducted several times daily between 10:15 A.M. and 5:45 P.M., from Memorial Day to Labor Day. For more information, contact McConnells Mill State Park, R.R. 2, Box 16, Portersville, PA 16051-9401, telephone (412) 368-8091 or 368-8811.

Geology. The 9-mile incision called Slippery Rock Creek Gorge was a mere scratch 20,000 years ago. At that time, a finger of the Wisconsinan glacier plugged the flows of Slippery Rock and Muddy Creeks, creating the twin lakes of Arthur and Edmund. When the glacier retreated, the lakes drained over a series of spillways, the first being Alpha Falls (in the park) followed by Grant City Falls (upstream on private property) and Kildoo Falls (downstream). Elephantine torrents rapidly downcut through layers of limestone, shale, coal and sandstone, some 400 feet below the preglacial level in a short period of geological time. Before glaciation, Slippery Rock Creek emptied into the St. Lawrence River watershed. The new channel routed water into the new Ohio River system. Undercutting loosened rocks and house-size boulders from the bedrock wall and sent them crashing into the streambed. In places, this glacial and slump debris is 45 feet thick below the stream.

Alpha Falls and Kildoo Falls are hanging valleys created at the end of the ice age. Slippery Rock Creek's downcutting was swifter and deeper than its tributaries. When the flow of the main stem subsided, the mouths of the tributaries were left hanging at the rim of the gorge.

Notice the crossbedding, or odd angles, in the horizontal layers of sandstone and conglomerate and in slump rocks. Crossbedding indicates stream currents, ripples, and offshore dunes when the rock was formed 300 million years ago. From top to bottom, Slippery Rock Creek has washed over bedrocks of Vanport limestone, Clarion shales, Brookville coal, Homewood sandstone, Mercer coal and shale, and currently, Connoquenessing sandstone.

Along Hell's Hollow Trail, the rill rushes through a unique limestone flume measuring 80 feet long and 5 feet deep. Here the channel has widened, smoothed, and deepened a natural fissure in the bedrock. Ahead, the trail goes through an abandoned limestone quarry.

Water and algae make rocks in the stream slippery. But the stream's name comes from one slippery rock on the east bank at the southern border of the park, opposite Camp Allegheny, a sandstone slab that became slippery from a natural oil seep. Other slippery rocks that appeared near the mouth of Hell Run led to oil drilling.

Wildlife. Shade-tolerant hemlocks keep the gorge green, cool, and shady, while atop boulders and ledges grow American yews. Hardwoods fill out the rest of the canopy.

Try to visit the park in spring, when the gorge and side ravines awaken with wildflowers. Look for painted and large-flowered trilliums, sharp-lobed hepatica, wild ginger, foamflower, jack-in-the-pulpit, wood sorrel, false miterwort, wild geranium, clintonia, Solomon's seal, yellow and blue violets, cut-leaved toothwort, cardinal flower, nodding onion, and Canada mayflower. Good eyes may find parasitic beechdrops beneath beech trees, as well as white Indian pipes. Hell's Run has prominent clusters of wild phlox, spring beauties, Canada lily, and wild columbine by the flume and limestone ledges.

Fern fanciers will find at least twenty species in the park—one of the best collections in western Pennsylvania. Common polypody grows luxuriantly like whiskers from rock pockets. Ebony spleenwort, marginal woodfern, cut-leaved grape, maidenhair, bulblet, and fragile ferns are easily seen along Kildoo Trail.

Birders may see the scarlet tanager, eastern phoebe, pileated woodpecker, rose-breasted grosbeak, and yellow and black-billed cuckoos. Warblers and wrens hang out in the hardwoods. Tom turkey gobbles echo in the chasm in April and May, and hikers may flush a ruffed grouse from its hiding place. Mammals include white-tailed deer, fox and gray squirrels, raccoons, and mink.

History. The industrial revolution came to the gorge in the 1840s. Lawrence Furnace was built into a cliff at Hell's Run Falls in 1846 and produced iron until 1875. The first miller was probably Daniel Kennedy, who rebuilt a mill destroyed by fire in 1868. Thomas McConnell bought the place in 1875 and modernized it to be one of the first rolling mills in the country. The mill processed corn, oats, buckwheat, and wheat until it closed in 1928. The property was transferred from Thomas Hartman to the Western Pennsylvania Conservancy and then to the state. McConnells Mill became a state park in October 1957. The U.S. Department of the Interior declared the gorge a national natural landmark in May 1974.

The covered bridge by the mill is one of only two in Lawrence County. It is a Howe truss bridge, built in 1874 and covered to protect it from the weather.

Miller Esker

From above, the snaking mound looks like an earthwork of the ancient Hopewell moundbuilders, but the Wisconsinan glacier made this sinuous jelly roll some 20,000 years ago. The mound is an esker, a Swedish word for serpent.

Ownership. Western Pennsylvania Conservancy.

Size. 32 acres.

Physiographic Region. Glaciated Plateau.

Nearby Natural Attractions. Jennings Environmental Education Center, McConnells Mill and Moraine State Parks, Fringed Gentian Fen, Wolf Creek Narrows Natural Area, and Schollard's Run Wetland.

Features. Miller Esker trends northwest-southeast a few miles north of Moraine State Park. Zero in on the intersection of Swope, West Liberty (SR 4008), and Mount Union Roads. The esker is the serpentine ridge north of West Liberty Road. Parking and trails are absent, but visitors can tramp on the formation if they like. The Western Pennsylvania Conservancy suggests parking off the north side of West Liberty Road (on the soft berm), west of Swope Road. Walk directly north along a treeline, over a brook, to the summit. Follow the naked ridgetop, which looks similar to a railroad bed, northwest to the second lone tree, then retrace your steps. The open water and wetland to the north is Tamarack Lake, a glacial kettlehole on private land.

You can view more of the esker by driving west on West Liberty Road. Just past the Miller farm (Key-stone Dairy), turn right on Dickey Road (T344), which tracks the southern slope nearly to I-79. Swope Road goes over the gravel ridge and passes Tamarack Lake on the left.

Geology. Dr. Frank W. Preston, geologist and founding father of the Western Pennsylvania Conservancy, explained how this esker formed at the edge of the Wisconsinan glacier 20,000 years ago: "Eskers are apparently made in a tunnel excavated at the base of the ice. As the glacier

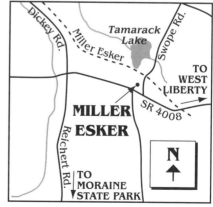

113

nears its end or margin, and its ice is melting, streams form on its surface, but generally manage to tumble down a crevasse and get to the contact between ice and ground below. The water dissolves some of the ice and makes a tunnel, and there the small stones originally embedded in the ice are deposited. Then the water has to dissolve more ice to make way for itself and so it continually enlarges the tunnel and deposits more stones."

Miller Esker is a half-mile section of 7.5-mile West Liberty Esker, sometimes called a hogback. It winds from west of West Liberty northwest across I-79 to Elliots Mills. In places, it reaches 40 feet in height and 360 feet in width at the base. The conservancy's holding is the best preserved segment. Erosion, farming, and gravel mining have reduced other stretches. The ridge, cut by Slippery Rock Creek and Taylor Run, is divided into three segments. Cross sections of the esker show the layers arranged in domes.

Tamarack Lake, directly north of Miller Esker, is glacial kettle-hole, a mere drop of a once-larger lake. It formed at the end of the ice age when huge slabs of ice broke off the face of the glacier. These ice chunks were the size of several big city blocks and as tall and as heavy as the buildings standing on them. Sediment-laden meltwater from the glacier enwrapped the ice chunk and created a basin. The ice eventually melted to form a kettle lake.

Wildlife. Folks come here for a geology lesson, not for wildlife. Still, you may see a hawk hovering above the esker, or barn swallows, bobolinks, deer, or groundhogs. The treeline route to the crest displays goldenrod, joe-pye weed, and dogwood blossoms. Bring binoculars for spotting waterfowl from the ridgetop.

History. The Western Pennsylvania Conservancy acquired this half-mile portion of the esker in 1975.

Moraine State Park

Moraine State Park is a full-service state park smack in the middle of the western third of the state and right off an interstate. It's a fine base camp for exploring the glacier-made natural wonders in the neighborhood.

Lake Arthur, the 3,225-acre centerpiece to the state park, is a geological re-creation and the brainchild of Dr. Frank Preston, a geologist who determined that Muddy Creek Valley once contained a lake.

Ownership. Pennsylvania Department of Conservation and Natural Resources, Bureau of State Parks.

Size. 15,848 acres.

Physiographic Region. Glaciated Plateau.

Nearby Natural Attractions. McConnells Mill State Park, Jennings Environmental Education Center, Miller Esker, Fringed Gentian Fen, Schollard's Run Wetland, and Wolf Creek Narrows Natural Area.

Features. Located right off I-79, Moraine State Park is one of Pennsylvania's busiest parks. It offers plenty of recreation facilities

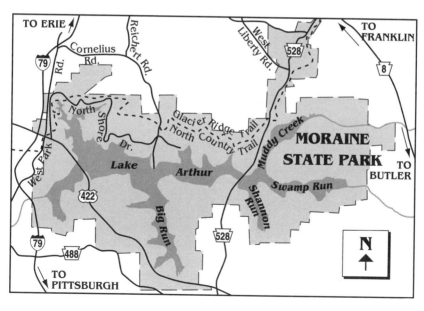

115

for hikers, boaters, campers, bicyclists, horseback riders, anglers, swimmers, picnickers, hunters, cross-country skiers, and snowmobilers, most of them in the western two-thirds of the park. Get a park guide for more information. People seeking solitude and wildlife usually head for trails on the east side of the park, notably Glacier Ridge Trail, east of Reichert Road, and Wyggeston Trail on the south shore. Their routes are shown on the park brochure.

Glacier Ridge Trail is a 14-mile path running on the north side of the park and extending northeast, parallel to PA 528, to the Jennings Environmental Education Center. Trailheads with parking are located on North Shore Drive east of the West Park Road entrance, Reichert Road north of North Shore Drive, Mount Union Road, and PA 528, south of Lindey Road by a park road heading to a boat ramp. This blue-blazed route is also a portion of the 3,200-mile North Country National Scenic Trail. Yellow blazes mark side loop trails named Lakeshore and Davis Hollow. At the PA 528 trailhead, hikers cross to east side of the highway and follow the northbound extension to Jennings Environmental Education Center.

Wyggeston Trail starts on the north side of Old Route 422, which branches west from PA 528 just north of US 422. Another trailhead is found on Christley Road, off PA 528. This lasso-shaped path wanders for 4.2 miles. Shorter nature trails on the south shore are the Sunken Garden Trail, off Pleasant Valley Road, and Hill Top Nature Trail, off Big Run Road north of the park office.

Hunting and trapping are permitted, except in posted areas. A game propagation area at the east end of Lake Arthur is off limits to humans.

Geology. At the end of the ice age, about 10,000 to 20,000 years ago, the edge of the Wisconsinan continental glacier advanced to a point roughly marked by PA 8 and PA 108, running from Harrisville to Slippery Rock and Elliots Mills. A finger of the ice mass curled eastward and blocked the flow of Muddy Creek exactly where a dam now stands. The icy plug created ancient Lake Arthur and backed up water as far east as Thorn Crossing. The rising lake breached a summit at Queen Junction and drained south over a waterfall into Stony Run and Connoquenessing Creek, leveling at an elevation of 1,260 feet, roughly 70 feet higher than its current level. The glacier also clogged Slippery Rock Creek, which grew into Lakes Edmund and Redmond at higher elevations to the north. Lake Edmund emptied into Lake Redmond through a spillway between West Sunbury and Thorn Crossing.

Warmer temperatures caused the glacier to retreat northward, reopening the outlets of the lakes via Muddy and Slippery Rock Creeks. The massive draining of the lakes created Slippery Rock

Creek Gorge, which can be seen in adjacent McConnells Mill State Park. The old lakes vanished, and Lake Arthur shrank to Muddy Creek. The Wisconsinan glacier left its signature in the form of a terminal moraine, a snaky mound of gravelly till marking its farthest advance. The park was named for this now-obscure formation north of Lake Arthur.

Muddy Creek Valley had a brief oil boom in the late nineteenth and early twentieth centuries. Coal mining in the first half of the twentieth century left the land pitted, scarred, and polluted. During park construction, coal mines and oil and gas wells had to be reclaimed so that an earthen dam could be built to make a new Lake Arthur. Today the lake has 40 miles of shoreline and is fed by Muddy, Big, Swamp, and Bear Runs plus seventy-five intermittent creeks.

Wildlife. The park's bird checklist names 239 species that have been observed in the park. Lake Arthur attracts many kinds of waterfowl, including common and red-breasted mergansers, green-winged and blue-winged teals, common loons, goldeneyes, black ducks, lesser scaups, ruddy ducks, northern pintails, tundra swans, and snow and Canada geese. Calm coves along the lakeshore harbor great blue herons (PA threatened), bitterns, and other waders, plus kingfishers and communities of barn and cliff swallows. The propagation area at the eastern point of the lake contains prefab osprey nests. These endangered birds were reintroduced in 1993, and by 1996 a pair fledged three youngsters. Please don't disturb these finicky nesters.

Check meadows for the prairie warbler, meadowlark, goldfinch, yellow-breasted chat, white-eyed vireo, and grasshopper, field, and savannah sparrows. Imperiled sedge wrens nest here, and their habitat is protected. Forested spots have indigo buntings, cedar waxwings, cuckoos, and warblers. Park naturalists and birders have placed bluebird boxes in the park. Gamebirds include ruffed grouse, northern bobwhite, and wild turkey.

The park is heavily wooded with oaks, maples, beech, black cherry, sycamores, aspen, hemlocks, and planted pines. Lake Arthur contains walleye, muskellunge, northern pike, channel catfish, bass, and panfish. Frogs, newts, turtles, and water snakes live along the shore.

History. Eyebrows must have been raised when Frank Preston suggested that a wasteland ruined by coal mining and oil and gas wells be resurrected as Lake Arthur and a state park. Nevertheless, the Western Pennsylvania Conservancy, cofounded by Preston, bought his dream, as well as the 1,000 acres that became the seed of the state park. Costly reclamation projects reversed pollution and got the land on the road to recovery. The dam was finished in 1969, and the park opened on May 23, 1970.

Lake Arthur and glacial Lake Edmund were named after a Pittsburgh attorney, the late Edmund Watts Arthur (1874–1948), who also dabbled as a geologist, naturalist, and writer. Like Preston, he specialized in this area's natural history, and he was on Preston's geological study team.

39

Mount Davis Natural Area

The state caretaker of this site describes it as follows: "Mt. Davis is not a prominent hill nor a mountain, but rather the top of a large rock lying on the nearly level rock-strewn summit of Negro Mountain, which is one of the shortest [in length] of Pennsylvania's famous northeast-southwesterly oriented ridges." What you see on this summit are flat stretches of rocky rubble, scarred-over clear-cuts, and runt trees beaten down by the weather. Many people swear that other cobbles are taller. Think of this place as a high plateau.

Ownership. Mount Davis Natural Area is in Forbes State Forest, owned by the Pennsylvania Department of Conservation and Natural Resources, Bureau of Forestry.

Size. 605 acres.

Physiographic Region. Allegheny Mountains.

Nearby Natural Attractions. Ohiopyle State Park, Bear Run Nature Reserve, Fort Necessity National Battlefield, and other sites in Forbes State Forest.

Features. You can walk or drive to the 40-foot Mount Davis Observation Tower. Hikers start at the state forest picnic area on SR 2004, across from a radio tower. Go to the high (west) side of the picnic area, and take the High Point Trail southwest. In a quarter mile, you'll arrive at the junction with the eastbound Tub Mill Run Trail. The quickest route is straight ahead (southwest) on High Point Trail, which ends at the tower a mile from the start. Climb the tower, weather permitting, enjoy the view, and read the interpretive signs around the base before returning. Walkers with more ambition and curiosity should take the 5.8-mile clockwise circuit consisting of the Tub Mill Run, Timberslide, Shelter Rock, and Mount Davis Trails. This loop can be halved by taking the abandoned Shelter Rock Road, branching right (south) off Tub Mill Run Trail, to Shelter Rock Trail, which forms the eastern boundary of the natural area. Motorists reach the landmark by going west from the picnic area on SR 2004 half a mile, then left (south) on South Wolf Rock Road, following the signs. Baughman Rocks, an outcrop of sandstone and conglomerate, can be reached via a short trail heading north from a small parking area on the north side of SR 2004, midway

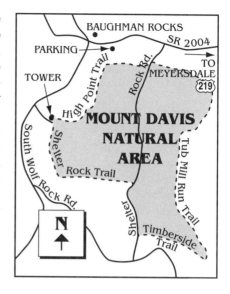

between the picnic area and North Wolf Rock Road. Rest rooms and drinking water are available at the picnic area.

For more information, contact Forbes State Forest, P.O. Box 519, Laughlintown, PA 15655, telephone (724) 238-9533.

Geology. Like its cousins to the west, Laurel and Chestnut Ridges, Negro Mountain was formed during the Alleghenian Orogeny, a mountain-building event that occurred 290 million years ago in which the North American and Gondwana crustal plates collided, creating the Appalachian Mountains to the east as well as the elongated anticlines known as the Allegheny Mountains.

Mount Davis's summit is littered by small, concentric rock rings caused by frost heaving, a process in which water repeatedly seeps into rock cracks and expands when freezing during winter, eventually breaking the stone. Each stone ring encircles a spot on the ground where the dirt is soft, loose, and slightly humped. Over thousands of years, fractured rocks on the slopes of these humps have slid outward to the margins of the mounds. This odd formation is best seen from the observation tower. At ground level, the terrain looks like someone stood slabs of sandstone on their ends and then shoved them into the ground to create stepping stones 20 feet above the forest floor.

Frost heave is responsible for sculpting several "rock cities" around the summit. Baughman Rocks, north of SR 2004, consists of a large ledge and blocks of white to gray sandstone and conglomerate dating back 300 million years to the Pennsylvanian Period. The formation is 50 yards long and 75 feet wide. Although cracks may be 20 feet deep, gaps between blocks rarely exceed 2 feet. Small trees struggle between some cracks, and a spring seeps below the ledge. Shelter Rocks, a similar formation, is located in the southern part of the natural area off South Wolf Rock Road, west of old Shelter Rock Road. A spring also seeps from Shelter Rocks. Vought Rocks overlook, on Vought Rock Road north of the picnic area, is on private property. The natural area is drained by Tub Mill Run, a tributary of the Casselman River.

Wildlife. According to early-twentieth-century botanist Dr. Emma Lucy Braun, author of *The Deciduous Forests of the Eastern North America,* the locale is a meeting place of the mixed mesophytic forest type and the southern arm of the northern beech-birch-maple-hemlock type. Logging, forest fires, and other intrusions changed the forest into a blended oak type with significant representation by species belonging to the northern hardwood forest. Happily for nature lovers, the timber here doesn't interest commercial loggers. It is marginal at best, because of the high elevation, thin and rocky soil, short growing season, and harsh climate. Trees are brushy, short, twisted, and severely deformed by strong winds and winter ice storms. Summit trees consist of quaking aspen, black and yellow birches, black cherry, pitch pine, black gum, red maple, sassafras, fire and black cherries, serviceberry, and red, scarlet, and bear (scrub) oaks. Witch hazel and American chestnut sprouts occupy the understory. Ground vegetation and shrubs around the observation tower are mostly mountain laurel, rhododendrons, greenbrier, club mosses, and painted trillium, which favor acidic soils. Lower elevations feature some of the above, along with cucumber magnolia, eastern hemlock, white oak, and mountain ash. Striped maple is abundant.

History. Negro Mountain honors an African-American man of unknown name who lived on the ridge in pioneer days. Stories abound of the mountain man's fate. He may have been killed by Indians, white bounty hunters (the 30-mile-long mountain stretches into Maryland, a slave state before the Civil War), or a black bear or other predator. Mount Davis was named after the surveyor, John N. Davis, who determined it to be Pennsylvania's highest point. Davis also pointed out the unusual rock rings and listed the resident flora and fauna.

According to local storytellers, Baughman Rocks was the scene of a ghastly crime in earlier times. Henry Baughman, the ill-tempered landowner, was hunting the woods for escaped cows with his sons when he became enraged that August, his youngest son, was holding up the search. Baughman knocked August unconscious with a stick, and thinking the boy was dead, he concealed the body in the rocks, now known as Baughman Rocks. When Baughman returned later, August's body had disappeared. On the testimony of his oldest son,

Baughman was convicted of second-degree murder, but the whereabouts of the body remain a mystery.

Logging was done on a small scale on Mount Davis during pioneer days. Commercial timbering occurred in the first two decades of the twentieth century. One short-lived company built a 4-mile railroad up Tub Mill Run.

Mount Davis became a state forest natural area in 1974. This designation prohibits logging and development for perpetuity. The observation tower was constructed in 1976 by the Pennsylvania Youth Conservation Corps.

◆ 40 ◆

North Park

Allegheny County's largest park is filled with natural diversity, from open water to dark forest, marsh, and meadow. The park's nature center, an old dairy farm, seems wonderfully detached from busier and noisier sections.

Ownership. Allegheny County Department of Parks, Recreation and Conservation.

Size. 3,010 acres.

Physiographic Region. Low Plateau.

Nearby Natural Attractions. Beechwood Farms and Frick Woods Nature Reserves, Barking Slopes and Dead Man's Hollow Wildlife Preserves, the Flower and Wildlife Preserve, and Harrison Hills and Boyce Parks.

Features. Nature enthusiasts tend to gather at Marshall and North Park Lakes, Latodami (la-TOD-a-mi) Nature Center, a restored dairy barn, off Brown Road in the northwestern corner of the park, and at the hub for eight trails by Pie Traynor Field on South Ridge Drive in the southeastern section. Ladotami Nature Center offers programs, exhibits, and activities. The grounds feature a small pond, several interpretive trails blazed by local scouts, parking, and rest rooms. Trails from the barn visit recovering farmland, an old orchard, young

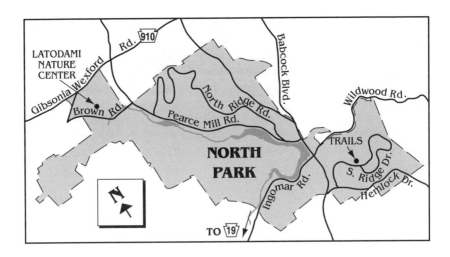

forest, and meadows with the rusty tower of a windmill or cluttered with new birdhouses. Across Brown Road, the Nature Access Trail helps visually handicapped hikers travel a half-mile loop through a hardwood ravine, guiding them by ropes along a tributary of the North Fork of Pine Creek.

The South Ridge Road trail hub marks the easiest entry to the Rachel Carson Trail, a 33-mile orange-blazed path between North Park and Harrison Hills Park. The late Rachel Carson, a celebrated and influential environmentalist and author, lived nearby for many years. The trail goes west and east from this port. Eight other trails are described on a wooden board by the trailhead. The red-blazed South Ridge Trail loops for 2.3 miles through woodlands bordering South Ridge Road. Here you can also pick up the Perimeter Trail, unblazed for most of its 8 miles, for destinations elsewhere in the park. Unfortunately, printed trail guides are not available, and blazing becomes careless in places.

The park, open 8 A.M. to dusk, offers picnic areas, golf, a swimming pool, boating, a bike trail, tennis and platform tennis courts, ballfields, playgrounds, an ice-skating rink, a horse show arena, a basketball court, open play areas, and rest rooms. For more information, contact the Allegheny County Department of Parks, Recreation and Conservation, Penn-Liberty Plaza, 1520 Penn Ave., Pittsburgh, PA 15222, telephone (724) 935-1766, or Latodami Nature Center, (724) 935-2170.

Geology. The high-ridged terrain is characteristic of the region—a plateau floored by 300 million-year-old Pennsylvanian Period bedrock deeply incised by creeks. Dams plugging the North Fork of Pine Creek were built in the 1930s. The impoundments created Marshall Lake and the hook-shaped North Park Lake. Pine Creek slices through Pittsburgh before dumping into the Allegheny River.

Wildlife. The park's many habitats support 250 species of birds, including the American goldfinch, dark-eyed junco, eastern meadowlark, brown-headed cowbird, Baltimore oriole, savannah and Henslow's sparrows, Louisiana waterthrush, scarlet tanager, eastern towhee, rose-breasted grosbeak, red-eyed and warbling vireos, ruby-crowned kinglet, wood thrush, cedar waxwing, barn swallow, white-breasted nuthatch, Carolina wren, yellow-shafted flicker, Acadian and least flycatchers, eastern phoebe, red-bellied woodpecker, chimney swift, common nighthawk, black-billed cuckoo, common snipe, spotted sandpiper, killdeer, American kestrel, red-tailed hawk, bufflehead, hooded merganser, wood duck, mute swan, and green heron. Warblers include the Kentucky, hooded, Cape May, Tennessee, magnolia, yellow-rumped, prairie, blackpoll, black-throated green, and common yellowthroat.

Wooded areas off South Ridge Road hold white oaks that sprouted during the American Revolution, one of ninety some woody species in this 3,000-acre cornucopia. Other specimens include black cherry, flowering dogwood, red maple, catalpa, tulip tree, yellow birch, white ash, red oak, and black locust. Sugar maples yield enough sap for a month-long maple syrup festival in late winter. Mountain laurel, the state blossom, and great rhododendron occupy acidic soils.

Park naturalists and volunteers are still counting the wildflower species, now over 100 varieties, including trilliums, mayapple, spring beauty, jack-in-the-pulpit, and violets. Later bloomers include bluets, joe-pye weed, yarrow, ironweed, Queen Anne's lace, milkweed, and wetland orchids. Sweetflag, a state-endangered emergent resembling a small cattail, has established a thriving colony in North Park.

History. This land was extensively farmed, grazed, and logged before the county purchased it in the 1930s. Acquisitions over time made this the largest park in the county system. The 300-acre Latodami Farm, a dairy operation until 1968, was added in the early 1970s. The name Latodami was derived from the first names of the former owner's children.

Ohiopyle State Park

Wild, serpentine whitewater boils through a rocky slit furred by hemlocks and hardwoods. Roiling rapids and waterfalls remain indomitable and postcard pretty. Imperiled and isolated plants survive amid hundreds of native species on a knob above a river called the Yough (Yock), short for Youghiogheny (yock-a-GAY-nee). Come here for waterfalls pinched by walls of ravines, for a long bike ride through the gorge, for sage trout, for trails to heights and hollows, and for campfires below pinecones or stars.

Ownership. Pennsylvania Department of Conservation and Natural Resources, Bureau of State Parks.

Size. Pennsylvania's largest land state park measures 18,719 acres.

Physiographic Region. Allegheny Mountains.

Nearby Natural Attractions. Quebec Run Wild Area, Laurel Ridge State Park, Laurel Caverns, Bear Run Nature Reserve, Friendship Hill National Historic Site, State Game Lands 51 and 111, and Fort Necessity National Battlefield.

Features. Two million visitors annually come to Ohiopyle State Park for its boisterous river, steep and scenic gorge, whitewater

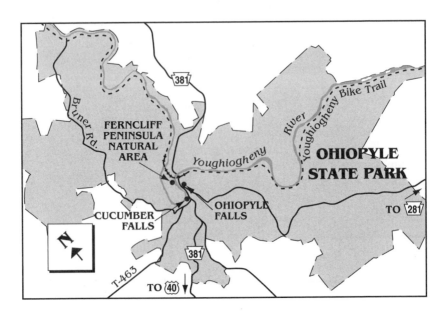

thrills, waterfalls and rapids, excellent trails, and natural wonders. More than 100,000 boaters ride the rapids of the Youghiogheny River, making it the busiest whitewater river east of the Mississippi.

Splashing, paddling, bouncing, and bucking in a whitewater boat is undoubtedly the best way to experience the wild, 18-mile Youghiogheny gorge. Start your trip at Ohiopyle Falls, seen safely from a deck in the village or more intimately from ledges along the Ferncliff Trail. The cascade separates the mild Middle Yough (upstream to the dam at Confluence) and the wild Lower Yough (downstream to Bruner Run). The 11-mile Middle Yough is a gentle, easy journey with Class I and II waves, though you may hang up on rocks in low water. Experienced canoists should have no difficulty. The Lower Yough, with a dozen set of rapids in the Class III to IV range, keeps kayakers, rafters, and canoeists hooting and hollering. The Yough remains high enough for year-round boating. Six rapids are crammed in 1.7-mile horseshoe bend below Ohiopyle Falls, a famed stretch known as The Loop. Boaters who take out after The Loop (a.k.a. Ferncliff Peninsula) are less than half a mile from their starting point.

The state park tightly regulates boating on the Yough to prevent overcrowding, accidents, and river degradation. The Loop, for example, may not be soloed until 3 P.M., fifteen minutes after the launching of the last raft caravan. A park brochure explains all rules, launch and take-out locations, and registration procedures. Outfitters sell river guides. Take a couple of guided tours before soloing.

Although whitewater boating is the star attraction, adventurers on foot have 60 miles of trails to explore. Besides the featured routes below, hikers find rewards on the Sugarloaf, Baughman, and Jonathan Run paths, and on the southern end, the Laurel Highlands Trail, running more than 5 miles from Ohiopyle northeast into and beyond State Game Lands 111.

Ferncliff Peninsula Natural Area, 100 acres, was dedicated a national natural landmark by the U.S. Department of the Interior in 1972. Almost 3 miles of footpaths traverse this botanical bounty, the longest being the perimeter Ferncliff Trail, measuring 1.7 miles. The trail follows the inside lane of The Loop. Trailhead parking is found on the west side of PA 381 in Ohiopyle, north of the bridge over the river. Look for the trail sign for orientation. The state park has a trail map and interpretive guide, but it's not always available at the trailhead.

After completing The Loop, the trail makes a hairpin turn right heading back to the terminus. Walkers eager to return to the start continue on this trail. Others can go left at the sharp turn and walk several hundred feet to another path going right, the take-out path across the neck of the peninsula. Go left on the bike trail and cross the river on an old railroad bridge. Follow signs to the Great Gorge Trail, a flat, easy trail going upstream.

On lazy summer days, this path has sunbathers baking like iguanas on rocks beside the rapids. In a mile, the trail forks. Great Gorge splits to the right, crosses SR 2019 above Cucumber Falls, and traces Cucumber Run to a trailhead on Chalk Hill Road (T463). Meadow Run Trail goes left along the riverbank and drops into a ravine at the mouth of the Cucumber Run. After rock-hopping across the brook, take the short side path to Cucumber Falls, which tumbles 30 feet. Return to Meadow Run Trail, then continue upstream to PA 381 in Ohiopyle. There are plenty of rocks for watching boaters in the rapids.

The Youghiogheny River Bike and Hike Trail is an easy 28-mile bike and hike trail on the riverbank from Confluence downstream to Dawson. It rides atop an abandoned Western Maryland Railway bed and is an alternative way to experience the gorge. This southern segment of the Youghiogheny River Trail is part of a larger 300-mile trail from Washington, D.C., to Pittsburgh. In the state park, trailheads with parking are located at Ramcat Boat Launch on T880 near Confluence (east terminus); the old train station and visitors center in Ohiopyle; the Ferncliff Peninsula Natural Area in Ohiopyle; and Bruner Run take-out at the end of Bruner Road. From Ramcat to Bruner Run, the elevation drops 300 feet.

Waterfall lovers will find rhododendron festooned cascades along Jonathan Run Trail, Sugar Run, and Meadow Run. (See Geology section.).

The state park boasts a 226-site campground, trout fishing, picnic areas, trails for snowmobiling and Nordic skiing, hunting, nature programs, boat launches, sledding, backpacking, mountain biking, overlooks, and ballfields. The village of Ohiopyle has many outfitters offering guided or unguided whitewater tours, boat and bike rentals, gear, and refreshments.

For more information, contact Ohiopyle State Park, P.O. Box 105, Ohiopyle, PA 15470-0105, telephone (724) 329-8591.

Geology. Ohiopyle State Park is cradled between Chestnut Ridge and Laurel Ridge, which were formed during the Alleghenian Orogeny. The bedrock seen at Ohiopyle is Pottsville sandstone, dating back 300 million years to the Pennsylvanian Period. Beneath it lie rocks of the Mississippian Period (330 million years ago) and Devonian Period (375 million years ago).

The Youghiogheny River has cut through Laurel and Chestnut Ridges at weak spots, creating spectacular gorges at each end of the park. Consequently, it has exposed a cross-section of rock spanning 75 million years. The river flows over slabs of hard Pottsville sandstone in Ohiopyle, forming the park's centerpiece falls and rapids. The river's downcutting has been slowed by this erosion-resistant layer. From the falls, Pottsville sandstone slants upward to the east and west, arching over Laurel and Chestnut Ridges. The Yough washes over it again in Confluence, east of the park. Pottsville sandstone also forms the stiff upper lips of waterfalls at higher elevations in the gorge, notably cascades on Cucumber, Sugar, and Jonathan Runs.

From the Fayette-Somerset county line downstream to the Flats (formerly Bidwell Station to Victoria Station on the old railroad line), the Yough slices into older Devonian Period bedrock, around 350 million years old. Pottsville sandstone, once the sandy bottom of an ancient sea, now lies well above the river. Mississippian rocks (the middle layer) appear in road cuts, ravines, and railroad grades in the park.

Ferncliff Peninsula, the horseshoe-shaped riverbend at Ohiopyle, stands atop a knob of Pottsville sandstone. On the Ferncliff Trail, the riverside path facing the falls, look for potholes scoured by the current and for magnum fossils of lepidodendron, a scaly tree that grew in the Pennsylvanian Period.

Wildlife. Botanists tout the Ferncliff Peninsula's unusual flora, discovered by Dr. O. E. Jennings between 1920 and 1940. The area was later designated as a national natural landmark. Several southern species, having traveled up the Yough, reach their northernmost limit here, such as large-flowered marshallia (PA endangered), Carolina tassel-rue (PA rare), umbrella magnolia (PA rare), and buffalo nut (PA rare). Meanwhile, Canada buffalo-berry (PA endangered) and Canada plum, a northern tree, secure their southernmost beachhead on the peninsula. Curtis' goldenrod and slender blue iris (both PA endangered) grow here too. Ferncliff is also home to arrow-leaved violet, dwarf cinquefoil, fairy wand, gray beardtongue, hairy Solomon's seal, jack-in-the-pulpit, white clintonia, spotted coral root, sweet flag (PA endangered), marsh bluebell, panicled hawkweed, and turtlehead. Fern species include dissected grape, grape, long beech, marsh, lobed spleenwort, rattlesnake, royal, and cinnamon. Cucumber Run has botanical significance because it is home to American bugbane (PA rare) and blue monkshood (PA threatened).

Several other imperiled plants grow elsewhere in the park. These include hard-stemmed bulrush, single-headed pussytoes, slender goldenrod, slender spike-rush, umbrella flatsedge (all PA endangered); lettuce saxifrage (PA rare); purple fringe-less orchid and small headed rush (both PA threatened); and Pursh's goldenrod (PA in decline).

Ohiopyle appeals to birders looking for wood warblers (thirty-four species), raptors (eleven kinds), sparrows (fourteen kinds), swallows (six varieties), and woodpeckers, including the red-headed, red-bellied, and pileated. The olive-sided flycatcher, a species believed to have been extirpated in the state, occasionally shows up in spring and autumn. It is one of ten flycatchers seen in the park. The bird checklist includes 162 species.

Everybody knows about the Yough's trout, but walleye, rock bass, eel, and northern pike are here too. Naturalists have counted fourteen types of reptiles and sixteen amphibians, including timber rattlesnakes (PA endangered), common snapping turtles, and mountain dusky and spotted salamanders. The forests are home to twenty-four kinds of mammals, notably the bobcat, (a rarity nowadays), snowshoe hare, mink, flying squirrel, and black bear.

Woody plants are plentiful. The mixed oak forest holds fifty-three varieties of trees, plus twenty-six species of shrubs and eleven vines, including white mulberry, butternut, pussy willow, autumn olive, catalpa, cucumber magnolia, quaking aspen, and smooth sumac. The park office has checklists for trees, wildflowers, and birds, and a beginner's field guide to the Ferncliff Peninsula.

History. The Monongahela, Erie, Lenni-Lenape, Shawandase, and Seneca intermittently hunted, fished, and settled in the gorge of the Youghiogheny, which some say means "a stream flowing in a contrary direction" or "in a roundabout way" in one these native dialects. Others define it from Indian words loosely translated as "bumpy ride" or "daredevil stream" (appropriate enough), or "four swift streams," referring to the meeting of tributaries upriver at Confluence.

Ohiopyle derives from an anglicized Indian expression "ohiopehhle," meaning "white, frothy water." The falls and rapids presented an obstacle to George Washington in 1754, dashing his hopes of an easy waterborne transport route to Fort Duquesne (now Pittsburgh).

Though Ohiopyle has had its share of gristmills, tanneries, factories, sawmills, mines, and farms, the gorge and the falls have been the mother lode. In the early twentieth century, Ohiopyle was a resort town with hotels, boardinghouses, a railroad station, and assorted spinoff businesses. By the far the glitziest lodging was the Ferncliff Hotel, located at the neck of the Ferncliff Peninsula. Tourism declined during the Great Depression. Hard times also killed plans to build a monumental dam across the gorge at Ohiopyle.

Between 1961 and 1968 the Western Pennsylvania Conservancy obtained 10,000 acres in the gorge as the seed of a state park. The land was conveyed to the Bureau of State Parks in 1968. The park opened on May 31, 1971. Ohiopyle has again become a major recreation destination in southwestern Pennsylvania.

Oil Creek State Park

Drake Well Museum

Oil Creek doesn't sound pleasant, at first. Images of a modern ecological disaster come to mind—crude oil dripping from birds, fish
wallowing in shiny black ooze, oil derricks rather than trees occupying the slopes. Indeed, that was the scene from 1860 to 1875, during
America's first oil boom. Today, hardwoods have reclaimed the gorge
and concealed ghost towns. Trout spawn in the creek again, and bicyclists and hikers quietly tread on a road once plied by noisy locomotives. The gorge celebrates nature's vast healing power. Oil Creek is a
place of possibilities.

Ownership. Oil Creek State Park is owned and managed by the
Pennsylvania Department of Conservation and Natural Resources,
Bureau of State Parks. The Pennsylvania Historical and Museum
Commission runs Drake Well Museum.

Size. 7,075 acres.

Physiographic Region. Pittsburgh Low Plateau at the edge of
the glaciated plateau.

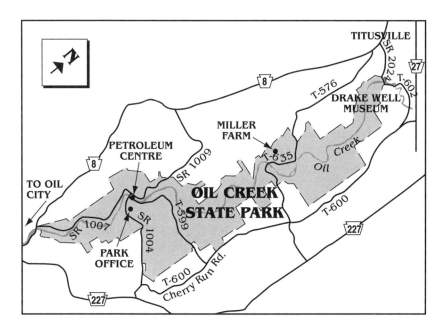

Nearby Natural Attractions. Two Mile Run County Park, Allegheny National Forest, and Allegheny Gorge (Kittaning State Forest), State Game Lands 39, 45, 47 and 49.

Features. Oil Creek has 75 miles of trails for nature hikers, so plan to stay a few days. And prepare for cardiac climbs, rocky terrain, and soggy socks. The main route, the 36-mile Gerard Hiking Trail, is designed for overnight backpacking trips. Four connector trails divide the Gerard loop into shorter day hikes. Three hikes and a combination canoe-hike are described here, but there is a larger menu of variations.

Yellow blazes mark the 36-mile Gerard Hiking Trail, a challenging backpacking loop stretching from Rynd Farm, a historic site at the southern park entrance at PA 8, to Drake Well Museum at the north end. The trail was named after Ray Gerard, a park volunteer and Western Pennsylvania Conservancy member who designed the trail and maintained it for sixteen years. Trailhead parking areas are located at the park office in Petroleum Centre, Drake Well Museum, T635 on both sides of Oil Creek, T621 at Pioneer historic site, and Rynd Farm historic site. Four connecting trails (white blazes) enable hikers to plan day hikes of varying lengths. Hikers will encounter attractive waterfalls, scenic overlooks, steep climbs, creek views, and solitude. Two hike-in camps (Cow Run and Wolfkill Run areas) are located beside the trail. Each has half a dozen Adirondack-style shelters with fireplaces, four tent sites, rest rooms, and water. Contact the state park office for reservations and fee schedule.

The Petroleum Centre Loop covers 6 miles in the southern third of the park. Start at the park office in historic Petroleum Centre on SR 1004. Take the marked trail behind the office to the Oil Creek trail, watching for yellow blazes (just beyond a pole line). Bear left here and continue ahead, past cross-country skiing trails, trees toppled by a 1985 tornado, Hemlock Road (T599), and the headwaters of Hemlock Run, roughly 2.5 miles into the hike. Turn left on a white-blazed side trail, and go down Hemlock Run ravine. Near the mouth, the trail turns left, climbs and descends a cliff, and merges with the park's paved bike trail. A left turn here returns to the starting point via the hike-bike path, completing a 4.8-mile hike. A right turn crosses to the west side of Oil Creek. Take the white-blazed connector to a historic site called Pioneer. At the site's parking area, bear left on the white-marked trail. Go left when this path joins the Gerard Hiking Trail, designated by yellow blazes. Follow this route to Greg Falls, Pioneer Run, scenic railroad depot, Petroleum Center, and back to the starting point to finish a strenuous 7-mile adventure.

Oil Creek's 9.7-mile paved trail for bicyclists and foot travelers follows the abandoned level grade of the Oil Creek and Titusville

Railroad between Petroleum Centre and Drake Well Museum. The southern terminus starts on the east side of the SR 1004 bridge in Petroleum Centre, heads north on a township road for half a mile, then drops to the banks of Oil Creek. Nine miles later, you'll reach the museum. Interpretive signs along the route mark former settlements and farms and explain natural history. Benches, picnic tables, rain shelters, and close encounters with Oil Creek await strollers. Parking, toilets, and water are available at both ends of the trail, a latrine at the Miller Farm Road crossing. Petroleum Centre has a bike rental concession.

Canoe launches at both ends of the park make it possible to hike, bike, or ride a train from Rynd Farm upstream to Drake Well and return via canoe, bike, or hiking. Canoeing is best April through mid-June. Thereafter the creek gets too shallow for continuous paddling.

Oil Creek also offers picnicking, hunting, fishing, Nordic skiing, and an outdoor education classroom. Privately owned campgrounds are nearby. The Oil Creek and Titusville Railroad runs a scenic railroad on weekends from May through October. The 26-mile round-trip train between Titusville and Rynd Farm stops at Drake Oil Well and Petroleum Centre.

The Pennsylvania Historical and Museum Commission operates Drake Well Museum off PA 8 at the north end of the park. Six miles east of the park, the historical commission commemorates the brief heydey of Pithole, the country's first boom town. Trails, access areas, and public roads at Drake Well Museum remain open daily. Indoor exhibits and museum grounds are open Tuesday through Saturday, 9 A.M. to 5 P.M., Sunday, noon to 5 P.M. Closed on holidays except Memorial Day, the Fourth of July, and Labor Day. Admission is charged.

For more information, contact Oil Creek State Park, R.R. 1, Box 207, Oil City, PA 16301-9733, telephone (814) 676-5915, or Drake Well Museum, R.D. 3, Titusville, PA 16354, telephone (814) 827-2729.

Geology. Oil had always leaked like sap in this valley. It reached the surface through oil seeps, akin to water springs, and trickled into the creek. For a long time, Native Americans, and then early Euro-American settlers, gathered the goop for medicine and waterproofing. Hamilton McClintock collected twenty to thirty barrels a year from a seep on his farm south of Rouseville. So, Edwin L. Drake was not the first "oilman" in this valley, nor did he have any doubt that he would strike oil here in 1859, as he dug right next to a well-known seep.

Like coal, oil is a fossil fuel derived from organic material. Most oil deposits originated as marine sediment that accumulated on the bottom of stagnant seas, whereas coal started as ancient trees and plants piled up in swamps. Overlying strata of mud, clay and sand hardened into bedrock. Every layer increased the pressure and temperature of the organic "soup," which "cooked" into oil. Whereas coal baked into its own rock, oil soaked into neighboring porous sedimentary rock, forming the oil-rich bedrock oilmen call pools.

Oil here pooled in 345- to 395-million-year-old sandstones of the Devonian Period. Drake's first well tapped a thin, isolated layer 69½ feet deep. Later, wells were drilled to depths of 450 to 550 feet, holes considered shallow today. Successful wells pumped 1,000 to 4,000 barrels of oil a day. By 1875, however, they began drying up, and oilmen began clearing out.

The park still has thousands of unplugged oil and gas wells leaking tiny amounts of oil and brine. Occasionally, one of them will blow, spewing larger amounts for a day or so. Abandoned wells, some 20 to 30 feet deep, can be dangerous if stepped on by curious sightseers. More information on the region's oil industry is available at the state park office and gift shop at Drake Well Museum.

Fossilized marine creatures that swam in tropical Devonian oceans long ago can be found in a Corry sandstone outcrop beside the train station at Drake Well Museum. The ledge is packed with molds of brachiopods (lampshell mollusks), bivalves (clams), gastropods (snails), and crinoids (segmented coral), as well as the tracks, burrows, and trails of other animals. Lucky diggers might stumble upon an uncommon sponge named after this area, *Titusvillia drakei*. Though the outcrop stretches for a mile, fine examples lie on the ground by the museum entrance. Collectors should remember that trains use the railroad daily. This Devonian-era rock appears elsewhere in the valley, but fossils are not abundant at those locations.

Younger chunks of sandstone stand as a jumbled "rock city" in Wildcat Hollow, site of an outdoor classroom for school groups near Petroleum Centre. Frost heave and erosion are responsible for these structures, composed of 330-million-year-old Shenango sandstone of the Mississippian Period. During a freeze, precipitation expanded natural fractures in the rock, and repeated freezing and thawing eventually split it into blocks. Softer underlying shales and siltstones eroded, causing the heavy blocks to tumble or slide down the slope. Soil creep, the downhill crawl of soil, put the blocks in their present position. Most tributary waterfalls in the valley foam over Shenango sandstone.

The highest ridges in the park are capped by sandstone, shale, and thin coal beds representing the 300-million-year-old Pottsville Formation, from the Pennsylvanian Period. These were deposited by a great river system spreading deltalike across a coastal plain.

Today, Oil Creek drains from Lake Canadohta in Crawford County, 20 miles northwest of the the park. From there it rushes southeast to Titusville, then south through the park to its merger with the Allegheny River in Oil City. Before the ice age, Oil Creek was a sleepy, shallow stream whose headwaters originated near Boughton Run, roughly 2 miles south of Drake Well Museum. A hill north of the headwaters served as a drainage divide, separating Oil Creek from northwest-flowing Muddy Creek. Contemporary Pine Creek and Oil Creek, west of Titusville, were part of the Muddy Creek watershed at that time. Oil Creek's bed was 400 to 500 feet above its modern route.

The vanguard of a continental ice mass spanned Oil Creek near the historic Miller Farm about 250,000 years ago and obstructed the channel of Muddy Creek, northwest of the state park. Melted water pooled as lakes in front of the glacier until it crested the divide and emptied through Oil Creek. As the glacier retreated, meltwater escaping through Oil Creek deepened the valley. Simultaneously, the land, now relieved of the weight of ice, rebounded, thereby intensifying the erosive power of the current. This deep-cutting action exposed the oil seeps that gave the creek its name and fame.

Small side streams could not gouge their channels as swiftly as the main current. When Oil Creek's flow subsided, the mouths of these side-cuts were left hanging above the parent stream. Waterfalls on Miller, Boughton, Plum, Dungeon, and Pioneer Runs are prime examples of hanging valleys.

Wildlife. The original forest cover surrounding Oil Creek was removed by lumbering by the mid-1800s, well before the oil boom. That virgin forest consisted of oaks, chestnut, and hickories in the uplands, with hemlocks, white pine, beeches, and maples on the slanting slopes and cool hollows. Today a northern hardwood forest prevails, consisting of beeches, birches, maples, and hemlocks. Since the park straddles the western edge of this forest type, clusters of mixed oaks and hickories also thrive, as well as black cherry and ashes. Floodplain wetlands covering 1,400 acres of the park contain cattails, marsh grasses, alders, willows, aspen, sycamores, and aquatic plants, notably arrowhead and water plantain. All totaled, eighty-four species of trees and shrubs flourish in this recovering land.

Wildflower fanciers can count 305 varieties, including wood anemone, sarsaparilla, dwarf larkspur, homewort, bittersweet, marsh marigold, crooked-stemmed aster, boneset, American pennyroyal, several Saint-John's-worts, spotted jewelweed, miterwort, bee balm, Indian pipe, foxglove, beardtongue, mad-dog skullcap, various goldenrods, rattlesnake root, a dozen varieties of violets, painted trillium, golden Alexander, and Solomon's seal. Twenty-four kinds of ferns include rattlesnake, cinnamon, hay-scented, and adder's-tongue. Common fungi are fly agaric, chanterelle, artist's fungus, puffball, and scarlet cup. Grasses include poverty, big bluestem, orchard, barnyard, and velvet.

A wildflower trail at Drake Well features the state-imperiled spreading globeflower and Jacob's ladder; small whorled pogonia (PA endangered); and blue monkshood and showy lady's slipper (both PA threatened). Common flowers include large-flowered trillium, blue-eyed Mary, cardinal flower, jack-in-the-pulpit, wood sorrel, mallow, swamp milkweed, turk's cap lily, wild columbine, swamp pink, wild geranium, wood lily, yellow lady's slipper, rhododendron, and morning glory.

The bird list includes 155 species. Warblers are abundant in spring, including mourning, palm, chestnut-sided, blue-winged, Connecticut, bay-breasted, magnolia, Blackburnian, and cerulean. Savannah, white-crowned, swamp, vesper, chipping, and fox sparrows flit about, along with indigo bunting, golden-crowned kinglet, rough-winged swallow, and blue-gray gnatcatcher. The park manages a bluebird trail and also attracts rarities such as the great blue heron (PA threatened); bald eagle and osprey (both PA endangered); red-headed woodpecker; and Cooper's and red-shouldered hawks. Pick up a checklist at the park office.

Thirty-seven species of mammals include the black bear, red fox, porcupine, southern bog lemming, mink, masked shrew, beaver, and two kinds of flying squirrels. Twenty-two reptiles and twenty-two amphibians are found here, including the northern copperhead, timber rattlesnake (PA rare), five-lined skink, spotted turtle, stinkpot, black rat snake, hellbender, mud puppy, red-spotted newt, and four-toed salamander.

What a local newspaper reporter in 1877 called "the most filthy stream on God's footstool" now supports thirty-one kinds of fish, including shiners, darters, pike, and walleye. Thousands of trout are stocked in Oil Creek to boost reintroduced populations of brook, brown, and rainbows. Anglers also toss lines for smallmouth and rock bass.

History. Oil Creek's human history is long-winded and well documented. An explorer dubbed the stream Oil Creek in the 1780s. (Any Indian designation for the location has been forgotten.) Frontier soldiers apparently found great pleasure bathing in the greasy ooze, reported a Massachusetts magazine. They also drank the oil-laden water, believing it purged their bowels. The Brewer and Watson sawmill here cut 4,000 board-feet of timber a day. Crude oil was used to illuminate the mill and lubricate the machinery. Most of the lumber was rafted to Pittsburgh via the Allegheny River.

By 1850 Oil City, founded on land once granted to Cornplanter, chief of the Seneca Nation, had become a thriving town with mills, a steamboat landing, an iron furnace, and a hotel. Most of the hillsides had been lumbered when Edwin L. Drake, a former clerk and railroad conductor, came here for the Seneca Oil Company. The "colonel" before his name was a fake title concocted by his employer to elevate his prestige.

Drilling three feet a day, Drake struck oil on August 27, 1859, marking the start of the world's oil industry. Oil Creek quickly developed into a bustling valley of little boom towns, with Petroleum Centre at the hub. The village of Cornplanter was renamed Oil City. The scenery changed overnight. Trees were replaced by oil derricks. The valley became crowded with people, railroads, oil barrels, outbuildings, shacks, logjams, engines, and animals. Soot and smoke fouled the air, and shiny scum iced the creek. For awhile there was plenty of oil, plenty of jobs, and easy money. Some men, like sawmiller Jonathan Watson, got rich quick; others, notably Drake and a speculator named John Wilkes Booth, Lincoln's assassin, never profited. The heydey ended by 1875, with most wells barren and many men busted. The money men and their minions moved to the next mother lode, leaving the Oil Creek valley ruined. The place became a ghost town cluttered with the detritus and obsolete hardware of the early oil industry.

In 1864 Seneca Oil sold the Drake site to David Emory, whose family deeded it to the Daughters of the American Revolution in 1911. The American Petroleum Institute later acquired it and gave it to the state in 1933. Oil Creek's restoration started in October 1962 when Dr. Maurice Goddard, secretary of the Pennsylvania Department of Forests and Waters, took a wagon ride through the history-rich valley with Virginia and Alfred Hunt, local property owners. The Hunts regaled Goddard with colorful stories of oil's glory days. Goddard saw the location's potential as a state park soaked in history. The Western Pennsylvania Conservancy bought the first tract in 1966. By the end of 1970, the state had acquired more than 7,000 acres. The paved bike trail opened in 1979, followed in 1983 by the Gerard Hiking Trail and visitors center.

Drake Well Museum is a must-see for people interested in industrial history or linked to the oil business. It has a full-size replica of Drake's well and other early oil well operations.

Pine Ridge County Park

Many evergreens grow in Indiana County, but not here. Pine Ridge County Park is actually a hardwood haven at the bottom of a ridge once celebrated for its chestnuts. The name recognizes the county's pride as a top Christmas tree producer. Misnomer aside, the site is special for its deciduous delights, including a grove of maturing American chestnut trees that may be resistant to the fungus that has nearly exterminated the species.

Ownership. Indiana County Parks.

Size. 630 acres.

Physiographic Region. Pine Ridge County Park straddles the border of the Allegheny Mountain and Pittsburgh Low Plateau Provinces.

Nearby Natural Attractions. Yellow Creek State Park, Conemaugh Gorge, Blue Spruce and Hemlock Lake County Parks, State Game Lands 153 and 276, and Charles F. Lewis, Blacklick Valley, and Buttermilk Falls Natural Areas.

Features. Take the park entrance road off Old William Penn Highway (SR 2002) to its end at the Toms Run Picnic Area. The main drag for hikers is the mile-long Lodge Trail from the picnic area to Pine Lodge. Rest rooms are available at the picnic area.

After tracing Toms Run for a quarter mile, the bouldery path heads uphill through a second-growth hardwood forest to Pine Lodge, a rustic, two-story day-use lodge overlooking Pine Lake. To make a circuit hike from here, head west on a lane that parallels an intermittent run draining Pine Lake. About a half mile ahead, bear left at a fork, following a thin footpath that traces the descending rill. After passing boulders and a pipeline, the trail turns north and eventually joins the main park road. Go east on the park road to Toms Run Picnic Area to complete a 3-mile journey. You also can roam on abandoned logging roads branching from the lodge and park entrance road. Trails are open daily from 7 A.M. to dusk.

The gated driveway to Pine Lodge branches from Strangford Road. From Toms Run, head west on SR 2002, left on Chestnut Ridge Road (T724), and left on Strangford Road (T888). The lodge is open by reservation only to groups up to 150.

For more information, contact Indiana County Parks, Blue Spruce Park Rd., Indiana, PA 15701, telephone (724) 463-8636.

Geology. Pine Ridge is at the base of the western slope of Chestnut Ridge and a few miles north of the western gateway to Conemaugh Gorge. Hikers ascending the Lodge Trail from the Toms Run Picnic Area begin in the Pittsburgh Low Plateau physiographic region but finish in the Allegheny Mountain Province upon reaching Pine Lodge.

Most water here drains into Toms Run, which originates on Chestnut Ridge east of the park and flows west into the Conemaugh River. Weirs Run, another Conemaugh tributary, receives runoff from parkland north of US 22. The current in Toms Run remains clean enough for trout and other aquatic life, even though acidic drainage from an abandoned strip mine enters it via an unnamed brook east of the picnic pavilion and trailhead.

Natural gas lies beneath Pine Ridge's Pennsylvanian Period bedrock. Only one well, now orphaned, has been drilled in the park.

Wildlife. The diverse flora here includes 62 kinds of trees and shrubs and 166 wildflower varieties. When hiking the Lodge Trail, note the straightness and height of the tulip trees, factors that made this hardwood the favorite of log cabin builders. Tulip trees were not so abundant two centuries ago. American chestnuts (*Castanea dentata*) held sway on this ridge back then, hence the name Chestnut Ridge, and most tulips remained in the subcanopy. When a fungal blight began felling the chestnuts in the early twentieth century, tulip trees, among others, began to fill the forest vacancies.

Park officials keep their fingers crossed as they observe several seemingly healthy chestnuts that grow along the Pine Lodge road. The specimens measured 20 inches in diameter in 1997 and showed no signs of disease. The fungus usually girdles chestnut saplings at ground level before they reach this size. Chestnut roots remain immune and send up shoots, but this does not prevent the new growth from succumbing to the blight. Perhaps this grove has not been exposed to the fungus or maybe these trees are resistant and will save the species from extinction.

An 1877 geological and botanical survey of Indiana County also mentioned white and chestnut oaks on the flanks of Chestnut Ridge.

These trees still exist, but disturbances such as logging, development, agriculture, and mining removed the original forest, and pioneer varieties such as red maple, sassafras, black birch, and black cherry now occupy the ridge. Red oak, a species not on from the 1877 inventory, is now common in the park. This oak may have benefited from the disturbances or from the chestnut's decline. Salvage logging to remove trees and shrubs killed by a gypsy moth epidemic was done in 1995.

Climax-size sugar maples and beeches are anchored on a north-facing slope traversed by the Lodge Trail. These broad-leaved trees have shaded out undergrowth except for clumps of greenbrier and spicebush. Spring wildflowers led by large-leaved trillium generously decorate this section of the forest. Other plants include wild geranium, mountain anemone, butter-and-eggs, smooth Solomon's seal, jewelweed, mad-dog skullcap, New York ironweed, and mouse-eared chickweed (PA endangered). Fourteen species of ferns include silvery spleenwort, maidenhair, long beech, and cinnamon.

Members of the Todd Bird Club of Indiana have sighted ninety-eight bird species, including the American kestrel; red-tailed, broad-winged, and sharp-shinned hawks; Blackburnian, magnolia, pine, mourning, and golden-winged warblers; ruby-crowned and golden-crowned kinglets; and warbling and red-eyed vireos.

Toms Run supports fourteen kinds of fish, notably brown, brook, and rainbow trout. Minnows known as blacknose dace, creek chub, and stoneroller constitute the largest population.

History. European explorers in the 1700s noted Indian "forts" along the Conemaugh River. (Use of the word *fort,* rather than *village,* would get the attention of colonial administrators east of the Appalachians.) In 1952 archaeologists with the Carnegie Museum of Natural History found the remnants of one of these settlements near Blairsville, 3 miles west of the park. Conemaugh supposedly derives from an Indian expression meaning "otter creek."

Stone foundations, piles of rocks, and locust tree fence posts point to an agricultural past, but not likely a lucrative one, given the stony ridgetops and steep terrain. Loggers cut the original forest, and miners briefly removed coal from banks above Toms Run.

Pine Lodge once was a privately owned camp, now renovated, and Pine Lake, the 1-acre pond beside the dwelling, was a pay-to-fish lake. The parkland was purchased in 1966–67. An estimated 90,000 people visited in 1997.

Pine Swamp

Pine Swamp is a damp, cool bog that seems more appropriate to northern Canada than to northwestern Pennsylvania. Carnivorous animals and plants are concealed here in this uncommon wetland and reminiscent of Pleistocene-era museum dioramas with tusked mammoths knee-deep in muck, the chill and scent of glacier ice in the wind.

Ownership. Pine Swamp is part of State Game Lands 130, owned by the Pennsylvania Game Commission.

Size. 395 acres.

Physiographic Region. Glaciated Plateau.

Nearby Natural Attractions. Pymatuning Wetlands, Wallace Woods, Schollard's Run Wetland (State Game Lands 284), and Maurice K. Goddard State Park.

Features. Pine Swamp has become overgrown since the game commission took ownership. Vegetation has erased trails maintained by the former owner, Western Pennsylvania Conservancy, and a roadside farmhouse that once served as a landmark has been demolished. Still, experienced hikers can discern old paths or follow new ones blazed by deer. You're free to explore this soggy realm. If you lose your bearings, head south until you reach PA 965, where there's a parking area. From there, an old farm lane heads north through tall grass and shrubs to forest and swamp. To the east is a pond popular with local anglers. The southern tip of the wetland and the headwaters of Wolf Creek are on the left. Pine Swamp trends north-south. A wet forest protects its eastern frontier.

A small parking pulloff on Parker Store Road gives hikers access to the northern reaches. To get there, continue east on PA 965, then go north on PA 173 and left on Parker Store Road. The game lands are open daily from sunrise to sunset. Hunting and fishing are permitted.

Geology. Pine Swamp started when meltwater and precipitation

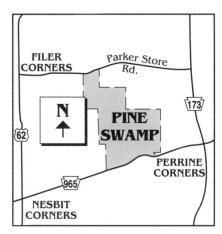

filled a scratch made by the Wisconsinan glacier 15,000 years ago. Rainwater is still the chief recharger of the swamp. The wetland is the source of south-flowing Wolf Creek, which trickles from the southern end and later squeezes through a narrow gorge near Slippery Rock in Butler County. The north end of the swamp feeds Fox Run, which heads southwest into Yellow Creek.

The fishing pond near the highway is man-made. The embankment of the old farm lane impounds the water, though some percolates into Wolf Creek.

Wildlife. Forty acres of swollen, spongy no-man's-land lie in the middle of the wetland. Growing there are white pines, aspens, willows, black birch, chokecherry, alder, swamp rose, willows, nannyberry, and highbush blueberry. The accumulation of dead vegetation over thousands of years has caused this insular kingdom to crest along its spine like a surfacing whale. It's because of this humpback that Fox Run circles around the north edge of the mound.

The swamp has been called a barrens, a misnomer based on its inaccessibility and low commercial value to humanity. More fittingly, the patch is a peatland, with rich peat soil derived from the buildup and compaction of organic material.

Reaching this little wilderness requires plunging across an uneven waist-deep moat covered with webs of sphagnum moss, wild cranberry, clumps of cotton grass and Virginia chain fern, marsh Saint-John's-wort, and bladderwort, a yellow-flowering carnivorous plant that captures tiny water insects and crustaceans in submerged bladders. The mire contains other surprises—frogs, turtles, waterfowl, mink, and perhaps a beady-eyed Pleistocene holdover.

Most people stay in the safer and drier swamp forest, with its chaotic collection of high-rising hemlocks, red maple, white oak, beeches, white pine, and sugar maple. Below these thrive sassafras, hawthorns, mountain laurel, blackhaw, hobblebush, maple-leaved viburnum, and highbush blueberry, which sustains the black bear and other vertebrates. The forest floor is cluttered with large-flowered and painted trilliums, trout lily, skunk cabbage, bloodroot, jewelweed, hepatica, cut-leaved toothwort, Canada mayflower, wild blue iris, wintergreen, and goldthread, or canker-root. Royal, cinnamon, sensitive, and Christmas ferns wave their fronds. Huckleberry, another heath plant capable of growing on mineral-poor soil, thrives on the grounds, too. Look for partridgeberry, bird's-foot trefoil, various goldenrods and violets, arrowwood, running pine club moss, and beechdrop, a parasitic plant that finds nourishment from beech tree roots.

Chipmunks and wild turkeys go bonkers on beechnuts in autumn. You might flush deer and ruffed grouse on your hike. Beavers can be spotted at dusk. From time to time, wildlife officers have to destroy a beaver dam that chokes a culvert. Gray squirrels, woodchucks, and cottontail rabbits also inhabit the spot. Birders can scope for great blue herons (PA threatened), which nest in a rookery in the northern reaches of the swamp, as well as red-winged blackbirds, common yellowthroats, black-capped chickadees, and downy woodpeckers.

History. The Western Pennsylvania Conservancy acquired the parcel piecemeal between 1974 and 1981. Ownership was transferred to the Pennsylvania Game Commission in the 1990s.

45

Powdermill Nature Reserve

Powdermill started as a biological field station in the mid-1950s, a wild setting in the Laurel Highlands exclusively for scientific research. In nearly half a century of discovery, scientists have unlocked secrets as varied as the winter struggles of insectivores, the wanderings of thousands of birds, and a cheap and natural way to remove lethal pollution from bleeding, abandoned coal mines. In the 1980s, following construction of a nature center, education became another mission at the reserve. Researchers now share their bounty of knowledge and land with the next generation of scholars, be they fifth graders or octogenarians.

Ownership. Carnegie Museum of Natural History.

Size. 2,200 acres.

Physiographic Region. Allegheny Mountains.

Nearby Natural Attractions. Forbes State Forest, Linn Run, Laurel Mountain, Laurel Ridge, Laurel Hill, and Kooser State Parks.

Features. Trails and education programs are concentrated in a 17-acre area around the Nimick Nature Center. The rest of the property is a nature sanctuary and wildlife research area. Black Birch Trail snakes for 0.75 mile through mostly bottomland forest, the highlight being an encounter with Powdermill Run. An interpretive guide available at the parking lot trailhead adds to the enjoyment.

The Florence Lockhart Nimick Nature Center features an exhibit consisting of dioramas of local habitats and a videotape on the reserve.

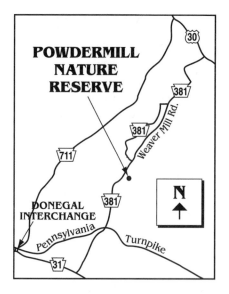

Staff offices, rest rooms, and class-rooms are also located around the center. Butterfly and herb gardens flank the building. The center is open when staff is available. Call ahead for nature center hours and programs. Nature education programs occur almost daily and every weekend during the warm months. Trails are open daily from sunrise to sunset.

The reserve offers conference and dining rooms, five rustic cabins, and a laboratory-dormitory facility for researchers. Powdermill can accommodate forty-five overnight visitors and has hosted many scientific conferences and workshops. The center is the field station for the Carnegie Museum of Natural History.

For more information, contact Powdermill Nature Reserve, HC64 Box 453, Rector, PA 15677-9605, telephone (724) 593-2221.

Geology. The reserve spreads out in the Loyalhanna Creek Valley (also called Ligonier Valley), flanked by Laurel Ridge to the east and Chestnut Ridge to the west. Though technically part of the Appalachian (or Allegheny) Plateau, these steep, parallel ridges were jostled into their current northeast-southwest orientation during a tectonic event called the Alleghenian Orogeny, 290 million years ago. The place is underlain by bedrock made during the Pennsylvanian Period, 300 to 325 million years ago.

Powdermill, Laurel, and White Oak Runs merge in the reserve and flow into Loyalhanna Creek, which heads northeast to Ligonier, then northwest through a gap in Chestnut Ridge. At Latrobe it goes north and meets with the Conemaugh River at Saltsburg to form the Kiskiminetas River, a tributary of the Allegheny River.

Wildlife. Over the years Powdermill researchers have studied woodland lilies, bird migration, forest composition, acid rain pollution, spiders, butterflies, stink bugs, caddisflies, gypsy moths, land snails, wood turtles, frogs, Acadian flycatchers, Kentucky warblers, Louisiana waterthrushes, chickadees, and white-footed mice. They have specialized in bird banding and the lives of small mammals.

Birders can look for the Swainson's thrush (PA rare), gray catbird, blue-gray gnatcatcher, tufted titmouse, red-winged blackbird, red-eyed vireo, woodcock, Lincoln's sparrow, ruby-crowned kinglet, yellow-bellied flycatcher (PA threatened), pine siskin, indigo bunting, downy woodpecker, and black-and-white, Wilson's, and yellow-rumped warblers. Ponds built in the 1960s attract great blue herons (PA threatened) and other waders.

Butterflies commonly seen are the tiger, black, and pipevine swallowtails; regal, great spangled, silver, and bordered fritillaries; question mark; wood nymph; harvester; and spring azure.

Spring wildflowers of note are turk's-cap lily, large-flowered and red trilliums, blue phlox, foamflower, dwarf ginseng, trout lily, spring beauty, mayapple, halberd-leaved violet, and wood, rue, and mountain anemone. Summer blossoms include joe-pye weed, ironweed, thistle, milkweed, Indian pipe, cardinal flower, jewelweed, and elderberry. Along Powdermill Run and its contributing rill, White Oak Run, look for skunk cabbage, false hellebore, marsh marigold, and tall meadow-rue. Buffalo Nut Sanctuary, a 53-acre parcel near Stahlstown that became part of the reserve in 1971, protects the buffalo nut, a rare shrub.

Most of the reserve consists of mixed deciduous trees such as American beech, tulip tree, sugar maple, red oak, hemlocks, rhododendrons, yellow birch, cucumber magnolia, aspen, hickories, white oak, ironwood, witch hazel, and sycamores. Black Birch Trail is named after the tree growing along its route. Successional meadows are dominated by hawthorns, crab apples, black locust, black cherry, and dogwood.

The center has been an advocate and pioneer of passive treatment to restore streams polluted by acid mine runoff. When the reserve bought the neighboring 240-acre Friedline Farm in 1968, it inherited two small abandoned strip mines that were leaking toxic aluminum and iron into Laurel Run. Initial pollution-control steps using settlement ponds showed promise in the 1970s, and the strategy was improved in the early 1990s, Today the mine waste drips through a series of collection ponds, where natural processes combined with some technology filter out the poisons. Laurel Run may soon support trout again.

History. Back in the 1950s Dr. M. Graham Netting, director of the Carnegie Museum of Natural History, declared the museum's need for a field station. Netting's idea came to fruition in 1956 following a gift of 1,160 acres in the Laurel Highlands by Gen. and Mrs. Richard K. Mellon and Dr. and Mrs. Alan M. Scaife. In 1969 Cordelia S. May donated a nearby 133-acre tract known as Furnace Woods to the reserve, followed in 1971 by the acquisition of 53-acre Buffalo Nut Sanctuary from Ruth Scott and Mrs. Townsend Treese. The Magee family gave the reserve a 3-acre mature woodlot called Seminar Forest.

Over the years, ponds have been dug for wetland habitats, buildings and cottages have been restored, and educational facilities have been improved. The Florence Lockhart Nimick Nature Center opened in 1983, and a classroom was added in 1993.

46

Presque Isle State Park

Presque Isle's claw-shaped spit of land looks poised to scratch Erie. Its name comes from a French expression meaning "almost an island," and for most of its life it has been tethered to the mainland, although for 12,000 years it has been drifting eastward. Every so often, this skinny peninsula stretches its neck too far and snaps its umbilical cord, but nature—or lately humankind—always restores it. The park has sensational sunsets, intriguing trails, rich history lessons, lagoons and ponds, great birding, windswept dunes and natural beaches, and the best public swimming beaches in the state. Presque Isle is a stellar site and should be placed at the top of any list of places to visit.

Ownership. Pennsylvania Department of Conservation and Natural Resources, Bureau of State Parks.

Size. 3,200 acres.

Physiographic Region. Central Lowland.

Nearby Natural Attractions. Asbury Woods Nature Center, David M. Roderick Wildlife Reserve, and Siegel Marsh.

Features. Stull Interpretive Center, located near the entrance, should be your first stop, unless you are eager to plunge into Lake

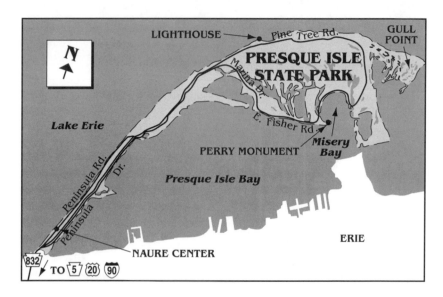

144

Erie. This former administration building and first-aid station was converted into a nature center with the help of the Presque Isle Audubon Society, Northwestern Pennsylvania Duck Hunters' Association, and the state park bureau. It is named after James and Jean Stull, longtime birders and banders on the spit. Here you will find exhibits on the park's natural history, geology, wildlife, and ecological zones. A quarter-mile interpretive trail leads to a sand dune and forest. Nature programs usually start at the center, open 10 A.M. to 6 P.M. daily from Memorial Day weekend to Labor Day, and 10 A.M. to 4 P.M. Thursday to Sunday in the spring and fall. The park is open daily from 5 A.M. to sunset. A park guide to the trails, beaches, and historic sites is available at the nature center.

Hikers can explore this national natural landmark on 13 miles of trails. The favorites of nature lovers are Dead Pond and Gull Point Trails. Dead Pond stretches for 2 miles between the parking lot for Beach 11 at the east end of the park and the Sidewalk Trail near its terminus at the lighthouse. Dead Pond Trail traipses across several sand dunes and swamps, through an oak-maple forest and pines, over sandy plains, and beside Niagara Pond. Inexplicably, it does not visit Dead Pond.

Birders head for the 1.5-mile Gull Point Trail, which starts at a kiosk in the parking lot for Budny Beach (Beach 10). The loop travels through Gull Point Natural Area, at the easternmost snout of the spit. At the turnback curve, take the side trail to an observation platform overlooking Gull Point Special Management Area. The sanctuary beyond the platform is off-limits to humans from April to November 30.

Three trails have historic importance. Sidewalk Trail tracks the 1.25-mile path lighthouse keepers followed from the old Misery Bay boat dock to the Presque Isle Lighthouse. Grave Yard Pond Trail runs 0.75 mile along the shore of Grave Yard Pond, the final resting place of sailors who died of smallpox during the winter of 1813–14. The ruins of a field lab used by famed biologist Dr. O. E. Jennings, who studied plant succession on Presque Isle, are found on 0.75-mile Pine Tree Trail.

The paved Multi-Purpose Trail stretches 5.8 miles from the park entrance to Perry's Monument. En route, it passes the nature center and the Niagara and East Pier boat ramps. Hikers, bicyclists, joggers, skaters, and visitors in wheelchairs share this popular south shore lane, designated a national recreation trail.

Millions of humans swarm to the eleven beaches that ring the peninsula's Lake Erie shore. The park also has a marina, boat launches, boat rentals, a dozen boat landings, picnic areas, a pavilion, rest rooms, food concessions, and a Coast Guard station. Naturalist-led boat tours are offered three times daily from Memorial Day to Labor Day. Register at the nature center for the forty-five-minute ride to a lagoon. Hunting and fishing are permitted in the park. Check park restrictions for boating, hunting, fishing, and diving.

For more information, contact Presque Isle State Park, P.O. Box 8510, Erie, PA 16505, telephone (814) 833-7424, website www.dcnr.state.pa.us, or the Stull Interpretive Center, (814) 833-0351.

Geology. At the end of the ice age, 13,000 years ago, the last finger of the retreating Wisconsinan glacier poked southwest as far as Erie, plugging the St. Lawrence outlet and impounding a fresh-water sea, a predecessor of Lake Erie. Meanwhile, meltwater laden with sediment consisting of gravel, sand, and clay piled up in front of the ice, creating a ridge called a terminal moraine. This broad moraine swelled above the water level and stretched across the width of the lake.

About 5 miles off today's shore, probably where the ridge narrowed to a neck, stream erosion cut through the moraine, disconnecting the ridge attached to Ontario from a broad platform, or swollen beach, bulging northeast from Pennsylvania. As the glacier melted and filled the Lake Erie basin, the shoreline migrated across the bulge and eventually submerged it. To the west, waves and wind eroded sandy bluffs, and eastbound longshore currents deposited the sediment on the platform, creating successively bars, peninsula, and recurved sand spit. The mass moves eastward half a mile per century. Easterly waves strike the spit at an oblique angle, so sand is removed from the thin neck, carried along the shore, and redeposited at the northern and eastern ends where the current slows. Gull Point, the easternmost tip, has grown nearly a mile during the twentieth century. Several dozen ponds have formed in depressions between sand dunes that once marked the eastern extent of the spit. The spit shifts and stays attached as long as sand deposition continues faster than erosion.

Since 1819 storm waves have broken through the narrow neck four times, turning the place into a true island. One break lasted thirty-two years, until natural siltation and human intervention closed it. Shoreline development west of the peninsula had exacerbated the erosion by reducing natural sand deposition. Since 1955 sand that would have filled fifty-five football stadiums has been dumped on the park's beaches. Detached artificial reefs called break-walls, perpendicular walls called groins, seawalls of stone or broken concrete called revetments, and beach nourishment, in which lost sand is replenished, all have been employed to stop erosion and protect park facilities, wildlife, and Erie's harbor. The idea is to halt or manage Presque Isle's dynamic natural forces.

Wildlife. Presque Isle is a celebration of wildlife diversity and rare and delicate habitats. The spit bulges with life because it has six ecological zones: the Lake Erie shoreline and bay; sandy plains and new ponds (Gull Point); sand dunes and ridges; old ponds and swamps; shrubs and young forest; and climax forest. Note the successional stages of these zones while walking along paths.

Presque Isle harbors the only populations in Pennsylvania of silverweed, dragon's mouth and elk sedges, branching bur reed, variegated horsetail, and white-stemmed pondweed (all PA endangered). Another rarity is Kalm's lobelia (PA endangered), which blooms in July and August. Look for yellow flax, buttonbush, beach pea, lupine, lyre-leaved rock cress, wormwood, spotted touch-me-not (jewelweed), blue flag iris, winter cress, milkweed, New England aster, wild raspberry, and royal, marsh, and bracken ferns.

Eighty-eight percent of all bird species counted in Pennsylvania, or 323 varieties, have been spotted in the park. Of these, 45 are species of special concern, including the osprey, sedge wren, and black tern. Birdwatchers know the park is a hot spot during spring and fall migrations. In fact, birding magazines rank it one of the top locations in the nation, right up there with Hawk Mountain Sanctuary in eastern Pennsylvania. Take along binoculars and checklists to observe and identify the many gulls, herons, bitterns, woodpeckers, flycatchers, warblers, vireos, birds of prey, and waterbirds, including the common loon, least bittern, great blue heron (PA threatened), black-bellied plover, Hudsonian godwit, solitary sandpiper, red-headed woodpecker, dunlin, prothonotary warbler, chuck-will's-widow, and short-billed dowitcher.

Gull Point, a bird sanctuary since 1927, attracts shorebirds and winter guests like the snowy owl and northern shrike, which impales its victims on thorns. Raptors are likely to be seen along Dead Pond Trail during migrations. Look for owls in the pines near Budny Beach.

Thousands of monarch butterflies collect here in late summer and early autumn, after flitting across Lake Erie from Canada, on their way to their wintering grounds in Central Mexico.

The protected waters off Gull Point safeguard freshwater mussels and fish. Blanding's turtle, an imperiled animal, lives in the park along with deer, raccoons, muskrats, and fox squirrels.

History. The Erie Indians who lived here in the sixteenth century believed Presque Isle to be the fabled spot where the Great Spirit had extended his arm to protect his favorite people from a storm. The sheltered bay, however, could not stop an Iroquois takeover in 1655. A century later, a well-armed French force landed on Presque Isle, perhaps as a beachhead for an invasion into the Pennsylvania–New York frontier. The Iroquois sent a delegation to protest, but the French ignored it.

During the War of 1812, Presque Isle sheltered a small American fleet commanded by Commodore Oliver Hazard Perry. The commander's flagship, the *Lawrence,* and five other ships, including the *Niagara,* were built in Erie Bay with local trees. Perry left the bay in September 1813 to head off an eastbound British fleet. The fleets clashed near Put-in-Bay, off Sandusky, Ohio, on September 10. Two hours into the bombardment, damage to the *Lawrence* forced Perry to board the *Niagara.* Perry won the battle an hour later, reporting for posterity, "We have met the enemy and they are ours."

Perry docked the fleet in Presque Isle after the battle. During the winter, many sailors contracted smallpox and were quarantined in an inlet aptly called Misery Bay. Victims who succumbed to the disease were laid to rest in a nearby pond, also aptly known as Grave Yard Pond. Perry purposely sunk his fleet in Misery Bay in 1850, ostensibly to "preserve and protect them [the ships] from the weather," according to the park guide. They were raised around 1913, and the *Niagara* has been restored and docked at Erie harbor. It is Pennsylvania's official flagship in "tall ship" events. The Perry Monument, a statue of the commodore in Misery Bay, was erected in 1926.

Presque Isle Lighthouse, the second built on Lake Erie, first steered ships clear of the 7-mile-long peninsula on July 12, 1873. The U.S. Coast Guard still keeps the light flashing. The tower stands 70 feet above a ten-room red brick home now used as a park residence. Nine men and their families served as lighthouse keepers between 1873 and 1927, working from sunset to sunrise April through November.

Two man-made square ponds midway up the peninsula recall Waterworks Park, part of the water system for the city of Erie. Water piped from the lake went to the settling basins before being pumped to the city. The waterworks operated from 1917 to 1949.

Presque Isle was acquired for a state park in 1921. The United States Department of the Interior designated the spit a national natural landmark in 1967.

Pymatuning Wetlands

This swamp near the headwaters of the Shenango River has always been a paradise for myriad wild creatures and a breadbasket for human hunters and gatherers. Though changed by a dam and development, the Pymatuning Wetlands remain a cradle of life for aquatic, feathered, and fur-bearing creatures. All that restorative power rubs off on people who pass some hours here.

Ownership. The area includes State Game Lands 214 (Pymatuning Swamp), owned by the Pennsylvania Game Commission, and Pymatuning State Park, run by the Pennsylvania Department of Conservation and Natural Resources, Bureau of State Parks.

Size. State Game Lands 214 totals 5,398 acres, and Pymatuning State Park, the state's largest park, comprises 21,122 acres, most of it water.

Physiographic Region. Glaciated Plateau.

Nearby Natural Attractions. Conneaut Marsh, Tryon-Weber Woods, Woodcock Creek Lake, Erie National Wildlife Refuge, and Wallace Woods.

Features. Nature lovers tend to congregate in the eastern third of the lake-wetland, between Linesville and Hartstown. Outdoor recreationists flock to park attractions along the western crescent extending from Linesville to Jamestown.

For birding, Pymatuning is among the "best in the west." A checklist names 267 species, from the tiny ruby-throated hummingbird to the double-crested cormorant. For starters, go to the state park visitors center on Ford Island, off the Linesville Causeway (Linesville-Hartstown Road) south of US 6. A brown clapboard house built in 1938 serves as a wildlife museum, with more than 400 stuffed specimens

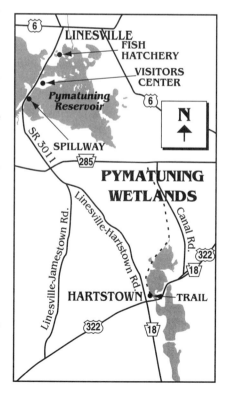

behind glass. Five spotting scopes allow you to observe live bald eagles raising their young in nearby nests. They are most active in April and May. A quarter-mile path running from the center to the parking lot has interpretive signs identifying local shrubs and trees. The free museum is open March through November, 8 A.M. to 4 P.M. Monday through Friday and 10 A.M. to 6 P.M. on weekends. For more information on the museum, call (814) 683-5545.

Birders can explore the area in the comfort of their cars by following a 25-mile route designed by the game commission. Figure on spending one to two hours on birding sites between Linesville and Hartstown. Pick up an itinerary at the museum, where the adventure begins.

Some 3,670 acres of state parkland and lake water east of Ford Island has been designated a wildlife propagation area, off-limits to humans. Migratory waterfowl and raptors gather in this protected area during spring and autumn migrations. The game commission also maintains the Pymatuning Waterfowl Management Area, east of Linesville-Hartstown Road between Tea Kettle Road and its office. These refuges are shown on state park and game commission maps.

North of the state park visitors center, also off Linesville-Hartstown Road, the Pennsylvania Fish and Boat Commission operates the Linesville Fish Culture Station and Robert J. Bielo Visitors Center. More than 100 ponds and open tanks hold walleye, largemouth and smallmouth bass, lake and brown trout, coho salmon, tiger muskellunge, channel catfish, paddlefish, steelhead, panfish, and muskellunge. Shorebirds swoop down to the ponds when they are drained in late summer. The visitors center has exhibits on fish and wetlands animals and a video on hatchery operations. Try to visit in early April, when staffers are making millions of walleye fry. Birders with binoculars can also scan the lakeshore and islands there for bald eagles, ospreys, great blue herons, and wood ducks. The hatchery visitors center is open daily 7:30 A.M. to 3:30 P.M. For more information, call the Pennsylvania Fish and Boat Commission, Linesville Fish Culture Station, telephone (814) 683-4451.

The University of Pittsburgh, Department of Biological Sciences, operates the Pymatuning Laboratory of Ecology, a biological field station next to the fish hatchery. Teaching and lab facilities are located on the shore of Sanctuary Lake within the wildlife propagation area. Call (814) 683-5813 for more information.

Hundreds of people stop to feed carp and waterfowl at the "spillway soup kitchen" south of Ford Island. Parking lots are on both sides of Linesville-Hartstown Road, and concessions sell food for fish and people. Picture thousands of monstrous, human-dependent carp packed gill-to-gill like sardines fighting for scraps tossed by amused people. Canada geese and mallard ducks walk on the backs of these corraled fish for bread crumbs, but shrieking, agile ring-billed and herring gulls are likely to snatch the bits from their bills or from human hands.

Hikers can use the abandoned towpath of the Erie Extension Canal, which cuts across Pymatuning Swamp between US 6 and US 322 in Hartstown, on the eastern leg of the horseshoe. Find the railroad tracks crossing US 322 at the eastern edge of Hartstown. Turn north on the east side of the tracks, following a potholed dirt road. In half a mile, the road forks right, and the tracks point north. Ahead, less than half a mile, park beside a gate blocking the towpath. Head north for 3 miles to PA 285, passing a reservoir on the right and the swamp on the left. Water impounded by the towpath was used by the canal. The northern trailhead of the towpath is found at a gate on the south side of PA 285, a bit east of the railroad tracks. Most people hike between these highways, a 6-mile round-trip. The game commission owns the right-of-way north to Conway Road, a quarter mile north of PA 285. From here to US 6, the cleared towpath crosses private property.

Hikers and bicyclists can also use an abandoned railroad bed that parallels Linesville-Hartstown Road across the spillway. Enter at the spillway or across the road from the visitors center entrance.

The local office of the Pennsylvania Game Commission is located on Linesville-Hartstown Road south of PA 285. For more information, contact the Pennsylvania Game Commission, Northwest Region Headquarters, P.O. Box 31, 1509 Pittsburgh Rd., Franklin, PA 16323, telephone (814) 432-3187.

Pymatuning State Park provides camping in four locations, cabins, fishing, a swimming beach, hunting, winter sports, picnicking, boating facilities, and trails for hikers, cross-country skiers, and snowmobilers. Similar accommodations are offered at a state park on the Ohio side of the lake. For park information, contact Pymatuning State Park, P.O. Box 425, Jamestown, PA 16134, telephone (814) 932-3141.

Geology. Pymatuning stems from an Iroquois expression meaning "crooked-mouth man's dwelling place," a crooked-mouth man being someone deceitful. Shenango was the name of a Lenni Lenape camp on the river. Here, Pymatuning is the name of the lake and swamp behind a dam impounding the Shenango River. In eastern Ohio, Pymatuning Creek flows into another impoundment of the Shenango River called Shenango River Lake, north of Sharon. The swamp flanking Pymatuning Creek in Ohio is known as Shenango Swamp, part of the Shenango State Wildlife Area.

The Shenango River does take a crooked, zigzag course from its headwaters in Pymatuning Swamp to its merger with the Beaver

River in New Castle. Pymatuning Swamp also is the source of Crooked Creek, which feeds the Little Shenango River north of Greenville.

It is likely that ice age glaciers altered the original northward drainage of the Shenango River and its tributaries. The river starts northward, then bends west and south, as if it had bounced off an obstacle. The obstruction was the retreating Wisconsinan glacier, which diverted the river onto its present course.

Wildlife. The waters in the wildlife propagation area, also called Pymatuning Sanctuary, provide the natural breeding stock for fry raised in the hatchery. Just before spawning season in early spring, adult walleye, muskellunge, northern pike, largemouth bass, and tiger muskies are rounded up in nets. After their eggs and sperm are extracted, the fish are given back to the sanctuary. Northern pike arrive in the spawning streams just after ice-out, followed by walleyes and muskies. Bass and panfish are netted in May. More than 100 million walleye eggs will be collected and fertilized here annually. Lake trout, steelhead trout, and paddlefish are also raised here.

Newborn walleyes, or fry, are put in culture ponds, about 150,000 per acre of pond. In two months, some 30,000 of these grow to fingerling size. After release, it will take three to five years for these gamefish to reach "keeping" size.

Before a dam was constructed in the river, W. E. Todd, curator of the Carnegie Museum of Natural History in Pittsburgh, dispatched ornithologist George M. Sutton to inventory the wildlife in Pymatuning Swamp before it became a lake. He found a soggy, surreal wilderness— a 25-mile sponge of lush, shallow bog with a clear stream winding through it; marshes bristling with reeds and cattails, wispy tamaracks, and carnivorous plants; and more than 200 species of birds.

Sutton listed 134 nesting species and 74 migrating ones, including the bald eagle. These birds didn't stay here to nest because of the lack of open water and sufficient food in some cases. But the lake that formed behind the dam gave those birds, as well as coots, Canada geese, and some ducks and shorebirds, a habitat for permanent residency. Bald eagles settled within three years. Fields of grain planted by the game commission lured geese.

Migratory birds zero in on Pymatuning. Spring and autumn bring 25,000 to 30,000 ducks and geese to the wetlands. Imperiled birds such as the osprey, northern harrier, and peregrine falcon make appearances. Winter guests are the rough-legged hawk, short-eared owl (PA endangered), horned lark, and white-fronted and snow geese. Shorelines attract great blue herons and great egrets (both PA threatened). Warblers congregate in woodlands, including mourning, hooded, pine, common yellowthroat, cerulean, yellow-rumped, and blackpoll. Other state-imperiled birds seen here include the sedge and marsh wrens, American bittern, black tern, olive-sided flycatcher, Swainson's thrush, yellow-bellied flycatcher, least bittern, common tern, and king rail.

At stops on the auto nature tour, look for nesting platforms for geese, boxes for eastern bluebirds and American kestrels, turtles, and muskrat and beaver lodges. Deer and foxes also inhabit the area. Swampy spots may contain carnivorous wildflowers called round-leaved sundew and northern pitcher, and plants like poison sumac, pink lady's slippers, and royal ferns. Trees leaning over the Erie Extension Canal hiking path include cottonwood, chokecherry, black walnut, cucumber magnolia, aspen, sassafras, white oak, shagbark hickory, black locust, elms, red maple, and various willows.

History. The hiking path is a section of the Erie Extension Canal towpath, built in the 1840s from the Ohio River, up the Beaver River watershed, to Lake Erie. Some of the small lakes crossed by the towpath served as feeder reservoirs for the canal.

Flooding along the Shenango and Ohio Rivers reduced an ancient, impenetrable marsh important to both beast and naturalist.

Gov. Gifford Pinchot presided at the dedication of the dam in 1933. Behind it swelled a horseshoe-shaped, 17,000-acre impoundment with 70 miles of shoreline, straddling the Pennsylvania-Ohio border and pointing toward the Great Lakes.

Quebec Run Wild Area

Fecundity and deep solitude come to mind when I remember Quebec Run Wild Area, a remote 4,765-acre forest near the Mason-Dixon Line in Fayette County. Gurgling brooks enter tunnels made by overhanging rhododendrons and hemlocks. During the spring nesting season, the woods resound with choral birdsong from dawn to dusk. Old logging roads and abandoned country lanes crisscross the verdant tract, once thought to be a hideout for Confederate border raiders. Today the loot is the land itself and its natural abundance.

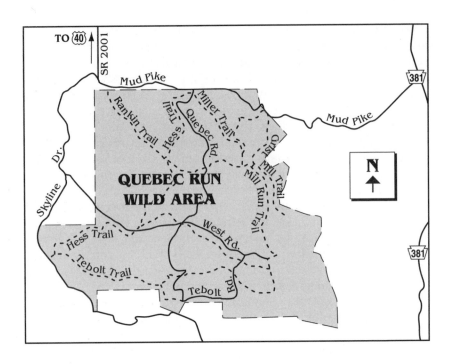

Ownership. Pennsylvania Department of Conservation and Natural Resources, Bureau of Forestry. The wild area is part of Forbes State Forest.

Size. 4,675 acres.

Physiographic Region. Allegheny Mountains.

Nearby Natural Attractions. Ohiopyle State Park, Youghiogheny Lake, Fort Necessity National Battlefield, Laurel Caverns, Bear Run Nature Reserve, and Friendship Hill National Historic Site.

Features. Quebec Run Wild Area occupies the eastern slope of Chestnut Ridge near the West Virginia border. It has six hiking trails measuring 14 miles, plus 8 miles of abandoned country roads. These roads, the widest and easiest paths, can easily be combined with other foot trails. The closing of these dirt roads (Quebec and Tebolt Roads) makes the wild area the largest "roadless" region in southwestern Pennsylvania. All trails are blazed in blue, and most intersections have signs. Hikers are urged to get a topographic trail map of the wild area from the District Forester, Forbes State Forest, P.O. Box 519, Laughlintown, PA 15655, telephone (724) 238-9533. Primitive backpack camping (permit required), hunting, and fishing are allowed.

Access is tricky. From Uniontown, travel east on US 40 to the top of Chestnut Ridge. Upon reaching Mt. Summit Inn, turn right on Skyline Drive (also called Seaton Road, SR 2001), the same road that leads to Laurel Caverns. The aptly named Skyline Drive offers panoramic views from two state forest overlooks, on the right side of the road, and Pondfield Fire Tower. Follow Skyline Drive to an intersection 6.5 miles from US 40 (past Laurel Caverns), then turn left on Mud Pike (T345). A sign at the junction may name the lane Quebec Road.

Two parking areas will appear ahead on the right. The first, about 1.3 miles from the turnoff, serves a trailhead for the Miller and Hess Trails and the abandoned and gated Quebec Road, heading south into the wild area. Another parking area is a mile east, after a hairpin right turn. Mill Run Trail starts at the parking area, and Grist Mill Trail branches southbound from the road a quarter mile east of the lot.

Three other parking areas are available. For access to the southwestern corner of the area, turn right at the Skyline Drive–Mud Pike junction, then left at the split ahead, continuing on SR 2001 (labeled Skyline Drive on some maps). Half a mile after reentering state forest land, look for a small parking lot on the left, providing access to the Tebolt and Hess Trails. Four-wheel-drive vehicles are recommended for the other two parking sites, shown on the state forest brochure of the wild area.

A quick hike of a little more than 2 miles departs from the easternmost parking lot on Mud Pike. Take the Mill Run Trail, then go left on the Miller Trail, and left again on Rankin Trail. After crossing Quebec Run and Mill Run via bridges, go left on Grist Mill Trail to Mud Pike, and then left to the parking lot. The ruins of an old gristmill are located on Mill Run Trail, a few steps south of its intersection with Grist Mill Trail. These paths lead through hemlock and rhododendron ravines and young hardwood forests.

Maintenance of these mountain roads is not a high priority in winter. I negotiated Mud Pike in a minivan two days after several inches of snowfall. The road had not been plowed, but gravity safely propelled me eastbound down the slope of Chestnut Ridge. Traveling west up the hill would not have been possible that day.

From the Bruceton exit on I-68 in West Virginia, Quebec Run can be reached by taking WV 26 north to Brandonville, then north on a state highway that becomes PA 381 at the border. Travel north to Elliottsville, left (west) on SR 2004, then straight (west) on Mud Pike (SR 2004 and T345).

Geology. Quebec Run Wild Area lies on the steep eastern slope of Chestnut Ridge, the westernmost anticline in a group of elongated, southwest-northeast rolls that form the Allegheny Mountains. Like the

Appalachian Mountains to the east, Chestnut Ridge took shape during the Alleghenian Orogeny. 290 million years ago, this mountain building event occurred when the Gondwana (Africa and South America) and North America tectonic plates collided, buckling and changing the bedrock to form the Appalachian Mountains. Farther west, weaker shocks bent and swelled the bedrock into the Allegheny Mountains.

Like the neighboring Laurel Ridge, the summit of Chestnut Ridge is broad and flat. Bedrock consists of alternating layers of gray sandstone, conglomerate, and shales of the Pottsville Formation, from Pennsylvanian Period (300 million years ago) atop similar members of the Mauch Chunk Formation, from the Mississippian Period (330 million years ago). Small cliffs and rock outcrops appear on the summit and along walls of ravines.

The wild area protects the entire watersheds of Quebec and Tebolt Runs and much of Mill Run. The streams drain into Big Sandy Creek, a tributary of the Cheat River in West Virginia.

Wildlife. The woods are a mixed mesophytic hardwood blend, with sugar and red maples and tulip trees prevailing on north- and east-facing slopes and oaks dominating the warmer and drier hills, usually facing south and west. Hemlocks and rhododendrons cluster in moist, shaded ravines. Mountain laurel, sassafras, dogwoods, black cherry, blueberry, greenbrier, and wintergreen have found niches.

In spring, creek banks and lowlands nurture large-leaved wildflowers such as skunk cabbage, a March bloomer, followed by swamp buttercup in April and false hellebore in May. The slopes above the creeks host jack-in-the-pulpit, large-leaved trillium, foamflower, perfoliated bellwort, halberd-leaved violet, and phlox, a splashy, five-petaled flower of blue or pink. Observant eyes will spot dwarf ginseng, a white-flowered cousin of wild ginseng. Rhododendron puts on its show in late June and early July. Lichens and liverworts grow on sandstone ledges. A globally rare and state-endangered plant, white monkshood, struggles on state forest land just west of the wild area. Only one other community of the white, helmet-shaped flower exists in the state. Medicine derived from this poisonous plant treats neuralgia and sciatica.

Woodland birds arrive to nest in May, notably black-and-white, Blackburnian, black-throated blue, and black-throated green warblers. Solitary and red-eyed vireos dart among trees. Also look for the scarlet tanager, indigo bunting, ovenbird, wood thrush, blue-gray gnatcatcher, and great horned owl.

Quebec Run is home to deer, black bears, bobcats, squirrels, ruffed grouse, foxes, and coyotes. Wild turkeys are enjoying the fruits of a habitat improvement project partly funded by the National Wild Turkey Federation. Streams in the wild area hold native and stocked trout. Quebec Run is designated a wilderness trout stream.

History. There's talk of gold in these hills. Not veins of gold, or dust panned from the streams, but cached gold reportedly stolen from southwestern Pennsylvania banks by Confederate raiders during the Civil War. The "gold mine," located along Hess Trail north of Rankin Trail, was dug by feverish searchers after the war. Nobody reported finding gold. The real gold mine is the land itself, last extensively logged in 1940 by the Summit Lumber Company of Uniontown. Parcels were acquired by the Western Pennsylvania Conservancy and transferred to the Bureau of Forestry.

Raccoon Creek State Park

A renowned wildflower reserve here triumphs with 500 varieties of flowering plants within a small plot of land. The floral celebration begins with the emergence of skunk cabbage in March and finishes with the green tendrils of witch hazel in November. Such a bountiful bouquet probably has more healing power than the min-

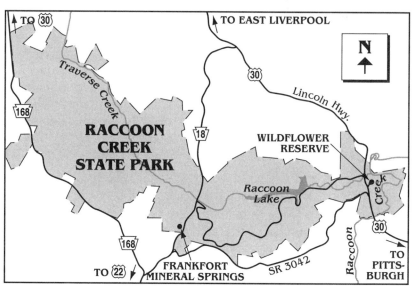

eral-rich spring water that once attracted thousands to a park waterfall 4 miles away.

Ownership. Pennsylvania Department of Conservation and Natural Resources, Bureau of State Parks.

Size. Wildflower Reserve is a 314-acre sanctuary within the 7,323-
acre Raccoon Creek State Park.

Physiographic Region. Pittsburgh Low Plateau.

Nearby Natural Attractions. Hillman State Park, Brady's Run
County Park, and Bradford Woods.

Features. The Wildflower Reserve off US 30 has six trails totaling 5 miles branching from the nature center. Grab a trail map and
blooming schedule before departing. Choose a route after asking park
staffers where flowers are blooming. Three popular trails commemo-
rate celebrated naturalists. The Jennings Trail commemorates Dr. O.
E. Jennings, a botanist from western Pennsylvania for whom the
Jennings Environmental Education Center was also named. The
Henrici Trail honors Max Henrici, a Pittsburgh nature and editorial
writer who touted the place. John James Audubon, the great birder
and wildlife artist, is remembered too. At the peak of the spring viewing season, late April to mid-May, your best strategy is to simply follow your eyes. For maximum time along Raccoon Creek, follow the
Jennings, Meadow, and Old Field Trails.

The interpretive center has parking, rest rooms, some exhibits,
and information. It's also the gathering ground for naturalist-led floral walks and other nature programs. Call ahead for nature programs and hours at (724) 899-3611.

The well-trodden loop path to Frankfort Mineral Springs and its
miniature waterfall starts from a parking area on the west side of PA
18, south of the park office. The spring water gushes from several
cavities in a cliff to the right of the trickling cascade. Note the rusty
stain deposited by iron in the water. In spite of its popularity and
avowed health benefits a century ago, park officials warn visitors not
to drink this spring water. It has not been tested for purity and may
contain pollutants associated with the modern era. On the north loop
of this half-mile trail, behind what used to be a museum, hikers will
find the mile-long, lasso-shaped Mineral Springs Trail.

Valley Trail traces Traverse Creek for 1.5 miles from PA 18, across
from the park office, to the western tip of Raccoon Lake. Foot travelers also can hike 16 miles of trails shared by horseback riders, Nordic
skiers, and snowmobilers. These more challenging trails stem from
Nichol Road in the western half of the park.

Raccoon Creek also offers family and group camping, boating,
fishing, swimming, hunting, horseback riding, cabins, a recreation
lodge, picnic areas, and playing fields. For more information, contact

Raccoon Creek State Park, 3000 State Route 18, Hookstown, PA 15050-1605, telephone (724) 899-2200.

Geology. Spring water has poured from the cliffs of Mineral Springs Hollow for thousands of years, refreshing animals, Native Americans, and European settlers alike. Between 1790 and 1912 thousands of people trekked to Frankfort Mineral Springs to drink cool spring water, believing that its fifteen minerals had healing power.

Springs appear wherever the groundwater flow meets the surface. Thank downcutting erosion by the adjacent trickling stream for that exposure here. Notice that the spring water spurts from rock fissures below the erosion-resistant sandstone caprock on the lip of the waterfall. Long ago, that sandstone ledge extended farther downstream (southeast) and probably covered the groundwater. Over many millenia, the erosion-prone layers beneath the sandstone eroded away, creating a cave behind a waterfall and weakening overlying layers. Eventually the sandstone lip broke off into the creek bed. This slow erosion process, or downcutting, continued upstream and opened the groundwater passages.

The amount of water in the spring depends largely on the amount of recent precipitation that seeps through soil, rock cracks, and permeable rock. Groundwater pools upon reaching nonporous rock and flows along the natural angle of the layer or through crevices and seams in the rock. The minerals in spring water—here heavy with iron and sulfur—are picked up from soluble elements in the soil and rock through which it percolates.

The spring water in Mineral Springs Hollow drips into Traverse Creek, then Raccoon Creek, the Ohio River, and the Mississippi River.

Wildlife. The wildflower reserve's fecundity stems from its location. It is situated at a biological crossroads where various plant realms converge and enjoy life at the margin of their ranges. The location boasts several habitats—an oak-hickory forest, pine plantations, abandoned fields, and fertile bottomland—much of it undisturbed acreage. What's more, Raccoon Creek takes a sudden and fortuitous hairpin course around a slender east-west-running rocky ridge, thus offering sunny southern and dim northern exposures for plants suited to those habitats.

A blooming schedule, available at the nature center, is helpful in identifying flowers, although nature never punches a clock. Snow trillium and coltsfoot usually appear in mid-April as skunk cabbage fades. Trout lily, bluets, mouse-eared chickweed (PA endangered), Dutchman's breeches, and others blossom in late April. The peak month for woodland flowers is May, when several varieties of trilliums and violets rise, along with blue cohosh, Greek valerian, marsh marigold, Virginia bluebell, Miami mist, dwarf larkspur, and

Solomon's seal. Late spring produces goat's beard, butterfly weed, Canada anemone, lily-leaved twayblade, and milkweed. Summer colors come from cardinal flower, orange hawkweed, lobelia, boneset, enchanter's nightshade, nodding ladies' tresses, ironweed, starry campion, and Saint-John's-wort. Closed gentian and witch hazel punctuate the blooming season. Among the twenty-eight species of ferns are notably grape, maidenhair, walking, ebony spleenwort, silvery, narrow-leaved, and cut-leaved.

History. King's Creek Cemetery, off PA 168, contains the remains of Levi Dungan, the first white settler in the area, as well as other pioneers. Dungan's original 1,000-acre tract, purchased in 1772, included the mineral springs, but in 1784 he sold 400 acres and the springs to Isaac Stephens. A few years later, Stephens sold 12 acres surrounding the springs to Edward McGinnis, a former riverboat sailor who bragged about being cured of some undisclosed ailment after sipping the water. McGinnis realized he actually had discovered a gold mine. In the late 1790s he built a three-story inn called Frankfort House to handle the "water worshipers." The nearby village of Frankfort Mineral Springs became a health spa. Summertime brought a steady stream of guests seeking the cure. A dance hall, guest cottages, orchards, a livery, an ice house, and a farm grew up around the inn. The stone house above the falls was one of the cottages of the health resort.

The good times ended when the spa closed in 1912. For a while, the water was bottled and sold as an elixir. Later, automobile batteries were filled with the filtered water. Everything shut down in 1932 when the Frankfort House was leveled by a fire of unknown origin.

Around the same time, the National Park Service bought some adjacent marginal farmland as the seed of a national park. Laborers working for the Civilian Conservation Corps and Works Progress Administration built much of the park's infrastructure before it was transferred to the commonwealth in 1945. Initial park improvements continued through 1956.

The Western Pennsylvania Conservancy bought the mineral springs acreage and restored the stone cottage, thanks partly to a gift from Thomas H. Walker of Sewickley. A group of nature-minded artists, teachers, and lawyers from Pittsburgh, known as the Hickory Club, protected the wildflower reserve before the conservancy acquired it. The conservancy has transferred the titles of these properties to the commonwealth.

David M. Roderick
Wildlife Reserve

Tucked in the northwest corner of Erie County, this reserve boasts the longest stretch of undeveloped Lake Erie shoreline between Buffalo and Toledo, 2.5 miles of wild, log-strewn beach, with undeveloped bluffs behind it. No trail, perhaps not even a footprint to follow. Shorebirds scurry away at your approach, and gulls hover overhead. And to think they almost put a steel mill here thirty years ago.

Size. This 3,131-acre tract is officially State Game Lands 314.
Ownership. Pennsylvania Game Commission.
Physiographic Region. Coastal Lowland.
Nearby Natural Attractions. Presque Isle State Park, Asbury Woods Nature Center, and Siegel Marsh.
Features. After parking on Lake Shore Road, your impulse will be to dash to the overlook for a sweeping view of Lake Erie. But first, find the stone monument commemorating the site.

The best walk is not on a trail, but along the beach. To reach the beach from the overlook, find an unmarked path descending into a hollow east of the grassy area. If you miss this rough route, go back to the intersection of Lake Shore and Rudd Roads and park off the road. Walk to the beach, and turn west (left) toward Ohio. This beach is not the uniform width of a park beach. In some places it's broad, in others narrow. The surface varies, sometimes sandy, soft clay, pebbly, or rocky. Trees and flotsam tossed onto shore add to the adventure but sometimes block your path.

When the lake looks like polished glass, the waves hardly cover your toes. Other times, waves 3 to 4 feet high slap the beach. Hiking can be dangerous when waves are hiphigh, especially around submerged, beached trees and where the beach narrows at the bottom of bluffs. Don't hike with small children when waves are high.

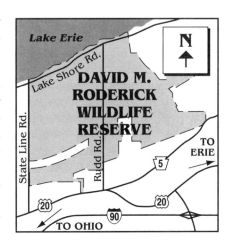

The bluffs are made of clay and silt, not rock. These soft deposits are easily worn down by the waves and human tread. Avoid hiking on the slippery bluff walls, if possible. Instead, walk in the shallow water, though this is not advised during a winter walk.

If you keep walking on the beach, you'll eventually enter Ohio and reach the mouth of Turkey Creek, about a mile across the state line. From here, you can retrace your steps or climb to a nearby concrete bridge and follow the abandoned road to the trail that leads to the junction of Lake Shore and State Line Roads. Follow Lake Shore east to your starting point. The beach route is about 3 miles.

The "inner trail" traces an old rail line through the center of the property. From the monument on Lake Shore Road, go west to State Line Road, then left (south) a mile to the trail entrance on the left. This overgrown, hard-to-discern trail passes through wetlands that form the headwaters of Turkey Creek and young forests of aspen, birches, red maple, beeches, and swamp oak. Follow the path to Rudd Road, and either return by the same route or turn left (north) on Rudd Road to Lake Shore.

Biking is permitted on the dirt roads but not on the inner rail-trail. You can picnick at Raccoon Park in the northeast corner of the reserve.

Geology. The silt and clay bluffs in the reserve are examples of the Erie Escarpment, a soft cliff that parallels the Lake Erie shore. I-90 rides atop this escarpment about 200 feet above the shore elevation. The sediments were made during the last stage of the ice age, roughly 12,000 years ago, when the Wisconsinan glacier was parked in the Lake Erie basin, pushing the water level farther inland. Silt and clay settled in large offshore deposits. When the glacier and water level retreated, the silt and clay became exposed. Lake Erie's waves and surface erosion now sculpt the coast.

Wildlife. Roderick Reserve is becoming a birding hot spot. For starters, the game commission is managing the tract as a haven for eastern woodcocks, which were abundant before shrubs took over the wet, grassy meadows. Game managers are trimming the shrubbery to open areas for woodcocks. Springtime visitors should linger until dusk to witness the male's unusual courtship ritual. He begins by spiraling upward and beeping eerily. At the top of the climb, he collapses his wings and tumbles toward earth, but flaps to a safe landing. The target of his affection watches in a clearing.

Look for bank swallows on the beach walk. These aerial acrobats nest in the clay banks, tunneling upward and as deep as 4 feet. They often swarm around the bluffs catching insects. Their relative, the cliff swallow, perches on utility lines. Bank swallows have V-shaped tails, while cliff swallows' tails have square ends.

At least 50 species of birds nest here, and 100 varieties have been identified. Bohemian and cedar waxwings eat the fruits on shrubs. Bald eagles, Mississippi kites, and peregrine falcons are sighted during migrations. Hawk viewing here is best when the wind blows from the southwest.

Another migrant to look for, especially in late August or early September, is the monarch butterfly, heading south for central Mexico. Some years you'll see more than others.

History. Steel baron Andrew Carnegie bought the property in 1900, built cottages on the bluffs, and used it for weekend retreats. USX, formerly U.S. Steel Corporation, later enlarged the Carnegie tract, tore down the bungalows, and rented the higher ground to local farmers.

Twice during the 1960s, USX announced plans to build a steel mill on the site. However, a decline in demand forced abandonment of the project. The Richard King Mellon Foundation bought the place the day before the retirement of David Roderick, head of USX and an avid outdoorsman. The foundation conveyed it to the Western Pennsylvania Conservancy, which then transferred the title to the Pennsylvania Game Commisssion. It was dedicated as a wildlife reserve on July 24, 1991.

51

Ryerson Station State Park

Two centuries ago Fort Ryerson was a remote frontier refuge during Indian uprisings. Today this outpost in the hilly southwestern corner of Pennsylvania serves humans as a refuge from the turmoil of modern living and wildlife as a refuge from humans.

Ownership. Pennsylvania Department of Conservation and Natural Resources, Bureau of State Parks.

Size. 1,164 acres.

Physiographic Region. Low Plateau.

Nearby Natural Attractions. Enlow Fork Natural Area, State Game Lands 302.

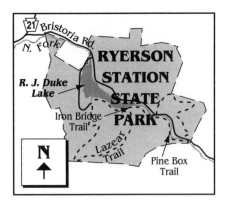

Features. To reach the hiking trails on the south shore of R. J. Duke Lake, follow the park road to the swimming pool and park in the lot at the end of the drive. Lazear Trail, named after a former landowner, at 2.6 miles is the longest individual trail in the park, and many hikers consider it the most rewarding. It starts with a semi-strenuous climb to an overlook 424 feet above the lake, wanders through a young forest ruled by oak trees three centuries old, and descends through picturesque Munnell Hollow. The final leg goes along the lakeshore. This hike can be truncated by trekking on the Fox Feather, Orchard and Tiffany Ridge Trails inside the Lazear loop.

Iron Bridge Trail stems from the eastern leg of Lazear Trail and goes upstream along Dunkard Fork to a bridge. Here you can cross the bridge and go north on the Iron Bridge Trail to the Deer Trail and campground or take the Pine Box Trail, a 2-mile loop along the creek and eastern side of the park. The Three Mitten and Polly Hollow Trails start on the north shore, on either side of the park office. The park brochure shows the trails.

R. J. Duke Lake, named for a former park superintendent, covers 62 acres and provides boating, fishing, and habitat for beavers, wood ducks, and great blue herons (PA threatened). Wetlands at the eastern end of the lake provide the best opportunities for wildlife viewing. Ryerson Station also offers camping, boating, fishing, swimming, picnicking, hunting, ice skating, and snowmobiling.

For more information, contact Ryerson Station State Park, R.R. 1, Box 77, Wind Ridge, PA 15380, telephone (724) 428-4254.

Geology. The park rests on bedrock 240 million (Permian Period) to 330 million (Pennsylvanian Period) years old. Sandstone, shale, limestone, siltstone, claystone, and coal of the Waynesburg Formation lie under R. J. Duke Lake. These late Pennsylvanian-aged rocks are exposed along the lakeshore, elevation 1,060 feet. Beds of younger sandstone, shale, flaky coal, and limestone, members of the Washington Formation, are visible in steep valleys of Munnell, Panther Lick, and Polly Hollows up to an elevation of 1,180 feet. Above them are Permian-age layers of similar rock belonging to the Greene Formation.

Visitors entering from the west will see a natural gas compression station at the park border. It processes gas from the Richhill gas field in the northeastern section of the park.

Wildlife. Park staffers have recorded 78 kinds of wildflowers, 45 trees and shrubs, 131 species of birds, 29 fish, 25 mammals, 15 amphibians, 11 reptiles, and a long list of invertebrates. Resident plants include the large-leaved waterleaf (PA endangered), yellow iris, dwarf larkspur, jack-in-the-pulpit, jewelweed, butter-and-eggs, fire pink, wild ginger, American pennyroyal, columbine, Virginia bluebell, gray-headed coneflower, and arrowhead.

During the spring migration, persistent birders usually glimpse an osprey, an endangered raptor that lately has been a regular drop-in around the lake. The great blue heron, Cooper's hawk, eastern bluebird, sharp-shinned hawk, and least flycatcher, all birds of special concern, also come to the park. In the oak-covered slopes surrounding the lake, look or listen for the pileated woodpecker, great horned owl, wild turkey, common whippoorwill, wood thrush, and yellow, yellow-throated, yellow-rumped, black-and-white, black-throated blue, black-throated green, and cerulean warblers. The checklist includes Swainson's thrush, pine siskin, scarlet tanager, cedar waxwing, eastern meadowlark, dark-eyed junco, golden-crowned kinglet, and eastern pewee. The lake attracts mallards, lesser scaup, ring-necked ducks, hooded mergansers, coots, grebes, tundra swans, and common loons.

Other residents include the beaver, flying squirrel, masked shrew, deer, mink, longtailed weasel, raccoon, Fowler's toad, red-spotted newt, pickerel frog, the eastern spiny softshell turtle, northern fence lizard, northern black racer snake, and northern copperhead, a seldom seen poisonous snake.

History. In colonial times the park land was located on land claimed by Native American nations, France, Virginia, and Pennsylvania. The frontier outpost of Fort Ryerson was constructed by Virginia to protect pioneers from raids and fortify its claim. After the Revolutionary War, while the two states argued over ownership, settlers talked about creating a new state called Westsylvania or Vandalia. Such talk ended in August 1785 when Pennsylvania won the claim. Indian attacks resumed in 1790 with the Davis Massacre, which claimed five victims. The Davis homestead was located near the park office. The bodies were buried nearby.

Remains of several Indians turned up in 1866 during construction of Jesse Lazear's residence, the historic home by the trailhead now used as the park superintendent's home. The bones strengthen Native American accounts of a permanent settlement in the area. The Lazear family owned the home until it was acquired by the commonwealth in 1958. Parkland purchases were completed in 1961, and the park opened in 1967.

52

Schollard's Run Wetland

An abandoned railroad bed provides a dry and elevated corridor for hikers traveling across a verdant mosaic of marshes, ponds, meadows, and woods. A striking waterfall sliding over sandstone slabs in a hemlock-lined ravine punctuates the northern end of the journey, and an extensive cattail swamp stirring with birds and bugs marks the southern tip.

Ownership. Pennsylvania Game Commission.

Size. Schollard's Run Wetland, totaling 1,200 acres, is officially known as State Game Lands 284.

Physiographic Region. Glaciated Plateau.

Nearby Natural Attractions. Wolf Creek Narrows Natural Area, Maurice Goddard State Park, Pine Swamp, Shenango River Lake, McConnells Mill and Moraine State Parks, Fringed Gentian Fen, and Jennings Environmental Education Center.

Features. The trail through Schollard's Run Wetland is an easy hike on a level, dry abandoned rail bed. It runs one-way for 2.75 miles and connects the hamlets of Springfield Falls, Schollard, and Drake.

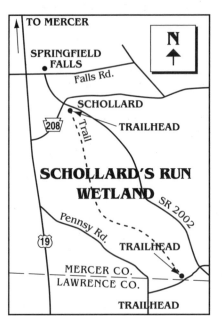

The northern, and larger, trail terminus is located at the intersection of PA 208 and Brent Road. The southern access, with perhaps room for two cars, is on Nelson Road at the Mercer-Lawrence County line. The game commission mows the path in the warm months. This trail goes by ponds, marshes, and steamy stream hollows, so summer hikers should protect themselves from biting insects by wearing long pants, caps and repellent. Horseback riding and mountain biking are permitted on the trail.

North of Schollard (PA 208), the rail bed is no longer on game commission land. The route is unmowed, occupied by utility pipes, and has a steep ravine now requiring a detour across a ford.

To reach Springfield Falls from the northern trailhead, return to US 19 and travel north a mile. Turn right (east) on Leesburg Station Road (SR 2002), north of Leesburg. In a quarter mile, where Leesburg Station Road bends sharply right, go straight on Falls Road. Look for a small parking lot on the right just a few feet up the road. Across the road, a 25-yard trail leads to the hemlock-lined Springfield Falls.

Hunters aiming for ducks and geese come to the state game lands in the fall. Check the dates of hunting season before hiking here. The site is open daily from dawn to dusk.

For more information, contact the Pennsylvania Game Commission, Northwest Region Headquarters, P.O. Box 31, 1509 Pittsburgh Rd., Franklin, PA 16323, telephone (814) 432-3187.

Geology. At Springfield Falls, Schollard's Run, a tributary of Neshannock Creek, tumbles over Connoquenessing sandstone of the Pottsville group. The rock goes back 300 million years to the Pennsylvanian Period. Walk to a perch overlooking the striking hemlock-lined glen. The cascade features several slabs dangling over a 60-foot precipice.

Upstream, Schollard's Run soaks through marshy wetlands in State Game Lands 284. The wetlands filter and recharge the water, purifying it enough for people to collect it in plastic jugs by the waterfalls.

Wildlife. The rail-trail serves as a dike with broad views of cattail marshes, beaver ponds, wet meadows, and thickets. Expect to see waterfowl such as Canada geese, mallards, and wood, black, and pintail ducks. Great blue herons (PA threatened) tiptoe in the shallows, stalking for frogs and fish. Nesting waterbirds include the Virginia, and sora rails (both PA rare) king rail (PA endangered), and common gallinule, identified by its bright red bill and snout. Red-winged blackbirds, marked by splashy red-orange epaulets, sing raucously by the cattail marshes, the same habitat to find muskrats and their dome-shaped lodges. Look for hawks perched on dead trees and belted kingfishers hovering at pond edges. Eastern woodcocks and ring-necked pheasants flush from meadows.

Tracks on the trail betray the presence of white-tailed deer, raccoons, opossums, cottontail rabbits, foxes, and skunks. Excavations on the cinder rail bed or mudflats surrounded by white flakes could be the sites of snapping turtle nests that were ransacked by raccoons or skunks. Painted turtles bask on logs and stumps, sometimes lined six or eight in a row.

Midsummer visitors may encounter surprisingly few mosquitoes if dragonflies, damselflies, swallows, and bats have been hungry and active, but take along repellent just in case. You'll hear frog song from spring peepers and others in spring. Summer evening song is dominated by owls, whippoorwills, and bullfrogs.

History. The Schollard Family operated an iron furnace below Springfield Falls in the 1840s. The wetland and nearby town bear their name. The railroad bed bisecting the property belonged to the Western New York and Pennsylvania Railroad.

Historic Johnston Tavern, built in 1983 with local sandstone, stands half a mile north of the waterfalls. The watering hole, once a stagecoach stop on the Pittsburgh to Erie route, was restored by the Western Pennsylvania Conservancy in the late 1960s. The conservancy acquired the tract in 1967 and transferred it to the state in 1973.

53

Sewickley Creek Wetlands

This small preserve is the fruit of a law, rooted in common sense, that requires humans to give back what they took from nature. Remove something here, restore it over there. Destroy a wetland for a road, make a new swamp beside it. That way nature's balance sheet stays level and human relations with nature improve.

Ownership. Westmoreland County Bureau of Parks and Recreation.

Size. 23 acres.

Physiographic Region. Pittsburgh Low Plateau.

Nearby Natural Areas. Twin Lakes and Cedar Creek County Parks, Powdermill Nature Reserve, Conemaugh Gorge, Forbes State Forest, and Laurel Ridge, Laurel Summit, Laurel Mountain, Linn Run, and Keystone State Parks.

Features. This small interpretive site north of New Stanton has trails and an observation deck overlooking a wetland. Flora and fauna are filling up this man-made wetland in spite of its location near busy highways and railroads. The preserve is open daily from sunrise to sunset.

For more information, contact the Westmoreland County Bureau of Parks and Recreation, R.D. 12, Box 203, Greensburg, PA 15601, telephone (724) 830-3950 or (800) 442-6926, ext. 3950.

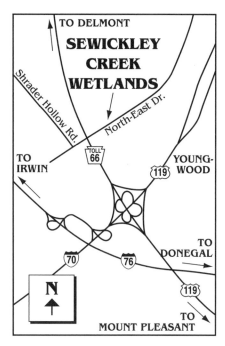

Geology. A tributary of Sewickley Creek weaves around four small man-made ponds and through a marsh, thus replenishing the wetland built by the turnpike commission. In spring and after heavy precipitation, this wetland acts like a sponge by absorbing and slowing flood water. Wetlands also control erosion, capture sediment that dirties water, filter pollution from water, and recharge groundwater fields.

Wildlife. Pennsylvania road masters drained a wetland to make way for a toll road and manufactured this one to replace it. Interpretive signs on wetland ecology stand beside an observation area, just steps from the parking lot. One sign explains that a wetland has hydric, or soggy, soils and supports plants that can live in high water during their growing season. It's a rich "farmland" for aquatic life, because it produces food, captures nutrients like nitrogen and phosphorus, and pumps oxygen into water. Marsh vegetation also provides shelter, food, and water for animals.

The preserve brightens with bulrush, teasel, cattails, and pickerelweed, a showy floating flower shaped like a bottle brush, with bluish or lavender blossoms. You'll find thickets of black willow, an early bloomer sought out by honey bees; flowering dogwood; and red osier, a shrubby dogwood distinguished by red or purple branchlets in autumn and winter. Red osier issues underground shoots, so a single plant quickly develops into a thicket. Pin and swamp white oaks also grow here.

Birders usually observe red-winged blackbirds, belted kingfishers, several kinds of swallows, and mallard ducks and Canada geese on the open water. Great blue herons (PA threatened) hunt here for frogs and tiny bluegills. Snapping turtles lurk in ponds. Eastern blue darners and other dragonflies feast on mosquitoes in summer. Raccoons, nocturnal marauders, leave their tracks on the trails. Muskrats build lodges with cattails and rushes. Deer come to the wetland to drink water and nibble on succulent plants.

History. The Pennsylvania Turnpike Commission disturbed the Sewickley Creek watershed during construction of PA 66. Because of a law stating that wetlands lost for new roads must be restored acre for acre, the PTC built the swampy site and donated it to the county for a nature preserve.

Shenango River Lake

This lengthy high-heel-shaped wetland straddling the Pennsylvania-Ohio border is becoming a refuge for wildlife, including the imperiled bald eagle and osprey. The old Shenango Trail plus new nature trails and wildlife-watching platforms on the south shore are avenues into the area's natural world.

Ownership. U.S. Army Corps of Engineers.

Size. 15,071 acres, including the portion in Ohio.

Physiographic Region. Glaciated Plateau

Nearby Natural Attractions. Schollard's Run Wetland, Pine Swamp, Pymatuning Wetlands, Brucker Great Blue Heron Sanctuary, Wallace Woods, and Maurice K. Goddard State Park.

Features. The 10-mile Shenango Trail wraps around the east-pointing "toe" of the Shenango River. Most of the path stays on the elevated towpath of the abandoned Erie Extension Canal. The northern access spot is at Kidd's Mill Road (SR 4012), site of a historic covered bridge east of Reynolds Heights and PA 18. The southern trailhead begins in a hamlet called Big Bend, where parking is at a designated area on North Bend Road, a tad southwest of its junction with Rutledge Road (SR 3022). New Hamburg is the midway point. Trail parking there is at the end of Stamm Road, branching from Baker Hill Road (SR 4024). Equestrians and mountain bicyclists also use the trail.

Follow white blazes when you can. Markings sporadically disappear along the section north of New Hamburg. Untrimmed briers, improvised detours, washed-out crossings, and other obstacles make

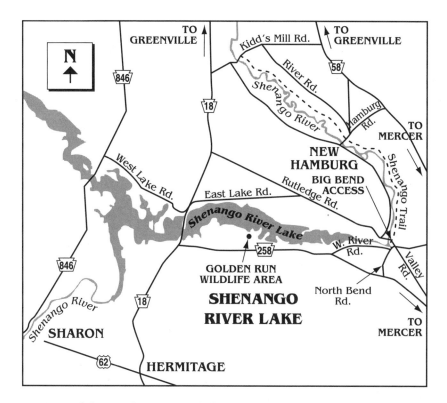

portions of the northern route difficult to read and negotiate. The route improves upon reaching the Kidd's Mill Trail for the last mile or so.

The river sometimes floods the better-maintained southern section in spring. During this season, hikers are advised to contact the corps of engineers about trail conditions, especially after heavy rain. Much of this section stays atop the old towpath of the Erie Extension Canal.

The sleepy Shenango River also can be viewed from a canoe. Put in at Kidd's Mill Road (SR 4012) and take out at the Big Bend public fishing access near the southern trailhead.

Wildlife viewing blinds and nature trails built in 1997 highlight the Golden Run Wildlife Area, off PA 258 (Lake Road) and east of PA 18 on the south shore. The gravel road into the wildlife area ends at a T intersection. Turn right to reach the Shore Viewing Area, left to find the Beaver Pond Viewing Area. Both sites were developed by local groups and the corps for dedication on National Public Lands Appreciation Day, September 27, 1997.

At the Shore Viewing Area, a short trail leads to an observation shelter with a sprawling view of the lake. A rough, unmarked west-bound fishermen's path continues along the shore for another stretch, but it finally vanishes among grass and shrubs. Be mindful of nesting birds. At Beaver Pond Viewing Area, the Eddie Patton Trail, a quarter-mile path honoring a Mercer County sportsman, leads to an observation shelter overlooking a snag-filled pond.

Two short nature trails, the Seth Myers and Coonie Trails, are located at the Shenango Recreation Area on the north shore off West Lake Road, west of PA 18. Other recreation facilities run by the corps of engineers include two public campgrounds, two swimming beaches, seven boat launches, picnic areas, an off-road vehicle area, and a marina. Boating, fishing, hunting, and trapping are allowed. The corps' property extends nearly a dozen miles into Ohio, where it's called Shenango State Wildlife Area.

For more information, contact U.S. Army Corps of Engineers, Shenango River Lake, 2442 Kelly Rd., Hermitage, PA 16150, telephone (724) 962-7746.

Geology. The Shenango River zigzags from its origin in Pymatuning Swamp to its confluence with the Beaver River in New Castle. Shenango supposedly was the name of a Lenni-Lenape camp on the river. Just above the dam, Pymatuning Creek trickles in from Ohio.

The Wisconsinan glacier undoubtedly changed the original northward flow of the Shenango River and its tributaries. Using a map, see how it starts northward, then sharply turns west and south, as if reflecting off a wall. The obstruction was the face of the glacier, which blocked the river's regular route. The current did an aboutface and found an outlet to the south.

Don't expect high ridges and bluffs along the lakeshore, except near Big Bend. Shenango River Lake is mostly a puddle spreading out in flatland. The corps of engineers drains the lake considerably in winter. The river's current is discernible then, and when the mudflats freeze on chilly days, you can easily hike to wooded mounds that are islands in summer. In a normal summer, the lake pool measures 11 miles long at an elevation of 896 feet and encompasses 3,560 acres. If necessary, the lake level can rise to 919 feet and flood 11,090 acres.

Wildlife. Bald eagles are "getting downright common here," say the rangers, proud that their restoration program (largely on the Ohio side) is paying off. Beyond this, the sedge wren, great blue heron (both PA threatened), and Virginia rail (PA rare) rely on the site. Ospreys (PA endangered) stop over during migrations. The woods, meadows, wetlands, and bottomlands host belted kingfisher, barred owl, American woodcock, yellow-shafted flicker, common snipe, American kestrel, Baltimore oriole, American redstart, and magnolia, chestnut-sided, black-and-white, bay-breasted, hooded, and Wilson's warblers. Open water appeals to the Canada goose (year-round), pied-billed grebe, double-crested cormorant, mallards, blue-winged teal, wood and black ducks, and hooded merganser. Late summer draw-downs bring in shorebirds, including seven varieties of sandpipers, three plovers, yellowlegs, ruddy turnstone, killdeer, ruff, and short-billed dowitcher.

The raptors, herons, and herring and ring-billed gulls prey on the lake's abundant fish, which include gizzard shad, darters, shiners, dace, minnows, three species of bass, black and white crappie, bluegill, northern pike, three kinds of suckers, bullheads, walleye, channel catfish, yellow and white perch, muskellunge, and grass pickerel. Spotted darter (PA endangered), bluebreast darter (PA threatened), black bullhead, warmouth, longear sunfish, and river redhorse (PA rare) have historically lived in Shenango waters. This aquatic supermarket explains why herons nest at nearby Brucker Great Blue Heron Sanctuary. Whatever the birds miss may end up in an angler's creel.

Woodlands from river to ridgetop contain sycamores, box elder, black cherry, black walnut, black willow, ironwood, tulip tree, shagbark hickory, yellow and black birches, white ash, basswood, beeches, silky and red osier dogwoods, speckled alder, black locust, hawthorns, and planted pines and spruces, as well as sugar, silver, and red maples and white, swamp white, and red oaks.

Imperiled rarities like downy willow herb (PA endangered) and the larger Canadian Saint-John's-wort (PA threatened) survive in the "project," along with Appalachian quillwort, pale sedge, speckled wood lily, woodland horsetail, flattened wild oat grass, and long beech-fern, all declining in number. Also look for jewelweed, arrowhead, skunk cabbage, marsh marigold, and bird's-foot trefoil.

Resident mammals include deer, striped skunks, beavers, muskrats, red and gray foxes, least weasels, mink, opossums, raccoons, mice, voles, shrews, and moles. Reptiles and amphibians are represented by snapping, eastern box, and painted turtles; northern water, black rat, and eastern milk snakes; hellbenders, red-spotted newts, and slimy salamanders; and spring peepers, bullfrogs, and Fowler's toads.

History. Shenango River Lake swells behind a 720-foot-long dam completed in Sharpsville in 1965. The flood-control and recreation-making project cost $38 million. Portions of the Shenango Trail utilize the abandoned towpath of the Erie Extension Canal. Built in the 1840s, the canal ran from the Ohio River, along the Beaver and Shenango Rivers, to Lake Erie. The canal crossed the Pymatuning Wetlands, too. Some of the small lakes crossed by the towpath served as feeder reservoirs for the canal. The well-preserved remains of Lock 10 are located in Sharpsville, a mile downstream from the dam.

Siegel Marsh

Primarily managed as a propagation area for Canada geese, the rolling fields, ponds, marshes, and woods of this state game lands attract an impressive collection of migrant waterbirds and other wildlife. Old farm roads, now footpaths, bring hikers close to wildlife.

Ownership. The Pennsylvania Game Commission manages this place as State Game Lands 218.

Size. 1,343 acres.

Physiographic Region. Glaciated Plateau.

Nearby Natural Attractions. Presque Isle State Park, Asbury Woods Nature Center, and David M. Roderick Wildlife Reserve.

Features. It's a good idea to obtain a sportsman's recreation map of the site from the game commission before visiting. Three-quarters of the property, found 6 miles southeast of Erie, is south of PA 8. The best access points are on Barton Road (SR 1005), which forms the western boundary, and May and Bennett Roads, the eastern border. Traveling south from PA 8 on Barton Road, take the second game commission road on the left to a hilltop observation area noted as a visitors center on the map. Although the visitors center is no longer standing, the promontory remains a decent viewing area. Take along binoculars. The walking trails shown on the map have vanished beneath vegetation, but you're free to roam.

For an improved trail, travel south on Barton Road to the next parking area on the left, and follow the gravel lane that winds around ponds, through woods, and across fields. If you follow this trail to its end, you'll come to another game commission parking lot at the end of Dyer Road, which branches off Turner Road. Rough lanes also stem from May Road, in the southeastern corner; Hill Road, between May Road and PA 8; and Bennett Road, north of PA 8. Trails shown on the game commission map have disappeared. Boaters can enter the largest pond, 200 acres, from the first parking area on Barton Road, south of PA 8, near the dam. Hunting and fishing are permitted. The park is open from dawn to dusk.

For more information, contact the Pennsylvania Game Commission, Northwest Region Headquarters, P.O. Box 31, 1509 Pittsburgh Rd., Franklin, PA 16323, telephone (814) 432-3187.

Geology. Though artificial dikes and dams have re-created and now regulate ponds and swamps, the marsh may look just like it did after the ice age. As the Wisconsinan glacier retreated 12,000 years ago, giant slabs of ice broke from its face. Sediment washing from the glacier enwrapped the ice, forming a high collar. When temperatures warmed, the ice melted into this basin, creating a kettlehole lake. Over time, sediment and vegetation filled the lake, transforming it into a marsh. The East Branch of LeBoeuf Creek drains from the main lake at Barton Road and flows into LeBoeuf Creek, a tributary of French Creek.

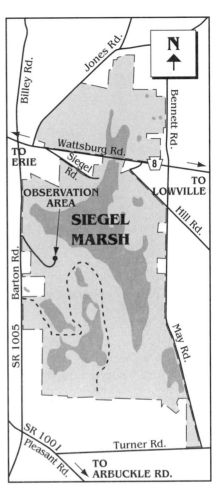

Wildlife. Standing atop the observation hill at dusk one late-April day, as one noisy, V-shaped squadron of geese splashed into the lake, followed by another, and another. I was reminded of a line in Aldo Leopold's *Sand County Almanac.* "One swallow does not make a summer, but one skein of geese, cleaving the murk of a March thaw, is the spring." Although their numbers peak during spring and fall migrations, geese are present here year-round, except when blizzards strike.

Snow and white-fronted geese also appear, along with hooded and red-breasted mergansers, mallards, buffleheads, blue-winged teal, and wood and black ducks. Low water levels in summer attract seventeen species of shorebirds to mudflats, including red-necked phalaropes, stilt sandpipers, and long-billed dowitchers. Great blue herons (PA threatened), green herons, and great egrets stalk for frogs and small fish. Other visitors include the black tern, American coot, killdeer, belted kingfisher, and several kinds of swallows. Red-shouldered, red-tailed, and rough-legged hawks circle above the fields and ponds looking for easy prey, such as rabbits, mice, and small birds. American kestrels, diminutive falcons, perch on utility lines, fence posts, and snags. Woodland species include the yellow and yellow-rumped warblers, northern flicker, wood thrush, and dark-eyed junco. Look for the American woodcock, goldfinch, bobolink, and savannah sparrow in meadows.

Deer, beavers, muskrats, rabbits, groundhogs, and many kinds of mice, voles, and moles live here. Meadow and marsh blossoms will fill the senses of wildflower fanciers.

Tamarack Swamp

Nature overflows with juxtapositions. Here, an acidic bog and an alkaline fen feed the headwaters of Brokenstraw Creek and nurture endangered plants and other wetland wonders. The ancestors of the swamp's namesake tamaracks migrated here from Canada during the ice age. In autumn, the green needles of these conifers turn to orange before falling to the ground.

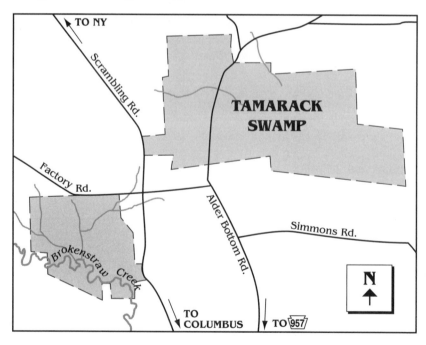

Ownership. The Pennsylvania Game Commission manages this place as State Game Lands 197.

Size. 670 acres.

Physiographic Region. Glaciated Plateau.

Nearby Natural Attractions. Allegheny National Forest, Anders Run Natural Area, Benson Swamp on US 6, in State Game Lands 306, and Akeley Swamp, along the Conewango River near the New York border, in State Game Lands 282.

Features. The U.S. Department of the Interior declared this wetland a national natural landmark in May 1977. The state-owned property is divided into two parcels. The larger northern section, known as Tamarack Swamp, is bisected by Alder Bottom Road north of Factory Road to the New York line. There are a few small parking areas on Alder Bottom Road, which tracks north from PA 957 east of Columbus. The southern parcel straddles Brokenstraw Creek off Factory Road and Schrambling Road, which also branches north from PA 957 east of Columbus.

The dirt roads are rough and lonely, like the location. You'll have to bushwhack or follow animal trails from the small parking lots. Dress for swampy terrain with biting insects. Knee-high rubber boots or waders, canteen, and compass are recommended, especially for newcomers.

Geology. In Columbus Township, the last ice age glacier, the Wisconsinan, edged as far south as what is now US 6 about 15,000 years ago. As the glacier began its slow northward retreat, enormous ice slabs broke off its face. Imagine icebergs aground in mud. Sediment-laden meltwater flowing off the glacier deposited till around the ice blocks, nearly burying them. Eventually, the ice melted into these basins, creating kettlehole lakes. Northwestern Pennsylvania was pocked with kettleholes after the ice age. Since then, many glacial teardrops have filled in by eutrophication, a natural process whereby a lake changes into a swamp and then a forest. Others were drained for various human enterprises. Tamarack Swamp is a former kettlehole lake in the stages of transition.

The "swamp" in the southern parcel is really a fen, a wetland recharged by spring water seeping from glacial till deposits. Both wetlands refresh the headwaters of Brokenstraw Creek, which snakes over the Pennsylvania–New York border before curling south into the Allegheny River at Irvine. Horseshoe-shaped ponds, or oxbows, add diversity to the southern parcel. These sickle-shaped puddles are abandoned channels of Brokenstraw Creek, which meanders in elongated S curves in this area. During times of high water, the creek crests over the narrow neck and cuts a new channel. The orphaned curve refills when the new channel overflows, but by midsummer many oxbow ponds become dry beds. Autumn rain often restores them.

Wildlife. The eastern half of Tamarack Swamp is a bog, a wetland replenished by precipitation and typically emptied by evaporation, though here a slack brook drains northwesterly into Brokenstraw Creek. Water in a bog becomes acidic due to the accumulation of decaying vegetation. Consequently, Tamarack Swamp supports plants that can thrive in a caustic habitat, such as the rare northern pitcher plant and round-leaved sundew, which survive in a low-nutrient world by devouring insects.

Part of the bog has brown, open water surrounded by floating rafts of sphagnum moss and rings of cattails. Elsewhere, hemlocks, white pine, alders, black cherry, aspen, and beeches grow on hummocks. The wetland is named for the tamarack, or American larch, one of only two conifers that shed their needles. It's a tall, wispy tree with scaly bark and tiny cones.

Water in the fen a mile away is alkaline, with vegetation specific to that harsh habitat. Because of a problem with plant poaching, the rarities found here will not be listed.

Wetland residents such as mink, beavers, and muskrats thrive here. Birders will find wood ducks, mallards, Canada geese, and other waterbirds.

History. The game commission began purchasing the swamp land in the 1960s. More acres were added in the 1980s. The Northern Allegheny Conservation Association, based in Warren, played a key role in the acquisitions.

Todd Sanctuary

Visitors' entries written in a guestbook at this site build on the wisdom of the late W. E. Clyde Todd, former bird curator at the Carnegie Museum of Natural History in Pittsburgh. Many visitors commented that the place was "quiet, peaceful, beautiful" and "breathtaking." Others shared special moments. "I saw eight turkeys out in the road!" wrote an exuberant hiker. "We liked seeing all the beautiful leaves," scribbled a young summer guest. Scientific observers entered, "Too bad about the web worms" and "Saw an eight-inch box turtle, female; ruffed grouse, deer." I put in my two cents: "Flushed two grouse, one doe deer; pond looks thirsty."

Ownership. Audubon Society of Western Pennsylvania.

Size. 176 acres.

Physiographic Region. Pittsburgh Low Plateau.

Nearby Natural Attractions. Crooked Creek Lake, Moraine State Park, Miller Esker, Jennings Environmental Education Center, and Harrison Hills Park.

Features. From PA 356, turn north on SR 2015 (Monroe Road). At the top of a hill, bear right on Kepple Road. Look for the preserve on the right at 1.8 miles. Small signs point the way from PA 356. From the parking area, follow a gravel service road to a wooden bridge that crosses Hesselgesser's Run. Stop to register at a wooden box beside a cabin that serves as headquarters for group hikes, nature programs, and staff. Trail maps are usually available in the box. Return to jot down your observations and comments in the registry after the hike.

The 2-mile, red-blazed Loop Trail forms a perimeter route through diverse habitats: oak and hickory forest, the crest of a hemlock ravine, a woodland pond, reverting meadows, and former pastures. Shorter paths crisscrossing within the Loop Trail—the Polypody, Indian Pipe, Meadow, Warbler and Hemlock Trails—can be taken to lengthen or shorten your hike. Some folks rate the 0.8-mile Ravine Trail, which descends into a boulder-clogged, hemlock-lined glen formed by Watson's Run, the preserve's best hike.

The well-marked footpaths are open daily from sunrise to sunset, except during deer hunting season, from late November to mid-December. Picnic tables stand by the cabin.

For more information, contact the Audubon Society of Western Pennsylvania, Beechwood Farms Nature Preserve, 614 Dorseyville Rd., Pittsburgh, PA 15238, telephone (412) 963-6100.

Geology. A quartet of trickling forest runs—Hesselgesser's, Knixon's, Spring, and Salamander—feed into diminutive Watson's

Run, which taps into Buffalo Creek less than a mile away. In 4 miles, Buffalo Creek drains into the Allegheny River.

The creek beds looked starved during my visit in September. However, judging from the depth of the ravine and the chunky blocks of 300-million-year-old sandstone blocking the current, these sleepy rills once had frothy, tree-toppling velocities.

Look for an old limestone quarry, now overgrown, on the Loop Trail, just west of the northern junction with the Warbler Trail. Stones from the pit became the foundations for local buildings, including the preserve's cabin.

Wildlife. The National Audubon Society designated the Buffalo Creek watershed an important bird area. The bird list includes 214 species. The relatively small area attracts a great diversity of avifauna, including large numbers of Blackburnian, hooded, prairie, blackpoll, magnolia, Kentucky, Canada, Nashville, northern parula, and Cape May warblers. Other birds spotted include the yellow-billed cuckoo, common whippoorwill, yellow-shafted flicker, golden-crowned kinglet, eastern meadowlark, horned lark, indigo bunting, scarlet tanager, Baltimore oriole, and eastern phoebe. Audubon members conduct annual nesting surveys and bird counts.

Great blue herons (PA threatened) have nested here, joining the summer residents such as the wood thrush, eastern pewee, ruby-throated hummingbird, cedar waxwing, and gray catbird, as well as the omnipresent black-capped chickadee, black crow, cardinal, and white-breasted nuthatch. A pond excavated in 1969 brought more waterbirds to the sanctuary. Pileated woodpeckers have excavated elongated, oval-shaped nesting holes in some snags.

The park is also home to typical Pennsylvania woodland animals, such as white-tailed deer, chipmunks, and gray squirrels.

Hemlock, Indian Pipe, and Polypody Trails reveal some of the vegetation found here. Eastern hemlock, black birch, ironwood, shagbark hickory, crab apple, Scotch pine, flowering dogwood, black cherry, black gum, and red, white, chestnut, and shingle oaks stand out along the Loop Trail. Small hemlocks grow atop sandstone slabs that have accumulated soil. Eventually their roots will snake over the edges to deeper soil below.

Indian pipe is a delicate, translucent white saprophytic plant that feeds on decayed matter in on the forest floor. The ghostly flower turns black when it dies. Woodland and meadow flowers are represented by Dutchman's breeches, large-flowered trillium, hepatica, trailing arbutus, bloodroot, pokeweed, mayapple, jack-in-the-pulpit, Solomon's seal, and false Solomon's seal. Skunk cabbage, foamflower, white clintonia, white baneberry, various violets and wood asters also color the scene. Except for a few asters and goldenrods, late-summer bloomers such as agrimony, joe-pye weed, ironweed, white snakeroot, and milkwort had faded when I tramped here in late September.

Polypody Trail honors the polypody ferns that spring from cracks in boulders. The trail map notes the location of the polypody rocks. Other ferns include rattlesnake, cut-leaved grape, Christmas, sensitive, and wood.

History. Dr. W. E. Clyde Todd spent many boyhood weekends exploring his grandparents' farm above Watson's Run. The old homestead stood in the vicinity of the pond. Ownership eventually passed to Todd, an ornithologist and curator of the Carnegie Museum of Natural History's bird collection. In 1942 Todd donated the first parcel to the Audubon Society, making it one of the first nature preserves in the greater Pittsburgh area. Additional acquisitions have increased the property's size to 176 acres.

Tryon-Weber Woods

This signature deciduous grove of stately American beeches and sugar maples may be the easternmost remnant of one of America's original floral communities: the beech-maple forest. Once common on glaciated soils west of the Appalachians, the realm has been reduced, in western Pennsylvania, to this 40-acre colony. The spring and summer greens of these trees and their associates give way to a colorful autumn palette. One of the preserve's namesakes, Dr. Clarence Archer Tryon, longtime director of the Pymatuning Laboratory of Ecology, studied the ecological relationships in this type of forest, as well as the forest's chipmunks, which bulk up on beechnuts before their long winter snooze.

Ownership. University of Pittsburgh.

Size. 84 acres.

Physiographic Region. Glaciated Plateau.

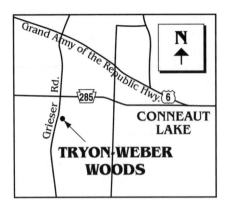

Nearby Natural Attractions. Erie National Wildlife Refuge, Conneaut Marsh, Pymatuning Wetlands, Wallace Woods, and Woodcock Creek Lake.

Features. Follow the trail from the parking lot on Grieser Road into the woods for 150 yards, then bear left at a fork. After crossing a small brook, look for a worn, fading wooden preserve sign on the left that reads "Friendship Is a Sheltering Tree." The path continues for a short distance before disappearing. You can roam around the woods, following deer routes and animal tracks. The preserve is open daily from sunrise to sunset.

For more information, contact the University of Pittsburgh, Pymatuning Laboratory of Ecology, 13142 Hartstown Rd., Linesville, PA 16424, telephone (814) 683-5813.

Geology. Ice age glaciers scoured and leveled northwestern Pennsylvania less than 15,000 years ago. Retreating glaciers, the last of which was the Wisconsinan, deposited layers of unsorted sediment called till, as well as orphaned mountains of ice, which later melted into lakes and ponds. A stream bisects the site and drains into Conneaut Lake.

Wildlife. American beeches and sugar maples—giants as well as saplings—share the site with chokecherry, black cherry, red maples, hornbeam, dogwood, sassafras, witch hazel, and spicebush. Spring wildflowers—large-flowered trillium, mayapple, violets, wild geranium, spring beauty, and bellwort—color the understory before the broadleaves block out the sunlight. Descendants of the eastern chipmunks observed by Tryon scamper along the cluttered forest floor with an incessant *che-ock, che-ock, che-ock.*

Like other natural communities, the beech-maple forest manufactures and recycles nutrients. Nitrogen, phosphorus, and potassium in the duff fuel the spring wildflowers. When these seasonal plants decay, their vital elements nourish fungi, mushrooms, and saprophytic beechdrops and Indian pipe. These plants break down soil nutrients, which the beech trees and other flora absorb through roots and transport skyward to buds and blossoms. In autumn, the small, triangular beechnuts, encased in burlike husks, fall to the forest floor to become food for chipmunks and other animals. The now-extinct passenger pigeons flocked to the beeches during autumn migrations. Nuts not consumed by beasts might germinate in the soil and sprout upward, though new beeches largely come from stump sprouts or sucker roots. Whatever their origin, only a lucky few will reach the sky with their ancestors. Unlike oaks and most pines, beech and maple seedlings are shade-tolerant, meaning they can grow in the shadow of their taller elders. Though clusters and individual beeches and sugar maples appear in forests throughout the state, their numbers are greatest in glaciated regions.

History. Arch Tryon (1911–73) was a world authority on chipmunks. Some of his studies for the University of Pittsburgh's Pymatuning Laboratory for Ecology were conducted in the forest that now partly bears his name. The Western Pennsylvania Conservancy purchased the tract from Dr. Robert G. Weber, an Allison Park dentist, in the 1970s and gave it to the University of Pittsburgh.

◆ 59 ◆

Twin Lakes County Park

Ann Rudd Saxman Nature Park

Nature enthusiasts can explore the wonders of woods and water in Westmoreland County's flagship park. Trees at the edge of their ranges, plus species imported from afar, have sunk their roots here. Centerpiece lakes that started as natural cooling tanks for blast furnaces now refresh flora and fauna, as well as humans.

Ownership. Westmoreland County Bureau of Parks and Recreation.

Size. Twin Lakes County Park is about 450 acres; Ann Rudd Saxman Nature Park is 65 acres.

Physiographic Region. Pittsburgh Low Plateau.

Nearby Natural Attractions. Cedar Creek County Park, Sewickley Creek Wetlands, Conemaugh Gorge, Powdermill Nature Reserve, Forbes State Forest, and Laurel Ridge, Laurel Summit, Keystone, and Linn Run State Parks.

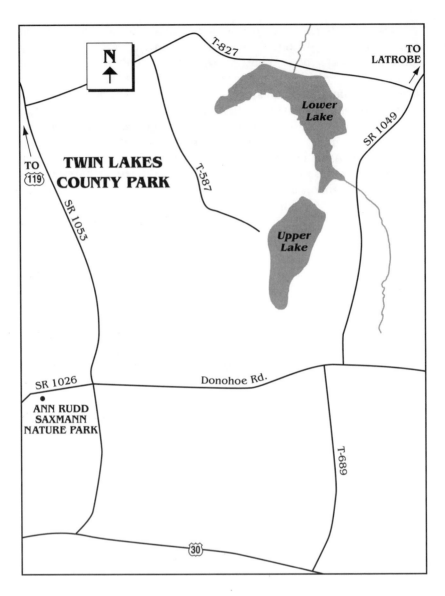

Features. The Twin Lakes are the centerpieces of this largely wooded park, which is bounded by SR 1049 on the east, T827 on the north, Georges Station Road (SR 1053) on the west, and railroad tracks on the south. Upper Lake is the southernmost and smallest, 24 acres. Downstream, the crescent-shaped Lower Lake measures 26 acres. Together, the lakes form a question mark, with the bottom pointing south.

Though the area is popular with humans, wildlife holds sway on roughly 80 percent of this site. Most human activity is concentrated in the eastern side of the park, between the eastern shores of Upper and Lower Lakes and SR 1049. The road provides access to parking lots for the boathouse, nature center, activities center, playground, and picnic pavilions. For a park brochure and peek at nature exhibits, stop at the John F. Laudadio Sr. Environmental and Nature Center, which also serves as the headquarters for nature programs.

Seven miles of trails await hikers. Tamarack Nature Trail is a 0.75-mile self-guided loop branching from the Tamarack Parking Lot on SR 1049. Trail signs explain natural wonders along the trail, including the tamarack, or larch, one of only two conifers on the continent that shed their needles in autumn. In fall, the needles look like orange whiskers. The tamarack's prime habitat is the northern boreal forest.

Wilderness Trail, a mile-long path in the southeast corner, loops through the valley of the unnamed creek feeding Lower Lake. This woodland trail begins at the East Parking Lot on SR 1049. A more challenging 2-mile route shared by horse riders and hikers wanders through forests west of the lakes. The trailhead is reached from the northern entrance (T587), off T827. The road leads to the park office and group camping areas. Drive to the end and park in the Wishing Well Parking Lot on the west shore of Upper Lake. Backtrack to trail entrances going north and south from the road.

An easy, barrier-free path, Upper Lake Loop, encircles Upper Lake for 0.9 mile. This handicapped-accessible walk continues along the east shore of Lower Lake. A foot trail leads from the North Picnic Area (off T827) along the west bank of Lower Lake to Upper Lake. A perimeter route around both lakes would cover 2 to 2.5 miles.

Twin Lakes also offers boat and cross-country ski rentals, fishing decks, a boat launch, ice skating, picnic areas (eight pavilions), two group camps, an activities building, nature programs, food concession, a lakeshore gazebo, rest rooms, volleyball, community garden plots, a stage, and playgrounds. Hunting is allowed in the southwestern and southeastern (Wilderness Trail) sections, as shown on the park brochure.

The Ann Rudd Saxman Nature Park is off SR 1026 (Donohoe Road) midway between Greensburg and Twin Lakes County Park. Park in the lot beside the Donohoe Center, which houses conservation agencies. A hiking trail begins by the parking lot. Take it into the woods, then choose among paths winding along a creek or into upland hardwoods. Benches are placed along trails for weary feet and wildlife watching. Hunting is not permitted here.

For more information, contact Westmoreland County Bureau of Parks and Recreation, R.D. 12, Box 203, Greensburg, PA 15601, telephone (724) 830-3950 or (800) 442-6926, ext. 3950.

Geology. Both parks spread just a few miles west of Chestnut Ridge, the westernmost syncline of the Allegheny Mountains. Shale and sandstone from the Pennsylvanian Period, some 300 million years ago, line the base of the shallow twin lakes. Sandstone for the dams in Twin Lakes Park was quarried from a valley between the lakes. The mining opened a spring that tumbles over the excavation, creating a waterfall in autumn through spring. The water flow stops during summer. The attraction is beside the paved trail that connects the lakes. Little Crabtree Creek feeds into the lakes, then empties into Crabtree Creek, a tributary of the Conemaugh River.

Wildlife. Twin Lakes supports an unusual collection of trees, both native and introduced. The coal company that once owned the place planted hundreds of pines and northern catalpas around the lakes to protect the watershed and enhance the landscape. Pines certainly thrive in Pennsylvania, but these occupy ground cleared of its original Appalachian oak forest. The northern catalpa is a native of the Mississippi Valley, likely planted here for its spring blossom and shade. Its gorgeous but nonfragrant, irislike white and blue flowers bloom in May. Large, heart-shaped leaves provide cool shade. In autumn it drops slender beanlike pods filled with seeds.

White birches clustered along the southern park boundary have extended their Pennsylvania range, thanks to a railroad company. Stones dumped during railroad construction probably held clumps of soil containing white birch seeds. These sprouted and spread into the park. Tamarack Trail is named for the resident tamarack trees, which normally grow in northern boreal climates. Hemlock and great rhododendron are represented, too.

Hardwoods of the old oak forest, led by white and red oaks, are regrouping on the higher slopes. These shelter spring wildflowers, including mayapple, large-flowered trillium, Dutchman's breeches, jack-in-the-pulpit, skunk cabbage, trout lily, various violets, and squirrel corn, a close relative of Dutchman's breeches whose root tubers resemble corn kernels.

Birders will find waterbirds around the lakes, including the coot, Canada goose, blue-winged teal, bufflehead, canvasback, and wood duck. Muted and whistling swans stay for several days during migrations. The park also has the pileated woodpecker, ruffed grouse, wild turkey, ring-necked pheasant, and eastern woodcock.

Largemouth bass, trout, bluegills, yellow perch, crappies, carp, channel catfish, and brown bullheads swim in the lakes. A local conservation club annually stocks these waters.

Ann Rudd Saxman Nature Park is a mixed hardwood forest heavily populated with American beech (some 150 years old) and sugar maple, along with lesser amounts of white, pin, red, and black oaks; sassafras; and black cherry. The short tree with large, paddle-shaped leaves is a pawpaw, here stretching its native range farther northeast. The pawpaw produces a strange-looking fruit resembling a cross between a banana and a pear. Deer reject pawpaw buds, so the plant sometimes rises in thickets. Wild grape and brier patches lace some trails. Wild geraniums, turtleheads, wood lilies, and yellow violets lead the spring wildflower procession.

History. The Twin Lakes location was previously owned by the Jamison Coal Company, which built the double impoundments across Little Crabtree Creek shortly after World War II. Water from the ponds cooled company-owned coke furnaces downstream at Luxor. The company used local rock for the dams and planted hundreds of pines and catalpa trees to improve and beautify the watershed. No coal was mined within the parkland. Westmoreland County acquired the property for a public park in 1969–70. The John F. Laudadio Sr. Environmental and Nature Center was dedicated in 1977. Its namesake was a local legislator.

Ann Rudd Saxman (1914–90) was a pioneer conservationist, botanist, landscape designer, and master gardener who served as associate director of the Westmoreland Conservation District and hosted a local radio show on gardening for many years. As a professional landscaper, she coordinated the relandscaping of Fallingwater, the home designed by architect Frank Lloyd Wright.

Saxman's connection to the land constituting the nature park began in 1940, when she married and moved to adjacent Twin Run Farm. She was instrumental in the formation of the nature park in 1960. Two years later, she married Harry Saxman, an executive at Latrobe Steel. In later years, she worked to keep encroaching suburban development from swallowing the site. In July 1996 a revitalized nature park was rededicated in her honor.

Two Mile Run County Park

Venango County residents call this place a hidden jewel. For thirty years this diamond in the rough was unknown to nature lovers heading to more celebrated sites nearby. But now the gem shines. There's lots of room for solitude seekers, pure gravel-based streams catering to mussels and trout, a 144-acre lake, 26 trail miles for foot and hoof, birding and fishing hot spots, and enough flora and fauna to keep naturalists busy for years.

Ownership. Venango County.

Size. 2,695 acres.

Physiographic Region. Pittsburgh Low Plateau near the eastern edge of the glaciated plateau.

Nearby Natural Attractions. Oil Creek State Park, Allegheny Gorge (Kittaning State Forest), Allegheny National Scenic River, and State Game Lands 39, 45, 47, 96, and 253.

Features. Seventeen trails totaling 26 miles visit every nook in the park. Pick up a trail map at the park office on PA 450 to choose destinations and paths. The longest route is the bridle trail (combined with the Raccoon Trail), which travels along the perimeter. Trail entrances can be found at the Lockwood Group Camp (west side); at Crosby Beach; along Cherrytree Road (PA 450), Speer Road (SR 4001), Pritchard Drive (T581), and Masterson Road (T567); at Justus Lake Dam (off Warren Road), and at the Top O'Flats, Pioneer Flats, and Daniel Boone Picnic Pavilions.

Human comforts and diversions include a family campground with fifty-three sites, a swimming beach, boat and ski rentals, miniature golf, a playground, picnic pavilions, a group camp, an activity center, two overnight cabins, a boat launch, a fishing pier, small ponds, hunting, and an observatory with an 16-inch telescope.

For more information, contact Two Mile Run County Park, R.D. 4, P.O. Box 320, Franklin, PA 16323, telephone (814) 676-6116.

Geology. Two Mile Run's dance is short and sweet. It actually courses about 8 miles from its headwaters in the northern end of the park to its confluence with the Allegheny River a couple miles upstream (east) of Franklin. The high-quality, pebble-based stream may have been born at the end of the ice age about 12,000 years ago, when the Wisconsinan glacier ran out of gas in northwestern Venango County. Sediment trapped in the ice washed over the area as the glacier melted. This gravel deposit serves as the bed for Two Mile Run. A dam across the run at the south end of the park created Justus Lake in 1971.

Wildlife. The land shows various stages of ecological succession, from recently cultivated fields to maturing second-growth woods dominated by oaks and black cherry. Flowering dogwood, several willows, and a shrub called ninebark thrive beneath the canopy. Such diverse settings support wildflowers like pink lady's slippers, arrow arum, swamp milkweed, bur reed, cattail, and Turk's cap lily, the largest native species, named for its elongated, recurved petals that resemble hats worn by medieval Turks.

The northern reaches of Justus Lake have become a birding hot spot. Ospreys (PA endangered) have camped here for two-month periods, and bald eagles (PA endangered) visit during migrations. Great blue herons (PA threatened) once had a rookery of half a dozen nests here, but they've moved elsewhere nearby. The herons that still frequent the site are believed to be members of that "lost" colony. Other waterbirds include the sora rail, common snipe, yellowlegs, Canada goose, sandpiper, and semipalmated plover, whose markings resemble a small killdeer, another park resident. The park's recovering forest attracts warblers and other woodland birds, even turkeys. Mourning doves, pheasants, and ruffed grouse prefer the meadows and shrubs. During my visit, I spied a great horned owl and heard the plaintive cry of a barred owl.

Beaver lodges are spaced along the bank of the lake and along Two Mile Run, especially below the dam. Quiet boaters stand a good chance of spotting these nocturnal builders at dusk. In summer and early autumn, bats, mostly big and little browns, also appear at twilight above the lakeshore and meadows. Many of these agile insectivores hibernate in old farm buildings. Tracks indicate the presence of raccoons, skunks, deer, gray squirrels, and rabbits. Black bears inhabit the woods from time to time.

Venomous copperhead snakes show up occasionally, but your chances of encountering the shy beast are remote. Most snakes are the harmless and common water snakes, the black rat, and small brown varieties. Although they have not been sighted, the park has ideal wetland habitats for the eastern massasauga rattlesnake, an endangered and poisonous reptile, and the hellbender, a giant salamander. Justus Lake hosts brown and rainbow trout, bass, walleye, muskellunge, and catfish.

History. The idea for this park originated in 1961 and incubated until Venango County planners found seed money in October 1964. The following year they started buying land from forty landowners. Back then, $20,000 bought them 2,700 acres. The park gates opened in August 1969. A funding crisis briefly closed the park in the mid-1990s. Crosby Beach honors Holmes Crosby, an architect who volunteered his services to the park project for a $1 annual salary. Justus Lake commemorates the contributions made by the Edith C. Justus Charitable Trust.

Wallace Woods

This is a cool, boreal hemlock forest thriving in open, flat, farmland. That makes this shady glen something of an anomaly, because hemlocks in Pennsylvania prefer steep-sided ravines that are shrouded from the sun. Biology students keep poking around, hoping this tad of tundra will reveal its secrets.

Ownership. University of Pittsburgh.

Size. 40 acres.

Physiographic Region. Glaciated Plateau.

Nearby Natural Attractions. Tryon-Weber Woods, Pymatuning Wetlands, Conneaut Marsh, Woodcock Creek Lake, and Erie National Wildlife Refuge.

Features. Wallace Woods is a field lab for staffers and students at the University of Pittsburgh, Pymatuning Laboratory of Ecology, located just a few miles away in Linesville. From US 6 in Linesville (at the firehouse), go north on Wallace Avenue, which becomes Russell Road outside town and ends at West Road. The nature preserve is on your left. You won't find trails or facilities. No sign notes its presence and there are no boundary markers. There are two unmarked sort-of parking spots on the west side of Russell Road, one 75 yards south of West Road (T605), the other 150 to 200 yards south of the first. Go to Pymatuning State Park for camping and other facilities.

For more information, contact the University of Pittsburgh, Pymatuning Laboratory of Ecology, 13142 Hartstown Rd., Linesville, PA 16424, telephone (814) 683-5813.

Geology. The hemlocks in Wallace Woods sink their roots in gravelly glacial sediments deposited by the retreating Wisconsinan glacier some 12,000 years ago. Linesville Creek washes through the woods before emptying into Pymatuning Reservoir. Note the various channels the creek has followed and forgotten over the years. In spring some abandoned channels get flooded and become vernal pools that sustain woodland aquatic life.

Geologists call the large, rounded boulders in the middle of the woods erratics. The glacier transported them from locations up north and left them here when it melted.

Wildlife. The eastern hemlock is the dominant tree in this swampy, shady forest. A strong presence of yellow birches, beeches, and red oaks indicates that this grove is a northern hardwood forest. Hemlocks, beeches, and yellow birches are shade-tolerant, meaning that they thrive with only a small amount of daily sunlight. Though hemlocks here reach the canopy, their successors compete in the understory and at seedling level.

All totaled, a blend of more than forty species of trees and shrubs have been recorded, including big-toothed aspen, shagbark hickory, black ash, basswood, black oak, hornbeam, red maple, slippery elm, tulip tree, spicebush, witch hazel, staghorn sumac, maple-leaved viburnum, common elderberry, and flowering dogwood.

At ground level, the flora includes jewelweed, jack-in-the-pulpit, skunk cabbage, blue cohosh, mayapple, enchanter's nightshade, wood sorrel, nodding mandarin lilies, Indian cucumber root, false Solomon's seal, purple trillium, and yellow clintonia and false hellebore, two typical boreal plants. The hardy Christmas fern grows here, as do interrupted, sensitive, rattlesnake, maidenhair, and lady ferns. Two kinds of horsetails and three club mosses occupy niches.

The fauna population is less well known. Tracks, scat, and other evidence reveal the presence of deer, raccoons, opossums, and chipmunks. Yellow-bellied sapsuckers leave straight-lined borings in birches. Other birds include dark-eyed juncos, and woodpeckers. Share your findings with the field lab.

History. The University of Pittsburgh bought the woods from Ralph Wallace in 1962.

62

Washington County Parks

Mingo Creek County Park
Cross Creek County Park

Set in rolling farmland, Washington County's park system offers more than 5,000 acres for outdoor recreation and nature study. Hikers and horseback riders go to Mingo Creek County Park for its forested trails. Cross Creek County Park appeals to anglers, hunters, slow boaters, and wandering nature explorers.

Ownership. Washington County Department of Parks and Recreation.

Size. Mingo Creek Park is 2,500 acres; Cross Creek Park is 2,600 acres.

Physiographic Region. Pittsburgh Low Plateau.

Nearby Natural Attractions. Enlow Fork Natural Area (State Game Lands 302).

Features. Fifteen miles of interconnected horse and hiking trails journey through forested *Mingo Creek County Park,* located in the eastern part of the county. Mingo Creek, a meandering tributary of the Monongahela River, bisects the site. Wooden covered bridges serve as scenic gateways at each end of the park. Trails maps are available at the park office. Picnic areas, a bike trail, playgrounds, and ballfields are concentrated along Mingo Creek, leaving the wooded uplands uncrowded for wanderers. Open every day from sunrise to sunset.

A 258-acre lake, constructed in the early 1980s, is the centerpiece of *Cross Creek County Park,* found in the west side of the county. A boat launch, a park office, picnic tables, and parking are located on the north shore at the end of Cross Creek Road, off PA 50 at Rea. A mile-long hiking path stems from the picnic area, but enthusiastic walkers will tramp more interesting footpaths made by shore anglers, like the one heading eastbound from the picnic area. Exploring 8 miles of lakeshore in a small boat (10-horsepower limit) can be rewarding for wildlife watchers. Shallow coves and no-wake zones attract waterfowl and kingfishers. Since May 1985 anglers have been casting for crappie, walleye, smallmouth and largemouth bass, and channel catfish. Hunters pursue deer, turkey, and grouse here.

The lake hits bottom at 50 feet near the west end dam but tapers to knee deep at the upstream eastern tip. Cross Creek dumps into the Ohio River south of Follansbee, West Virginia. The hills above the lake will be fully bearded in a decade or two. Look for more trails by then, too. The park is open daily 6 A.M. to 11 P.M. from the third Sunday in April to the third Sunday in October, and 8 A.M. to 5 P.M. daily the rest of the year. Anglers' maps are available.

For more information, contact Washington County Department of Parks and Recreation, Room 604, Courthouse Square, Washington, PA 15301, telephone (412) 228-6867.

Wolf Creek Narrows Natural Area

A nature photographer laden with equipment asked me if I had seen a showy orchis, one of five rare plants residing in this narrow gorge. We were surrounded by a coterie of wildflowers—bluebells and marsh marigolds mostly—but not a single settlement of the sought-after lavender blossom. The shutterbug seemed miffed, as if he had been sent on a wild goose chase or given a bum steer. He showed me a "treasure" map drawn on a napkin, so I could confirm that he was searching in the correct spot. His source had assured him two weeks earlier that the rarity lived at the X on his map. "Perhaps they have come and gone since then," I said. He growled disdainfully and tiptoed off the trail, looking for the needle in a haystack. I continued on the trail, enjoying the largesse before my eyes.

Ownership. Western Pennsylvania Conservancy.

Size. 125 acres.

Physiographic Region. Glaciated Plateau.

Nearby Natural Attractions. Miller Esker, Jennings Environmental Education Center, and Moraine and McConnells Mill State Parks.

Features. From the parking area, backtrack across the bridge to the 1.5-mile Narrows Trail, which begins on the left (north) side of West Water Street. Look for the site sign at the head of this old angler's path. The first 100 yards crosses a treeless floodplain thickened by willows, shrubs, and grasses. Proceeding upstream, the path

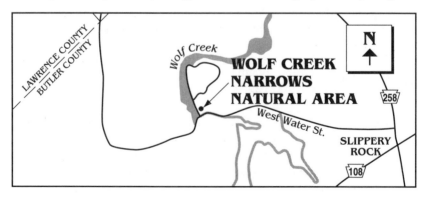

goes through a hemlock grove and touches the creek bank. Where the gorge narrows, the trail swings uphill to the top of the east bluff. It wanders through a black cherry and beech forest, then descends south and west back to Wolf Creek.

The Western Pennsylvania Conservancy sponsors group hikes during the peak of the spring wildflower season, often with a botanist. Local schools and conservation clubs also use the grounds for nature programs. Field guides on wildflowers come in handy.

For more information, contact the Western Pennsylvania Conservancy, 209 Fourth Ave., Pittsburgh, PA 15222, telephone (412) 288-2773.

Geology. Wolf Creek is a glacial-bred current. Its 20-mile-long journey begins at Pine Swamp, a glacial kettlehole lake and swamp northeast of Mercer, and ends at Slippery Rock Creek at PA 108. The headwater wetland, now State Game Lands 130, was originally purchased by the conservancy. Kettlehole lakes formed at the end of the ice age when enormous slabs of ice broke off the face of the withdrawing Wisconsinan glacier and melted into basins. The trickle flowing out of the lake, however, could not have carved the Wolf Creek Narrows.

After passing through Grove City, the creek increases its volume as it meanders southward across farmland. At PA 258, it seems that water should drain via lower ground to the east, not through the rocky narrows. Limestone walls in the gorge give away the secret. Wolf Creek once was Wolf Cave. Geologists figure that torrents of meltwater from the Wisconsinan glacier 15,000 years ago eroded the ceiling of a cave and scoured a path through 300-million-year-old limestone. The gorge, or narrows, may have been formed before the kettlehole lake. The outlet that was named Wolf Creek followed a path scratched by the glacier.

Wildlife. Wolf Creek gorge is noted for its wildflowers and ferns. Ninety kinds of blossoms have been found so far, including the endangered showy orchis, and the dwarf trillium and spotted coralroot, these declining in population. Showy orchis enjoys limestone-derived soils. Its pleasant fragrance comes from a syrup high in sugar. Spotted coralroot, a summer-blooming orchid, is saprophytic, drawing nourishment from fungi in woodland soils. Dwarf trillium, or snow trillium, emerges early in spring. It was transplanted here by conservancy scientists.

Violets are represented by eleven varieties, notably the smooth yellow, or Pennsylvania; arrow-leaved; long-spurred; and stemless, or dog tooth. A striking splotch of large-flowered trilliums brightens uplands above the creek Splashy flowers include turk's cap lily, painted and red trilliums, Dutchman's breeches, mayapple, spring beauty, hepatica, squirrel corn, bluets, skunk cabbage, trout lily, wood anemone, cut-leaved toothwort, bloodroot, celandines, and trailing arbutus.

Rare bulblet and walking ferns gracefully droop from the limestone cliffs. Bulblet ferns send wispy, lacy, streamerlike fronds from clusters in cracks and pocks. Walking fern, an evergreen, gets its name from its ability to leapfrog, as the arching tip of its long, tapered leaf sprouts roots when it touches ground. Fragile, or brittle, fern appears in early spring, shrivels in summer, then revives in autumn under moist conditions. Cinnamon and Christmas ferns also grow here.

Seventy years have passed since the last disturbance in the form of logging or farming on the forested slopes. Some individual giants may be the prodigy of virgin timber. American sycamore is the first tree you'll encounter. Before the hike ends, you'll also see hemlocks, American beeches, tulip tree, sugar maple, red oak, yellow birch, basswood, black gum, and black cherry.

Thirty species of warblers arrive in May. Focus on the orange-crowned and yellow-throated varieties. I watched a great blue heron and belted kingfisher going about their business along the stream.

History. The narrows property was part of a land grant issued after the American Revolution to encourage settlement beyond the Appalachian Mountains. Only three families owned and semi-preserved the spot before the Western Pennsylvania Conservancy purchased it in 1979. The 15-acre floodplain was acquired in 1983.

Woodcock Creek Lake

Framed by farmland and glacier-made hills, the recumbent Woodcock Creek Lake provides wildlife with myriad habitats and humans with outdoor entertainment. Like fiddles and cabernet, this place will improve with age.

Ownership. The U.S. Army Corps of Engineers owns the property. The eastern half of the property is leased to the Pennsylvania

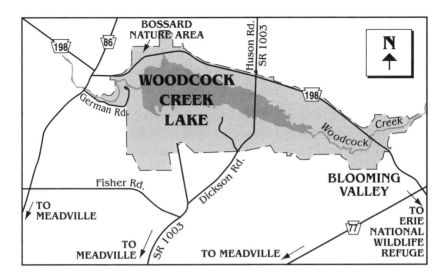

Game Commission for State Game Lands 435. Crawford County maintains Colonel Crawford Park on the south shore.

Size. 1,734 acres.

Physiographic Region. Glaciated Plateau.

Nearby Natural Attractions. Pymatuning Wetlands, Wallace Woods, Tryon-Weber Woods, and Conneaut Marsh. Woodcock Creek originates in nearby State Game Lands 69 and Erie National Wildlife Refuge.

Features. Bossard Nature Area is on the north side of PA 198, about a mile east of PA 86 and across from the site manager's office. Several miles of paths, designated as national recreation trails by the U.S. Department of the Interior, visit different habitats, including hemlock-shrouded Bossard Run. About 1,000 feet is paved for physically disabled hikers. Observation blinds offer concealment for wildlife watching. The underfunded and, therefore, underused nature center has outdoor toilets.

Colonel Crawford Park provides a campground, a swimming beach, a boat launch, hiking trails, and picnic areas. From Meadville, take PA 77, then turn left on Dickson Road (SR 1003). From Bossard Nature Area, go east on PA 198, then right (south) on Huson Road (SR 1003), which becomes Dickson Road on the south shore. Access to State Game Lands 435 is best from parking areas off Dickson Road (ramp) and PA 198. On game commission land, you're free to wander on unmarked paths or to bushwhack. The corps of engineers' Stainbrook Recreation Area below the dam has picnic areas, shelters, a playground, and fishing areas. To get there, take German Road from PA 86 or a park road from PA 198.

For more information, contact the U.S. Army Corps of Engineers, Resource Manager, Woodcock Creek Lake, P.O. Box 629, Saegertown, PA 16433, telephone (814) 763-4422

Geology. Woodcock Creek Lake lies among low, rolling hills atop land covered by glacial till. These gravel and sand sediments were deposited by the Wisconsinan glacier some 15,000 years ago. Dome-shaped hillocks, or kames, rise in state game lands property west of the PA 198 bridge over Woodcock Creek. Sediments pouring hourglasslike through cracks in the glacier account for the humped configurations.

Bossard Run has cut through the till and exposed the 300-million-year-old bedrock of the Pennsylvanian Period. Water in Bossard Run and Woodcock Creek drains into French Creek before reaching the Allegheny, Ohio, and Mississippi Rivers. The dam is located 4 miles above the creek's merger with French Creek.

Wildlife. Bossard Nature Area protects a northern hardwood forest ruled by the eastern hemlock, with a supporting canopy of yellow birch, black cherry, red maple, beeches, tulip tree, black walnut, white oak, bigtooth aspen, and red oak. The understory is occupied by sassafras, hornbeam, ironwood, flowering dogwood, and staghorn sumac, as well as saplings of the canopy trees.

Beyond this spot, the area features forested bottomlands, meadows in various stages of succession, marshes, shrub thickets, hedgerows, and woodlots. Sycamores stand shoulder to shoulder along Woodcock Creek below the tailwater. Elsewhere are habitats with sugar maples, bitternut hickory, white pine, witch hazel, ninebark, spicebush, white ash, speckled alder, crab apple, hawthorns, nannyberry, honeysuckle, black locust, quaking aspen, black willow, American elm, and wild grape. A comprehensive wildflower inventory has not been completed, but my cursory late-summer study turned up jewelweed, stinging nettle, boneset, joe-pye weed, smartweed, shrubby Saint-John's-wort, meadowsweet, and several asters.

Thickets conceal rabbits, eastern woodcocks, cuckoos, alder flycatchers, wrens, ruffed grouse, pheasants, chestnut-sided and yellow warblers, yellow-breasted chats, and indigo buntings. Groves of red and Scotch pine and Norway spruce, all planted, may conceal deer, pine siskins, red crossbills, pine warblers, and long-eared owls. Meadow dwellers include moles, mice, voles, and the hawks and snakes that prey on them, plus bobolinks, meadowlarks, savannah and grasshopper sparrows, and least weasels.

Muskrats and beavers live in the marshes, along with red-winged blackbirds, wood ducks, and flycatchers. Open water attracts migratory waterbirds, which over the years have included gulls, great blue herons (PA threatened), common loons, Canada geese, mergansers, scaups, teals, canvasbacks, and pintail, ring-necked, ruddy, and redhead ducks. Droughts that lower the lake level bring more shorebirds, notably various plovers, yellowlegs, and sandpipers.

Two 40-foot utility poles, serving as safe nesting platforms for endangered ospreys, were erected in January 1998, thanks to the Northwestern Rural Electric Cooperative, Pennsylvania Game Commission, and the corps of engineers. Raptors started building a nest that spring but then moved to another site. Bonding pairs may return to the site. Bald eagles (PA endangered) occasionally visit. They come here for the fish, which include muskellunge, walleye, yellow perch, black crappie, bluegill, largemouth bass, brown bullhead, white sucker, and minnows.

History. The corps of engineers built the Woodcock Creek dam to control flooding, improve water quality, enhance wildlife habitat, and provide outdoor recreation. The project was finished in 1973.

65

Yellow Creek State Park

Though fishing remains the major activity, birdwatchers flock here in ever increasing numbers. And it's no wonder—shallow shorelines and coves, reverting farmland, and quiet woodlands make this an attractive place for 240 species of birds.

Ownership. Pennsylvania Department of Conservation and Natural Resources, Bureau of State Parks.

Size. 3,140 acres.

Physiographic Region. Yellow Creek State Park is cradled in the Pittsburgh Low Plateau between two lobes of the Allegheny Mountains.

Nearby Natural Attractions. Blue Spruce and Hemlock Lake County Parks, Pine Ridge Park, Buttermilk Falls and Blacklick Valley Natural Areas, and the Conemaugh Gorge.

Features. Many public facilities—visitor center, park office, beach, bird blind, trails, and picnic areas—branch from PA 259 on

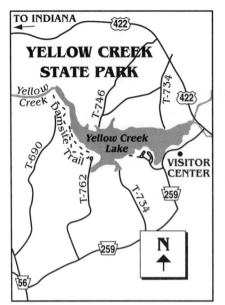

the south side of the park. The westernmost loop road, near the beach, has parking for a half-mile trail to a waterfowl observation blind. Rest rooms and water are nearby. The same loop road has parking for the 2-mile Ridge Top Trail, a more challenging route shared by snowmobilers in winter. Damsite Trail tracks the western shore of the lake for 2.5 miles. To get there from the beach area, return to PA 259 and turn right, going south and west. Take the second right, northbound on Hoffman Road (T762) to its end. From here, the path goes to the dam in the northwest corner of the park and back to the start.

The park offers boat rentals, lake fishing, a kids' fishing pond, ice skating, a sledding hill, and cross-country skiing. Camping is available in nearby private campgrounds.

For more information, contact Yellow Creek State Park, Box 145-D, Penn Run, PA 15765, telephone (724) 357-7913.

Geology. The bedrock beneath the park ranges from the shales, sandstones, coals, limestones, and siltstones of the Pennsylvanian Period (285 to 325 million years ago) to some gritty shale from the Mississippian Period (340 million years ago). The oldest Pennsylvanian rocks, layers of the Pottsville Group, surface in the western portion of the park. Above them lie sedimentary beds of the Allegheny and Conemaugh groups. The Allegheny Group contains the coal. Previous mining occurred in one small mine south of the dam. The park's oldest rock, sandstone originating in the Mississippian Period, is exposed along Yellow Creek south of the dam.

The park lies in the Brush Valley syncline between northeast-southwest trending anticlines called Chestnut Ridge and Laurel Ridge. One would expect Yellow Creek, which begins on Laurel Ridge, to flow parallel with the ridges, as do Brush and Little Brush Creeks to the south, but it seems to defy gravity by snaking through a gap in Chestnut Ridge and continuing westward to Two Lick Creek and the Conemaugh River. The same story applies to its southern brethren, streams called Blacklick, Conemaugh, Loyalhanna, and Youghiogheny. Chestnut and Laurel Ridges peter out a few miles northeast of the park. A dozen miles in that direction, streams drain into the West Branch of the Susquehanna River, en route to the Atlantic Ocean.

Chestnut and Laurel Ridges rose about 290 million years ago during the mountain-building event called the Alleghenian Orogeny. Land uplifted and buckled, and in weak places, the sedimentary bedrock layers of a plateau created Laurel and Chestnut Ridges. Existing sluggish streams on the plateau, now running faster and flooding, spilled over gaps in the ridges and quickly carved through the barriers.

Wildlife. Yellow Creek is becoming a birding hot spot, with an avian inventory of 240 species, and carefully maintained by the Todd Bird Club. The waterfowl blind is a excellent spot for observing ducks, geese, and other waterbirds. Charts in the blind help viewers identify puddle, or dabbling, ducks, which dip into water and put their tails skyward, and diving ducks, which dive below the surface and reappear elsewhere. Divers usually taxi to take off, but puddle ducks lift off the surface. Other good viewing spots are Gramma's and Grampa's Coves, and Damsite Trail. The park should develop a checklist for visitors. Waterbird sightings include the American wigeon, cattle egret, brant, Bonaparte's gull, double-crested cormorant, tundra swan, horned grebe, red phalarope, oldsquaw, and willet. Visitors include imperiled birds such as bald eagles, ospreys, loggerhead shrikes, and Virginia rails.

Boxes in fields are used by bluebirds, the intended resident, and sparrows. Warblers are represented by the orange-crowned, magnolia, Wilson's, yellow-rumped, bay-breasted, and others. Keep your eyes open for the horned lark, great horned owl, marsh wren, Hudsonian godwit, cedar waxwing, indigo bunting, and brown creeper.

Meadows gradually transforming into forest cover about 360 acres. These fields typically have yarrow, thistle, burdock, Queen Anne's lace, goldenrod, and brier patches. Wooded swamps and wet meadows account for 60 acres. Pin oak, red maple, jack-in-the-pulpit, skunk cabbage, and jewelweed are found here. All totaled, twenty-nine kinds of trees and shrubs and forty-six wildflower species grow in the park.

Shallow shores and coves are luxuriant with aquatic plants, including cattail, arrowhead, sweet flag, water milfoil, curly pondweed, spatterdock, and numerous algae. Sixteen kinds of ferns include fragile, ebony spleenwort, cut-leaved grape, and Goldie's. Take along a field guide to identify the twenty-nine types of fungi, such as stinkhorn, earthstar, fly agaric, giant puffball, and chantarelle.

Roughly 450 acres of the parkland is a mixed oak forest, consisting of second- and third-growth red and white oaks, hickories, black cherry, tulip tree, white ash, black locust, and some hemlocks. Flowering dogwood, young ashes, spicebush, firebush, multiflora rose, ironwood, and thickets of blackberries, grapevines, and blueberries occupy the understory. You'll also see planted pines.

Forty-two types of fish swim in park waters. Anglers come here for largemouth, smallmouth, and rock bass; brown, rainbow, and brook trout, especially below the dam; northern pikes; catfish; bluegills; crappies; yellow perch; and bullheads. Darters, shiners, chubs, and dace also are abundant.

Twenty-four varieties of amphibians conceal themselves here, including Jefferson, marbled, eastern slimy, and long-tailed salamanders. Watery spots entice the bullfrog, northern leopard and pickerel frogs, and snapping, spotted, and midland painted turtles. Be alert on trails for the poisonous northern copperhead and the eastern hognose snake. Southern bog lemmings, black bears, meadow jumping mice, striped skunks, and southern flying squirrels head a roster of thirty-seven mammals.

History. The park's eastern edge touches the Kittaning Path, a trade and traveling route used by the Lenni-Lenape, Shawandase, and later by European pioneers. US 44 somewhat follows the old Indian path. The commonwealth purchased land for the park from the 1960s to 1982. The dam creating the 720-acre Yellow Creek Lake was finished in 1969, and day-use facilities opened in 1976. The park name comes from the plugged stream, Yellow Creek, and the yellowish clay color of its water.

Pennsylvania's Scenic Rivers

Pennsylvania's scenic rivers program started in December 1972. To date, sixteen watercourses, totaling nearly 760 miles, have been designated as scenic rivers by the Pennsylvania Department of Conservation and Natural Resources or the federal government. Three of these currents, the Allegheny and Clarion Rivers and Bear Run, flow in western Pennsylvania. More than 140 miles of these flows have been designated.

The goal of the scenic rivers program is to safeguard sections of rivers that represent the state's and natural and cultural river heritage. Designation is based on the level of human development influencing the flow, water quality, natural diversity, land use, and the quality of the riparian habitat. Usually, only portions of a river meet the qualifications.

Pennsylvania has five designations for protected rivers: wild, scenic, pastoral, recreation, and modified recreation. Bear Run, the sole state-designated current in western Pennsylvania, is classified scenic. This designation means that the stream is free-flowing and must be capable of supporting water-based recreation, native fish, and other aquatic life. The view from the river should look wild, but some pastoral countryside and a few roads are permitted. Scenic river status does not change land ownership, increase taxes, or increase human use of the water. Activities on scenic rivers are subject to local restrictions, such as the launching of boats at prescribed locations.

For more information on state scenic rivers, contact the Pennsylvania Department of Conservation and Natural Resources, Division of Conservation Partnerships, P.O. Box 8475, Harrisburg, PA 17105, telephone (717) 787-2316. The management of the scenic Allegheny and Clarion Rivers is in the hands of the Allegheny National Forest, P.O. Box 847, Warren, PA 16365, telephone (814) 723-5150.

ALLEGHENY RIVER
The Allegheny is western Pennsylvania's longest and most famous river. The northern half of its journey across the commonwealth, the portion with national designations, traces the edge of the last ice age glacier. At Franklin, it turns south, carves a gorge, is fed by the Clarion and Youghiogheny Rivers, and joins the Monongahela to become the Ohio River.

Total Designated Miles. Acting on a report by the Department of Agriculture, Forest Service, the U.S. Congress designated three segments of the Allegheny River totaling 86.6 miles as wild and scenic in 1992.

Watershed. The Allegheny originates in western New York and flows 325 miles to its mouth in Pittsburgh. It drains an area of about 11,000 square miles. Major tributaries in Pennsylvania are Conewango Creek, Tionesta Creek, French Creek, Clarion River, Mahoning Creek, and Kiskiminetas River.

Designated Portions. The longest section, 47 miles, runs from the Buckaloons Recreation Area in Allegheny National Forest to Alcorn Island, just north of Oil City. A 31-mile portion is designated from Franklin to a refinery at Emlenton. The third segment is the 7 miles from the Kinzua Dam to the US 6 bridge in Warren.

Nearby Natural Attractions. Designated sections run through or near Allegheny National Forest, Anders Run Natural Area, Oil Creek State Park, Allegheny Gorge (Kittaning State Forest), and Two Mile Run County Park.

BEAR RUN AND BEAVER RUN

In June these runs carry the perfume of the great rhododendron shrubs blooming in Bear Run Nature Reserve. Bear Run's waterfall is one of the most photographed spills in North America because it tumbles beneath Fallingwater, the celebrated home designed by architect Frank Lloyd Wright.

Total Designated Miles. The Pennsylvania Department of Conservation and Natural Resources has designated 4.3 miles of the Bear Run watershed as scenic.

Watershed. The watersheds of both rills flow within Bear Run Nature Reserve in Fayette County.

Designated Portions. Bear Run is designated as scenic for 3.6 miles, from the 2,080-foot elevation where it becomes a perennial current to a railroad tunnel near its confluence with the Youghiogheny River. Scenic designation has also been given to Beaver Run, a tributary, from the Tree and Teaberry Trails in Bear Run Nature Reserve to Beaver Run's merger with Bear Run, a distance of 0.7 mile.

Nearby Natural Attractions. Bear Run Nature Reserve, Ohiopyle State Park, Laurel Caverns, Quebec Run Wild Area, and Fort Necessity National Battlefield.

CLARION RIVER

Indians knew it as the Tobeco, the French called it the Rivière au Fiel, and early pioneers named it Toby's or Stump Creek. Clarion stuck because the water is clear.

Total Designated Miles. Legislation signed by President Clinton in 1996 added 51.7 miles of the Clarion River to the National Wild and Scenic Rivers System.

Watershed. The west and east branches of the Clarion River are located in southern McKean County. From their confluence in Johnsonburg, the main stem runs about 100 miles southwest to the Allegheny River. Hundreds of small creeks contribute to the flow.

Designated Portions. The designated section begins at the Allegheny National Forest and State Game Lands 44 border below Ridgway, downstream to the backwaters of Piney Reservoir above Clarion. Nearly two-thirds of the land bordering the designated section is publicly owned.

Nearby Natural Attractions. Allegheny National Forest, Clear Creek State Park, Kittaning State Forest, Cook Forest State Park, Beaver Creek Nature Area and State Game Lands 28, 44, 54, 74, and 283.

Index

205